First World War
and Army of Occupation
War Diary
France, Belgium and Germany

40 DIVISION
Headquarters, Branches and Services
General Staff
1 June 1918 - 25 March 1919

WO95/2594/1

The Naval & Military Press Ltd
www.nmarchive.com
Published in association with The National Archives

Published by

The Naval & Military Press Ltd

Unit 10 Ridgewood Industrial Park,
Uckfield, East Sussex,
TN22 5QE England
Tel: +44 (0) 1825 749494

www.naval-military-press.com

www.nmarchive.com

This diary has been reprinted in facsimile from the original. Any imperfections are inevitably reproduced and the quality may fall short of modern type and cartographic standards.

© **Crown Copyright**
Images reproduced by permission of The National Archives, London, England, 2015.

Contents

Document type	Place/Title	Date From	Date To
Miscellaneous	WO95/2594/1 General Staff		
Heading	40th Division General Staff Mar 1918-1919 Mar		
Heading	War Diary 40th Division. General Staff Branch. From:- 1st June, 1918. To:- 30th June, 1918 Vol XXV		
Miscellaneous	Cover for Documents. Natures of Enclosures.		
Heading	War Diary 40th Division. General Staff Branch Vol. XXV. From:- 1st June, 1918. To:- 30th June, 1918		
War Diary	St. Omer.	01/06/1918	03/06/1918
War Diary	Lederzeele	04/06/1918	22/06/1918
War Diary	Renescure	23/06/1918	30/06/1918
Operation(al) Order(s)	40th Division Order No. 165	02/06/1918	02/06/1918
Operation(al) Order(s)	40th Division Order No. 166	14/06/1918	14/06/1918
Operation(al) Order(s)	40th Division Order No. 167	15/06/1918	15/06/1918
Operation(al) Order(s)	Schedule To Accompany 40th Division Order No. 167		
Operation(al) Order(s)	40th Division Order No. 168 Appendix 4	16/06/1918	16/06/1918
Operation(al) Order(s)	40th Division Order No. 169. Appendix 5	16/06/1918	16/06/1918
Operation(al) Order(s)	Schedule To Accompany 40th Division Order No. 169	16/06/1918	16/06/1918
Operation(al) Order(s)	40th Division Order No. 170 Appendix 6	17/06/1918	17/06/1918
Miscellaneous	40th Division Order No. 170. Appendix "A"		
Operation(al) Order(s)	40th Division Order No. 171. Appendix 7	20/06/1918	20/06/1918
Operation(al) Order(s)	40th Division Warning Order No. 172. Appendix 8	21/06/1918	21/06/1918
Operation(al) Order(s)	40th Division Warning Order No. 173. Appendix 9	21/06/1918	21/06/1918
Operation(al) Order(s)	40th Division Order No. 174. Appendix 10	22/06/1918	22/06/1918
Miscellaneous	Table to accompany 40th Division Order No. 174		
Miscellaneous	40th Division Order Of Battle.	25/06/1918	25/06/1918
Miscellaneous	Order Of Battle. 40th Divisional Headquarters.		
Miscellaneous	Army Service Corps. 40th Divisional Train A.S.C.		
Operation(al) Order(s)	40th Division Order No. 175	24/06/1918	24/06/1918
Miscellaneous	Appendix "A" to 40th Division Order No. 175		
Map			
Miscellaneous			
Operation(al) Order(s)	40th Division Order No. 176. Appendix 12	25/06/1918	25/06/1918
Operation(al) Order(s)	40th Division Order No. 177 Appendix 13	25/06/1918	25/06/1918
Heading	War Diary 40th Division General Staff Branch. Vol. XXVI From:- 1st July, 1918. To:- 31st July, 1918		
Miscellaneous	Cover for Documents. Nature of Enclosures.		
Heading	War Diary 40th Division General Staff Branch Vol. XXVI From:- 1st July, 1918. To:- 31st July, 1918		
War Diary	Renescure	01/07/1918	31/07/1918
Operation(al) Order(s)	40th Division Order No. 178. Appendix 7	07/07/1918	07/07/1918
Operation(al) Order(s)	Addendum No. 1 to 40th Division Order 178 dated 7th July, 1918	07/07/1918	07/07/1918
Operation(al) Order(s)	40th Division Order No. 179. Appendix. 2	10/07/1918	10/07/1918
Operation(al) Order(s)	40th Div. Order 180 Appendix 3	12/07/1918	12/07/1918
Operation(al) Order(s)	40th Division Order No. 182. Appendix 4	17/07/1918	17/07/1918
Miscellaneous	Appendix "A" To 40th Division Order No. 182		
Operation(al) Order(s)	Appendix "B" to 40th Division Order No. 158		
Map	G.3 5th Div 31/7/18		
Miscellaneous			

War Diary	War Diary. 40th Division. General Staff Branch. Volume XXVII. From 1st August, 1918. To 31st August, 1918		
Miscellaneous	Cover for Documents. Nature of Enclosures.		
Heading	War Diary. 40th Division. General Staff Branch. Volume XXVII. From 1st August, to 31st August, 1918		
War Diary	Renescure	01/08/1918	21/08/1918
War Diary	U.30.c.0.7. (Wallon Cappel)	22/08/1918	22/08/1918
War Diary	U.30.c.0.7	22/08/1918	31/08/1918
Operation(al) Order(s)	40th Division Order No. 183. Appendix 1	03/08/1918	03/08/1918
Miscellaneous	40th Division Instruction No. 1. for the occupation of the Army "Second Position" (West Hazebrouck Linos) Appendix 2	03/08/1918	03/08/1918
Miscellaneous	Appendix "A"		
Miscellaneous	Appendix 'B' Extracts from Defence Instructions of XI Corps.		
Operation(al) Order(s)	40th Division Order No. 184. Appendix 3	10/08/1918	10/08/1918
Operation(al) Order(s)	40th Division Order No. 185. Appendix 4	14/08/1918	14/08/1918
Operation(al) Order(s)	40th Division Order No. 186. Appendix 5	21/08/1918	21/08/1918
Miscellaneous	Table To Accompany 40th Division Order No. 186 dated 21/8/18	21/08/1918	21/08/1918
Operation(al) Order(s)	40th Div. Order No. 187. Appendix 6	22/08/1918	22/08/1918
Operation(al) Order(s)	40th Division Order No. 187. Appendix 7	22/08/1917	22/08/1917
Map	La Couronne		
Operation(al) Order(s)	40th Division Order No. 189. Appendix 8	22/08/1918	22/08/1918
Operation(al) Order(s)	40th Division Order No. 190. Appendix 9	24/06/1918	24/06/1918
Operation(al) Order(s)	40th Division Order No. 191. Appendix 10	24/08/1918	24/08/1918
Miscellaneous	XV Corps No. 636/27 G. 24th August, 1918. 40th Division.	24/08/1918	24/08/1918
Operation(al) Order(s)	40th Division Order No. 192. Appendix 11	25/08/1918	25/08/1918
Map			
Miscellaneous			
Miscellaneous	XV Corps No. 636/27/1.G.	26/08/1918	26/08/1918
Miscellaneous	XV Corps No. 636/27/2.G.	28/08/1918	28/08/1918
Miscellaneous	40th Div. No. 174/1 G. Appendix. 12	26/08/1918	26/08/1918
Miscellaneous	Account Of Attack On Bishops Corner, By 119th Infantry Brigade And 120th Infantry Brigade, On 27th August, 1918. Appendix 13	27/08/1918	27/08/1918
Miscellaneous	40th Div. No. 174. (G).	27/08/1918	27/08/1918
Diagram etc			
Diagram etc	Appendix A.2		
Operation(al) Order(s)	40th Division Order No. 193. Appendix 14	28/08/1918	28/08/1918
Diagram etc			
Operation(al) Order(s)	40th Division Order No. 194. Appendix 15	28/08/1918	28/08/1918
Miscellaneous	Account Of Operations Of 29th August, By 120th Infantry Bde. Appendix 16		
Diagram etc			
Operation(al) Order(s)	40th Division Order No. 195. Appendix 17	30/08/1918	30/08/1918
Operation(al) Order(s)	40th Division Order No. 196. Appendix 18	30/08/1918	30/08/1918
Map			
Heading	War Diary. 40th Division. General Staff Branch. Vol. XXVIII From 1st September, 1918. To 30th September, 1918		
Miscellaneous	Cover for Documents. Nature of Enclosures.		

Heading	War Diary 40th Division. General Staff Branch. Vol. XXVIII. From 1st September, 1918. To 30th September, 1918		
War Diary	U.30.c.0.7	01/09/1918	02/09/1918
War Diary	La Motte.	02/09/1918	29/09/1918
War Diary	36/A.21.b.3.8. (near Steenwerck)	30/09/1918	30/09/1918
Operation(al) Order(s)	40th Division Order No. 197. App. 1	04/09/1918	04/09/1918
Operation(al) Order(s)	40th Division Order No. 198 App 2	07/09/1918	07/09/1918
Operation(al) Order(s)	40th Division Order No. 199. App 3	10/09/1918	10/09/1918
Miscellaneous	Table to accompany 40th Division Order No. 199		
Operation(al) Order(s)	40th Division Order No. 200. App 4	10/09/1918	10/09/1918
Map	Sheet 36a N.E. 1/20,000		
Map	Belgium And Part Of France		
Miscellaneous	Glossary.		
Operation(al) Order(s)	40th Division Order No. 201. App. 5	10/09/1918	10/09/1918
Operation(al) Order(s)	40th Division Order No. 202. App 6	11/09/1918	11/09/1918
Operation(al) Order(s)	40th Division Order No. 203. App. 7	11/09/1918	11/09/1918
Operation(al) Order(s)	40th Division Order No. 204. App. 8	12/09/1918	12/09/1918
Miscellaneous	40th Division Instructions No. 2. App. 9	16/09/1918	16/09/1918
Miscellaneous	40th Division Instructions No. 3. App 10	17/09/1918	17/09/1918
Operation(al) Order(s)	40th Division Order No. 205. App 11	18/09/1918	18/09/1918
Operation(al) Order(s)	40th Division Warning Order No. 206. App 12	21/09/1918	21/09/1918
Operation(al) Order(s)	40th Division Order No. 207 App 13	22/09/1918	22/09/1918
Operation(al) Order(s)	40th Division Order No. 208. App 14	22/09/1918	22/09/1918
Operation(al) Order(s)	40th Division Order No. 209. App 15	23/09/1918	23/09/1918
Operation(al) Order(s)	40th Division Order No. 210. App 16	24/09/1918	24/09/1918
Operation(al) Order(s)	40th Division Order No. 211. App 17	25/09/1918	25/09/1918
Operation(al) Order(s)	40th Division Order No. 212. App. 18	25/09/1918	25/09/1918
Miscellaneous	War Diary	26/09/1918	26/09/1918
Miscellaneous	40th Division Instructions No. 4. App 19	25/09/1918	25/09/1918
Operation(al) Order(s)	40th Division Order No. 213. App 20	27/09/1918	27/09/1918
Miscellaneous	40th Division Instructions No. 5. App 21	28/09/1918	28/09/1918
Operation(al) Order(s)	40th Division Order No. 214. App. 22	30/09/1918	30/09/1918
Operation(al) Order(s)	40th Division Order No. 215. App 23	30/09/1918	30/09/1918
Miscellaneous	40th Division Daily Intelligence Summary, No. 10	02/09/1918	02/09/1918
Miscellaneous	40th Division Daily Intelligence Summary No. 11	03/09/1918	03/09/1918
Miscellaneous	Annexe to 40th Div. Daily Intelligence Summary No. 11		
Miscellaneous	Captured Enemy Order Of I.R. 140 at Croix Du Bac Timed 12.10 31st.		
Miscellaneous	40th Division Daily Intelligence Summary No. 12	04/09/1918	04/09/1918
Miscellaneous	40th Division Daily Intelligence Summary, No. 13	05/09/1918	05/09/1918
Miscellaneous	40th Division Daily Intelligence Summary, No. 14	06/09/1918	06/09/1918
Miscellaneous	40th Division Daily Intelligence Summary, No. 15	07/09/1918	07/09/1918
Miscellaneous	40th Division Daily Intelligence Summary, No. 16	08/09/1918	08/09/1918
Miscellaneous	Examination of Prisoner of the Bau Kompagnie I.R. 88-56th Division, captured at B.22.b.9.9., 7-9-18	07/09/1918	07/09/1918
Miscellaneous	40th Division Daily Intelligence Summary, No. 17. Period 6 a.m. 8th-6 am. 9th September, 1918	09/09/1918	09/09/1918
Miscellaneous	40th Division Daily Intelligence Summary, No. 18. Period 6 am 9th-10th September, 1918	10/09/1918	10/09/1918
Miscellaneous	40th Division Daily Intelligence Summary, No. 19. Period 6 am 10th-6am. 11th Sept. 1918	11/09/1918	11/09/1918
Miscellaneous	40th Division Daily Intelligence Summary, No. 20. Period 6 am 11th-6am. 12th Sept. 1918	12/09/1918	12/09/1918

Miscellaneous	40th Division Daily Intelligence Summary, No. 21. Period 6 am 12th-6am. 13-9-18	13/09/1918	13/09/1918
Miscellaneous	40th Division Daily Intelligence Summary, No. 22. Period 6 am 13th-6 am. 14th Sept. 1918	14/09/1918	14/09/1918
Miscellaneous	40th Division Daily Intelligence Summary, No. 23. Period 6 am 14th-6 am 15th Sept. 1918	15/09/1918	15/09/1918
Miscellaneous	40th Division Daily Intelligence Summary, No. 24. Period 6 am 15th-6 am. 16th Sept. 1918	16/09/1918	16/09/1918
Miscellaneous	40th Division Daily Intelligence Summary, No. 25. Period 6 am 16th-6 am. 17th Sept. 1918	17/09/1918	17/09/1918
Miscellaneous	40th Division Daily Intelligence Summary, No. 26. Period 6 am 17th-6 am. 18th Sept. 1918	18/09/1918	18/09/1918
Miscellaneous	40th Division Daily Intelligence Summary, No. 27. Period 6 am 18th-6 am. 19th Sept. 1918	19/09/1918	19/09/1918
Miscellaneous	40th Division Daily Intelligence Summary, No. 28. Period 6 am 19th-6 am. 20th Sept. 1918	20/09/1918	20/09/1918
Miscellaneous	40th Division Daily Intelligence Summary, No. 29. Period 6 am 20th-6 am. 21st Sept. 1918	21/09/1918	21/09/1918
Miscellaneous	40th Division Daily Intelligence Summary, No. 30. Period 6 am 21st-6 am. 22nd Sept. 1918	22/09/1918	22/09/1918
Miscellaneous	40th Division Daily Intelligence Summary, No. 31. Period 6 am 22nd-6 am. 23rd Sept. 1918	23/09/1918	23/09/1918
Miscellaneous	40th Division Daily Intelligence Summary, No. 32. Period 6 am 23rd-6 am. 24th Sept. 1918	24/09/1918	24/09/1918
Miscellaneous	News.		
Miscellaneous	40th Division Daily Intelligence Summary, No. 33. Period 6 am. 24th-6 am. 25th Sept. 1918	25/09/1918	25/09/1918
Miscellaneous	40th Division Daily Intelligence Summary, No. 34. Period 6 am. 25th-6 am. 26th Sept. 1918	26/09/1918	26/09/1918
Miscellaneous	40th Division Daily Intelligence Summary, No. 35. Period 6 am. 26th-6 am. 27th Sept. 1918	27/09/1918	27/09/1918
Miscellaneous	40th Division Daily Intelligence Summary, No. 36. Period 6 am 27th-6 am 28th September, 1918	28/09/1918	28/09/1918
Miscellaneous	40th Division Daily Intelligence Summary, No. 37. Period 6 am 28th-6 am 29th September, 1918	29/09/1918	29/09/1918
Miscellaneous	40th Division Daily Intelligence Summary, No. 38. Period 6 am. 29th-6 am 30th September, 1918	30/09/1918	30/09/1918
Miscellaneous	News		
Miscellaneous	40th Division Daily Intelligence Summary, No. 39. Period 6 am 30th Sept.-6 am 1st October, 18	30/09/1918	30/09/1918
Heading	War Diary 40th Division General Staff Branch Vol. XXIX From 1st October, 1918. To 31st October, 1918		
Miscellaneous	According To The Daily Summary		
Heading	War Diary 40th Division General Staff Branch Vol. XXIX From 1st October, 1918. To 31st October, 1918		
War Diary	36/A.21.b.3.8. Nr Steenwerck	01/10/1918	17/10/1918
War Diary	Armentieres	18/10/1918	19/10/1918
War Diary	Mouveaux F.21.c.7.7	20/10/1918	26/10/1918
War Diary	Lannoy	27/10/1918	31/10/1918
Operation(al) Order(s)	40th Division Order No. 216 App. 1	02/10/1918	02/10/1918
Miscellaneous	40th Division Instructions No. 6. App 2	05/10/1918	05/10/1918
Miscellaneous	40th Division Instructions No. 7. App. 3	06/10/1918	06/10/1918
Miscellaneous	40th Division Instructions No. 8. App 4	08/10/1918	08/10/1918
Miscellaneous	40th Division Order No. 217 App 5	10/10/1918	10/10/1918
Miscellaneous	40th Division Instructions No. 9. App 6	10/10/1918	10/10/1918
Operation(al) Order(s)	40th Division Order No. 218. App 7	13/10/1918	13/10/1918

Operation(al) Order(s)	40th Division Order No. 220 App 8	15/10/1918	15/10/1918
Miscellaneous	40th Division Instructions No. 10. App. 9	16/10/1918	16/10/1918
Miscellaneous	A Form. Messages And Signals. App 10		
Miscellaneous	A Form. Messages And Signals.		
Miscellaneous	A Form. Messages And Signals. App 11		
Miscellaneous	A Form. Messages And Signals. App 12		
Operation(al) Order(s)	40th Divisional Order No. 221	17/10/1918	17/10/1918
Miscellaneous	40th Division Instructions No. 11 App 14	17/10/1918	17/10/1918
Miscellaneous	A Form Messages And Signals App 15		
Miscellaneous			
Miscellaneous	A Form Messages And Signals.		
Miscellaneous	A Form Messages And Signals App 15		
Miscellaneous	A Form Messages And Signals App 16		
Miscellaneous	40th Division Instructions No. 12 App 17	18/10/1918	18/10/1918
Miscellaneous	A Form Messages And Signals. App 18		
Miscellaneous	A Form Messages And Signals. App 19		
Miscellaneous	A Form Messages And Signals. App 20		
Miscellaneous	A Form Messages And Signals. App 21		
Operation(al) Order(s)	40th Divisional Order No. 222. App 22	19/10/1918	19/10/1918
Operation(al) Order(s)	40th Division Order No. 223 App 23	23/10/1918	23/10/1918
Operation(al) Order(s)	40th Division Order No. 224 App 27	24/10/1918	24/10/1918
Miscellaneous	Movement Table to accompany 40th Div. Order No. 224		
Operation(al) Order(s)	40th Division Order No. 225. App 25	27/10/1918	27/10/1918
Operation(al) Order(s)	40th Division Order No. 226 App 26	31/10/1918	31/10/1918
Miscellaneous	40th Division Daily Intelligence Summary, No. 40 Period 6 am 1st-6 am 2nd October, 1918	02/10/1918	02/10/1918
Miscellaneous	40th Division Daily Intelligence Summary, No. 41 Period 6 am 2nd-6 am 3rd October, 1918	03/10/1918	03/10/1918
Miscellaneous	40th Division Daily Intelligence Summary, No. 42 Period 6 am 3rd-6 am 4th October, 1918	04/10/1918	04/10/1918
Miscellaneous	40th Division Daily Intelligence Summary, No. 43 Period 6.00 4th-6.00 5th October, 1918	05/10/1918	05/10/1918
Miscellaneous	40th Division Daily Intelligence Summary, No. 44 Period 6.00 5th-6.00 6th October, 1918	06/10/1918	06/10/1918
Miscellaneous	40th Division Daily Intelligence Summary, No. 45. Period 06.00 6th-06.00 7th October, 1918	07/10/1918	07/10/1918
Miscellaneous	40th Division Daily Intelligence Summary, No. 46. Period 06.00 7th-06.00 8th October, 1918	08/10/1918	08/10/1918
Miscellaneous	40th Division Daily Intelligence Summary, No. 47. Period 06.00 8th-06.00 9th October, 1918	09/10/1918	09/10/1918
Miscellaneous	40th Division Daily Intelligence Summary, No. 48. Period 06.00 9th-06.00 10th October, 1918	10/10/1918	10/10/1918
Miscellaneous	40th Division Daily Intelligence Summary, No. 49. Period 06.00 10th-06.00 11th October, 1918	11/10/1918	11/10/1918
Miscellaneous	40th Division Daily Intelligence Summary, No. 50. Period 06.00 11th October-06.00 12th Oct. 1918	12/10/1918	12/10/1918
Miscellaneous	40th Division Daily Intelligence Summary, No 51. Period 0600 12th-0600 13th October, 1918	13/10/1918	13/10/1918
Miscellaneous	News		
Miscellaneous	40th Division Intelligence Summary, No 52. Period 06.00 13th-06.00 14th Oct. 1918	14/10/1918	14/10/1918
Miscellaneous	40th Division Daily Intelligence Summary, No. 53. Period 0600 14th-0600 15th October, 1918	15/10/1918	15/10/1918
Miscellaneous	40th Division Daily Intelligence Summary, No. 54. Period 0600 15th-0600 16th October, 1918	16/10/1918	16/10/1918

Miscellaneous	40th Division Daily Intelligence Summary, No. 55. Period 0600 16th-0600 17th October, 1918	17/10/1918	17/10/1918
Miscellaneous	40th Division Daily Intelligence Summary, No. 56 Period 0600 26th-0600 27th October, 1918	27/10/1918	27/10/1918
Miscellaneous	40th Division Daily Intelligence Summary, No 57. Period 0600 27th 0600 28th October, 1918	28/10/1918	28/10/1918
Miscellaneous	40th Division Daily Intelligence Summary, No. 58. Period 0600 28th-0600 29th October, 1918	29/10/1918	29/10/1918
Miscellaneous	40th Division Daily Intelligence Summary, No. 59 Period 0600 29th-0600 30th October, 1918	30/10/1918	30/10/1918
Miscellaneous	40th Division Daily Intelligence Summary, No. 60 Period 0600 30th-0600 31st October, 1918	31/10/1918	31/10/1918
Miscellaneous	Examination of Prisoners of 8th Coy. 26th Bav. Inf. Regt., 12th Bavarian Division.	31/10/1918	31/10/1918
Map	Belgium And Part Of France		
Map			
Map	France		
Map			
Map	Belgium And Part Of France		
Map			
Miscellaneous			
Heading	War Diary. General Staff Branch. 40th Division. Vol. XXX From 1st November, 1918. To 30th November, 1918		
Miscellaneous	Cover for Documents Nature of Enclosures.		
Heading	War Diary General Staff Branch. 40th Division. Vol. XXX From 1st November, 1918. To 30th November, 1918		
War Diary	Lannoy	01/11/1918	24/11/1918
War Diary	Roubaix	25/11/1918	30/11/1918
Miscellaneous	A Form. Messages And Signals. App I		
Operation(al) Order(s)	40th Division Order No. 227. App 2	02/11/1918	02/11/1918
Operation(al) Order(s)	40th Division Order No. 228. App. 3	03/11/1918	03/11/1918
Miscellaneous	40th Division Instruction No. 13 App 4	04/11/1918	04/11/1918
Operation(al) Order(s)	40th Division Order No. 229 App 5	06/11/1918	06/11/1918
Miscellaneous	40th Div. No. 4/170 G. App 6	06/11/1918	06/11/1918
Operation(al) Order(s)	40th Division Order No. 230. App 7	09/11/1918	09/11/1918
Miscellaneous	App 8		
Miscellaneous	40th Div. No. 224 G. App 9	11/11/1918	11/11/1918
Operation(al) Order(s)	40th Division Order No. 231 App 10	11/11/1918	11/11/1918
Operation(al) Order(s)	40th Division Order No. 232. App 11	14/11/1918	14/11/1918
Operation(al) Order(s)	40th Division Order No. 233. App 12	15/11/1918	15/11/1918
Miscellaneous	40th Division Instructions No. 14 App 13	16/11/1918	16/11/1918
Operation(al) Order(s)	40th Division Order No. 234 App 14	20/11/1918	20/11/1918
Miscellaneous	To all recipients of 40th Division Order No. 234	21/11/1918	21/11/1918
Map			
Miscellaneous	War Diary		
Heading	War Diary General Staff 40th Division. Vol. XXXI From 1st December, 1918. To 31st December, 1918		
Miscellaneous	Cover for Documents. Nature of Enclosures.		
Miscellaneous	40th Division No. 34 (A).	21/01/1919	21/01/1919
War Diary	Roubaix		
Heading	War Diary 40th Div. General Staff Branch Vol. XXXII 1st Jan. 1919 to 31st Jan. 1919		
Miscellaneous	Cover for Documents. Nature of Enclosures.		
War Diary	Roubaix		

Heading	War Diary 40th Division. General Staff Branch. Vol. XXVIII. From 1st February, 1919. To 28th February, 1919		
Miscellaneous	Cover for Documents. Nature of Enclosures.		
War Diary	Roubaix	01/02/1919	28/02/1919
Heading	War Diary Of 40th Division. (General Staff Branch.) Vol. XXXIV. From 1st March, 1919. To 31st March, 1919		
Miscellaneous	Cover for Documents. Nature of Enclosures.		
War Diary	Roubaix	01/03/1919	24/03/1919
War Diary	Croix	25/03/1919	25/03/1919

WO95/2594/1
General Staff

40TH DIVISION

GENERAL STAFF
MAR 1918 - ~~MAR~~ 1919 JUNE MAR

CONFIDENTIAL. ORIGINAL.

WAR DIARY,

40th DIVISION.

GENERAL STAFF BRANCH.

FROM :- 1st JUNE, 1918.
TO   :- 30th JUNE, 1918.

VOL : XXV.

J. Ponsonby
Major-General,
Commanding 40th Division.

Army Form W.3091.

Cover for Documents.

Natures of Enclosures.

Notes, or Letters written.

WAR DIARY

40th DIVISION.

GENERAL STAFF BRANCH

VOL. XXV.

FROM :- 1st JUNE, 1918.
TO :- 30th JUNE, 1918.

INDEX

Pages 1 - 5   War Diary.
      6 - 33 Appendices.

Army Form C. 2118

WAR DIARY
or
INTELLIGENCE SUMMARY

(Erase heading not required.)

VOL: XXV.   40th DIVISION.

JUNE, 1918.

Instructions regarding War Diaries and Intelligence Summaries are contained in F. S. Regs., Part II. and the Staff Manual respectively. Title Pages will be prepared in manuscript.

Place	Date	Hour	Summary of Events and Information	Remarks and references to Appendices
ST. OMER.	1st		Divisional Headquarters continued at ST. OMER.	
,,	3rd		The undermentioned battalions, (training cadres) left the Division on transfer to the 34th Div. to assist in the training of American Troops :-	Appendix 1.
			21st Bn. Middlesex Regt. 13th Bn. East Surrey Regt. 10/11th Bn. Highland L. I. 14th Bn. Highland L. I. 13th Bn. Yorkshire Regt.	
,,	3rd.		Divisional Headquarters moved to LEDERZEELE.	
LEDERZEELE	4th. 5th. 6th. 7th. 8th.		Work on the WINNIZEELE and BALEMBERG Lines continued.	
,,	9th.		Instructions received of the formation of Infantry Garrison Guard Battalions, composed of men of categories lower than "A". As a temporary measure, some of these units are to be allotted to the 40th Division cadre.	
,,	10th.		119th Infantry Bde. H.Q. moved to N. E. of STUYVER. 120th Infantry Bde. H.Q. moved to LEDERZEELE.	
,,	10th.		The following Garrison Guard Battalions, forming one Brigade (under the 120th Infantry Brigade) are allotted to the Division, and Battalion Headquarters' moved into the LEDERZEELE Area :-	
			No. 6 Garrison Guard Battalion. No. 9 Garrison Guard Battalion. No. 7 Garrison Guard Battalion. No. 10 Garrison Guard Battalion. No. 8 Garrison Guard Battalion. No. 11 Garrison Guard Battalion.	
			When organised, this Brigade will be allotted to the W. HAZEBROUCK Line for work, and to man the line in case of necessity.	

Army Form C. 2118

WAR DIARY
or
INTELLIGENCE SUMMARY

(Erase heading not required.)

40th DIVISION.

JUNE, 1918.

Place	Date	Hour	Summary of Events and Information	Remarks and references to Appendices
LEDERZEELE	11th		The Garrison Guard Battalions are allotted permanent designations, to come into force on 12th June, as hereunder stated :-	
			No. 6 Garrison Guard Battalion becomes 11th Garrison Bn. Cameron Highlanders.	
			No. 7 -do- -do- 13th -do- R. Inniskilling Fusiliers.	
			No. 8 -do- -do- 13th -do- East Lancashire Regiment.	
			No. 9 -do- -do- 10th -do- King's Own Scottish Borderers.	
			No. 10 -do- -do- 15th -do- King's Own Yorkshire L.I.	
			No. 11 -do- -do- 12th -do- North Staffordshire Regiment.	
,,	12th) 13th)		Work on WINNIZEELE and BALEMBERG Lines continued and organization of Garrison Battalions proceeded with.	
,,	14th		Orders received that the 40th Division will be reorganized as a "Garrison Division" (semi-mobile) of 10 Garrison Battalions; four battalions being transferred from First Army. Light and Medium T.M. Batteries will be formed under Second Army arrangements and S.A.A. Section Divisional Ammunition Column under G.H.Q. arrangements. The Division will be required to hold a quiet Sector of the line and all efforts are to be concentrated on training with this object. The Division is withdrawn from work on Defence Lines; this will in future be undertaken by Major-General Kenyon. Orders are issued for the concentration of Brigades in training areas. The transfer of certain Garrison Battalions from the 120th to 119th Brigade, and the move of the Brigade Headquarters of the latter are ordered.	
,,	15th		Brigade Headquarters, 119th Infantry Brigade is established at NIEURLET. In case of enemy attack on the Second Army front, the 40th Division, with armed labour units in the area will be required to man the WEST HAZEBROUCK Line. Order 176 is issued. Subsequently orders are issued that formations, units, etc. must be prepared to act on Order 176 at short notice. Warning received that the undermentioned Garrison Battalions will join from 59th Division, First Army:-	Appendix 3.
			2nd Garrison Bn. Royal Irish Regt.	
			23rd -do- Cheshire Regt.	
			17th -do- Worcestershire Regt.	
			23rd -do- Lancashire Fusiliers.	

Army Form C. 2118

WAR DIARY
or
INTELLIGENCE SUMMARY
(Erase heading not required.)

40th DIVISION.

JUNE. 1918.

Instructions regarding War Diaries and Intelligence Summaries are contained in F. S. Regs., Part II. and the Staff Manual respectively. Title Pages will be prepared in manuscript.

Place	Date	Hour	Summary of Events and Information	Remarks and references to Appendices
LEDERZEELE	15th		The following is the allotment of Garrison Battalions to Infantry Brigades :-	
			119th Infantry Bde. 120th Infantry Bde. 121st Infantry Bde.	
			13th Gar.Bn. R.Innis.Fus. 11th Gar. Bn. Cameron Highrs. 2nd Gar. Bn. R. Irish Regt.	
			13th Gar.Bn. E.Lancs. Regt. 10th Gar. Bn. K.O.Scot.Bords. 23rd Gar. Bn. Cheshire Regt.	
			12th Gar.Bn. N.Staff. Regt. 15th Gar. Bn. K.O.Yorks.L.I. 17th Gar. Bn. Worcester Regt.	
			23rd Gar. Bn. Lancs. Fusrs.	
			Each Brigade is ordered to form one Light Trench Mortar Battery, consisting of 3 officers and 47 Other Ranks, from the personnel within Garrison Battalions.	
,,	16th		The 121st Bde. Headquarters is ordered to move from LE TOM to the ST. MARTIN-AU-LAERT Area.	Appendix 4
			Division Order 167 regarding the manning of the WEST HAZEBROUCK Line in case of emergency, in so far as it concerns the allotment of troops is amended. A fresh order is issued which shows the approximate number of armed men available to man the defences. Division Order 169.	Appendix 5
,,	17th		Division Order 167 is cancelled and a more comprehensive order (Division Order 170) regarding the manning of the WEST HAZEBROUCK Line is issued.	Appendix 6
			Battalion training staffs of the undermentioned units proceeded to England:-	
			10/11th Highland L.I. (from the 34th Division) for the 14th Division.	
			20th Middlesex Regt.) do. do.	
			14th Argyll & S. Hrs.) do. do.	
			12th Suffolk Regt. (from the 40th Division) for the 16th Division.	
			18th Welsh Regt.	
,,	18th		Nos. 3. and 4. Coys. 40th Divisional Train, rejoined the Division in consequence of the reorganization.	
,,	19th		The D.A.G., G.H.Q., inspected Garrison Battalions of the 119th and 120th Infantry Brigades.	
,,	20th		The embussing and debussing points for troops proceeding by bus. to man the WEST HAZEBROUCK Line are laid down, and also the route to be taken by the troops who march. Div. Order, 171.	Appendix 7

Army Form C. 2118

WAR DIARY
or
INTELLIGENCE SUMMARY
(Erase heading not required.)

40th DIVISION.

JUNE, 1918.

Instructions regarding War Diaries and Intelligence Summaries are contained in F. S. Regs., Part II. and the Staff Manual respectively. Title Pages will be prepared in manuscript.

Place	Date	Hour	Summary of Events and Information	Remarks and references to Appendices
LEDERZEELE	21st.		The 40th Division will move by march route on the 22nd instant, to the WEST HAZEBROUCK area. Warning Order No. 172 issued.	Appendix 8.
,,	22nd.		Orders received from Corps to postpone move. Warning Order issued that 40th Division less Artillery will move by road and rail on the 23rd inst. to the WEST HAZEBROUCK area. Warning Order 173.	Appendix 9.
,,	22nd.		The Division is transferred from VIIth to XVth Corps. Division Order No. 174 issued, with March Table etc. ordering move to WEST HAZEBROUCK Area.	Appendix 10.
RENESCURE	23rd		Divisional Headquarters opened at RENESCURE and troops arrive in the W.HAZEBROUCK Area.	
,,	24th		Field Marshal Sir Douglas Haig saw a battalion of each brigade at work.	
,,	25th		Consequent on move of Division into the W. HAZEBROUCK Area, Division Orders Nos. 170 & 171 are cancelled and a revised Order (175) is issued.	Appendix 11.
,,	26th		Practise manning of the W. HAZEBROUCK line carried out by the three infantry bdes; Labour and R. E. units did not attend.	
,,	26th		The 135th and 136th Field Ambulances rejoined the Division.	
,,	26th		A revised order showing the routes to be taken to assembly positions by troops manning the West HAZEBROUCK Line is issued, - No. 176.	Appendix 12.
,,	27th		Practise concentration of R.E. and Labour units who will man the W.HAZEBROUCK Line in an emergency is carried out.	Appendix 13.
,,	28th		The training cadre of the 12th Yorkshire Regt. (Pioneers) is absorbed into the 17th Garrison Bn. Worcestershire Regt. The latter unit becomes the Divisional Pioneer Battalion and ceases to be administered by the 121st Infantry Bde.	

Army Form C. 2118

WAR DIARY
or
INTELLIGENCE SUMMARY

40th DIVISION.

JUNE, 1918.

(Erase heading not required.)

Place	Date	Hour	Summary of Events and Information	Remarks and references to Appendices
RENESCURE.	29th.		Corps orders that for training purposes, one Battalion from each Brigade will, from 3rd July inclusive, occupy the EAST HAZEBROUCK Line, and will work under R.E. supervision in improving the position. Battalions to occupy the line for 3 or 4 days. All battalions of each Brigade to be detailed in turn.	
,,	30th.		The organization of the 119th Trench Mortar Battery being completed, it becomes a separate unit.	

(signed)

Lieut-Colonel.

General Staff, 40th Division.

Appendix I.   6

SECRET   Copy No. 25

        40th DIVISION ORDER NO.165.   2/6/18.

Ref. Map
HAZEBROUCK 5 A.
----

1. Headquarters of 40th Division will move from ST.OMER to LEDERZEELE, to-morrow 3rd June, 1918.

2. Offices will be closed at ST.OMER at 2 p.m. and will re-open at LEDERZEELE at the same hour.

3. ACKNOWLEDGE.

                          W. Carter, Major,
                          G.S. Lieut. Colonel,
                General Staff, 40th Division.

Issued at 10.30 a.m.   ****

Copy No. 1 to G.O.C.
     2   119th Inf. Bde.
     3   120th   ,,
     4   121st   ,,
     5   C.R.A.
     6   C.R.E.
     7   Signals
     8   A.D.M.S.
     9   A.P.M.
    10   Camp Commandant
    11   D.A.D.V.S.
    12   D.A.D.O.S.
    13   Gas Officer
    14   Train
    15   40th Div. M.T.Company.
    16   S.S.O.
    17   Major General KENYON.
    18   C.R.E. No.1 Sector.
    19   ,,   2,3 and 5 Sectors.
    20   VIIth Corps G
    21   ,,   Q
    22   ,,   C.E.
    23   40th Div. "Q"
    24   War Diary.
    25   ,,
    26   File
    27   Labour Commandant VIIth Corps.

Appendix 2

SECRET
Copy No. 24

40th DIVISION ORDER NO. 186.
14/6/18.

Ref. Hazebrouck Sheet.

1. The following battalions will be transferred from 120th Infantry Brigade to 119th Infantry Brigade on dates stated against each unit.

   13th Garrison Bn: Royal Inniskillon Fusiliers on 15th June.
   13th Garrison Bn: East Lancashire Regt. on 15th June.
   12th Garrison Bn: North Staff. Regt. on 15th June.

2. The ST.MOMELIN AREA is allotted to 119th Brigade and the ST.MARTIN AU LAERT AREA to 121st Infantry Brigade. Details of accommodation available will be forwarded later.

3. The following moves to the ST.MOMELIN AREA will take place to-morrow under arrangements to be made by G.O.C. 119th Bde.

   (a) 119th Inf. Bde. H.Qrs. to ST.MOMELIN.
   (b) H.Qrs. 13th Garrison Bn: Royal Inniskillon Fusiliers.
   (c) H.Qrs. 13th Garrison Bn: East Lancashire Regt.

4. The 12th Garrison Battalion North Staff. Regt. (which arrives at WATTEN station about 2 a.m. to-morrow 15th June) will be quartered at BROXEELE under arrangements to be made by 120th Infantry Brigade. This Battalion will move to the ST.MOMELIN Area on a date to be decided by G.O.C. 119th Inf. Brigade. The move will take place under Brigade arrangements.

5. Orders for the concentration of 121st Infantry Brigade in the ST.MARTIN AU LAERT Area will be issued later.

6. ACKNOWLEDGE.

Issued at 12.30 p.m.

Major,
General Staff, 40th Division.

Copy No.1 to G.O.C.
 2   119 Bde.
 3   120 Bde.
 4   121 Bde.
 5   C.R.A.
 6   C.R.E.
 7   Signals.
 8   A.D.M.S.
 9   A.P.M.
 10   Camp Commandant.
 11   D.A.D.V.S.
 12   D.A.D.O.S.
 13 Gas Officer.
 14 Div. Train.
 15. 40th Div. M.T.Company.
 16 S.S.O.
 17 VII Corps (G)
 18   "   (Q)
 19 40th Div. "Q"
 20 Area Comdt. ST.MOMELIN Area.
 21   "   ST.MARTIN AU LAERT.
 22   "   BROXEELE.
 23   "   LEDERZEELE.
 24 & 25. War Diary.
 26 File.

SECRET.

Ref: Map HAZEBROUCK.
Sh.27.
Sh.36A.

40th Division Order No. 167.

Appendix 3
Copy No.......
15/6/18.

1. In the event of an enemy attack on the Second Army front, the 40th Division and attached troops will man the West HAZEBROUCK Line from D.25.c. in the South to V.6.d. in the North, a distance of about 13,000 yards.

2. The Divisional Sector is divided into three Brigade Sections as shown on attached map.

3. The Sections will be held by the following troops :-

Southern Section.   120th Infantry Bde.
                      236th A. T. Company, R.E.
                      94th Labour Company.
                      12th Labour Company.

Centre Section.   121st Infantry Bde.
                      234th Field Coy. R.E.
                      224th Field Coy. R.E.
                      55th Labour Company.
                      13th Labour Company.
                      93rd Labour Company.
                      67th Labour Company.
                      178th Labour Company.

Northern Section.   119th Infantry Bde.
                      231st Field Coy. R.E.
                      164th Labour Company.
                      188th Labour Company.
                      111th Labour Company.
                      132nd Labour Company.
                      61st Labour Company.
                      133rd Labour Company.
                      147th Labour Company.

4. The 5th and 31st Labour Groups furnish the armed Labour Coys. troops who are detailed in para. 3.
  On the alarm being given, the Labour Commandant, VIIth Corps is notifying the Group Commanders who will order the armed Labour Troops to stand to, and will send an officer to each Brigade Headquarters for orders.
  Armed personnel will be attached to units in the Brigades. Each Labour Company has one officer per 100 men and at present the men are untrained.

5. A schedule is attached showing the location of all troops mentioned in this order.

6. Inf. Bns. of / The 40th Division will proceed from billets to the vicinity of the trench system by busses. "Q" 40th Division is arranging an embussing and debussing scheme.

7. Headquarters will be established as follows :-
     Divisional Headquarters,   - RENESCURE T.21.c.4.5.
     120th Inf. Bde. Hd. Qrs.   - C.9.d.90.35.
     121st Inf. Bde. Hd. Qrs.   - U.25.b.3.3.
     119th Inf. Bde. Hd. Qrs.   - P.31.d.50.75.

  The Divisional Signal Company will arrange forthwith for signal communication between the Headquarters mentioned above.

8. The line will be held in accordance with the principles laid down in S.S. 210 "The Division in Defence", so far as troops are available, but in any case, Brigades will so dispose their troops that they hold the Observation Line and the Main Line of Resistance.

It

2.

It must be clearly impressed on the troops that they are to hold the line in which they are posted, whether it be Observation Line, Main Line of Resistance or Reserve Line, to the last man and the last round of ammunition. No withdrawal of troops will take place even from the Line of Observation, until orders are issued from Divisional Headquarters to do so.

9. 120 rounds of S.A.A. will be carried by each man to the trenches, and 2,000 rounds per Lewis Gun.

10. Rations for the day and one Iron Ration, per man will be carried.

11. Reconnaissances of the line will be carried out by 119th and 120th Brigades and Battalion Staffs tomorrow 16th instant. Two busses will report at each Brigade Headquarters at 8. a.m.

The 121st Infantry Bde. will carry out the reconnaissance tomorrow also; a car will be sent to their Headquarters at 8.a.m. This car must be returned to Division by 2.30.p.m.

Battalion Staffs allotted to the 121st Brigade will, on the morning after their arrival in the area, carry out the reconnaissance.

12. Brigades will prepare a scheme for the occupation of their sections with the troops allotted under paragraph 3. These schemes should be so elastic that in the event of Battalions not arriving, modifications can be made.

13. Acknowledge.

Carter

Major.

General Staff, 40th Division.

Issued at 3. p.m.

Copy No. 1. to G.O.C.
2. 119th Inf. Bde.
3. 120th Inf. Bde.
4. 121st Inf. Bde.
5. Div. Sig. Coy.
6. O.C., No. 5 Labour Group.
7. O.C., No.31 Labour Group.
8. Labour Commandant, VIIth Corps.
9. C.R.E., 40th Division.
10. VIIth Corps, (G).
11. VIIth Corps, (Q).
12. XVth Corps (G).
13. XVth Corps (Q).
14. "Q" 40th Division.
15. 16. War Diary.
17. File.
18. C.R.E. No. 1 Sector.
19. C.R.E. 2.3.& 4. Sectors.
20. A.D.M.S.
21. D.A.D.O.S.
22. Div Train.
23. 40th Div. M.T.Coy.
24. S.S.O.
25. D.A.D.V.S.
26. A.P.M.
27. Camp. Comdt.
28. Div. Gas Officer.

SCHEDULE TO ACCOMPANY 40th DIVISION ORDER No. 167.

	Unit.	Location.	Labour Group.
Southern Section.	120th Infantry Bde.	LEDERZEELE.	
	236th A.T.Coy. R.E.	C.8.TERCUS	
	94th Labour Coy.	C.22.d.6.5.	No.5.
	12th Labour Coy.	C.5.d.9.5.	No.5.
Centre Section.	121st Infantry Bde.	H.36.d.2.5.	
	234th Field Coy.R.E.	U.1.b.6.7.	
	224th Field Coy.R.E.	H.33.b.6.5.	
	55th Labour Coy.	V.25.a.7.3.	No.5.
	13th Labour Coy.	V.13.d.2.2.	No.5.
	93rd Labour Coy.	STAPLE.	No.31
	67th Labour Coy.	U.5.c.8.9.	No.31.
	178th Labour Coy.	C.5.b.8.8.	No.5.
Northern Section.	119th Infantry Bde.	NIEURLET.	
	231st Field Coy.R.E.	V.15.a.5.1.	
	164th Labour Coy.	ST MARIE CAPPEL P.26.d.6.8.	No.5.
	189th Labour Coy.	P.25.b.central	No.31.
	111th Labour Coy.	V.15.a.7.3.	No.5.
	132nd Labour Coy.	P.36.a.9.2.	No.5.
	81st Labour Coy.	V.3.c.8.3.	No.5.
	133rd Labour Coy.	P.15.b.2.6.	No.31.
	147th Labour Coy.	P.17.c.2.2.	No.31.

Reference Maps, Sheet 27., 36A., and HAZEBROUCK.

Appendix 4.

SECRET   Copy No. 22

40th DIVISION ORDER NO. 168.   16/6/18.

Ref. map HAZEBROUCK.

1. 121st Brigade Headquarters will move to the ST.MARTIN AU LAERT Area during the afternoon of 17th June, under arrangements to be made by Brigade direct.

2. Completion of move and location of new Headquarters to be reported by wire.

M.M.Chapman Capt.
G.S.
for Major,
General Staff, 40th Division.

Issued at 2 p.m.

```
Copy No. 1   to G.O.C.
        2       119 Bde
        3       120 Bde
        4       121 Bde
        5       Div. Signal Coy.
        6       C.R.E. 40th Division.
        7       VIIth Corps    G
        8         ,,           Q
        9       XV Corps       G
       10         ,,           Q
       11       A.D.M.S.
       12       D.A.D.O.S.
       13       Div. Train.
       14       40th Div. M.T.Coy.
       15       S.S.O.
       16       D.A.D.V.S.
       17       A.P.M.
       18       Camp Commandant
       19       Div. Gas Officer.
       20       Div. Claims Officer.
       21       40th Div. "Q".
    22 & 23     War Diary.
       24       File
       25       Area Commandant, ST.MARTIN AU LAERT.
```

SECRET   Copy No. 25

40th DIVISION ORDER NO. 169.   16/6/18.

1. With reference to 40th Division Order No. 167 dated 15/6/18, cancel Para. 3 and substitute –

"3. The sections will be held by the following troops :–

Southern Section.   Approx. No. of rifles.

120th Infantry Bde.	3,000
236th A.T. Company.	130
94th Labour Coy.	270
12th Labour Coy.	270
3rd Labour Coy.	30
	3,700

Centre Section.

121st Infantry Bde.	
234th Field Coy. R.E.	70
224th Field Coy. R.E.	50
229th Field Coy. R.E.	130
55th Labour Coy.	270
13th Labour Coy.	270
67th Labour Coy.	50
170th Labour Coy.	270
4th Labour Coy.	40
35th Labour Coy.	40
48th Labour Coy.	40
156th Labour Coy.	40
173rd Tunnelling Coy. (3 Sections)	100
	1,370

Northern Section

119th Infantry Bde	3,000
231st Field Coy. R.E.	90
164th Labour Coy.	270
188th Labour Coy.	50
111th Labour Coy.	270
132nd Labour Coy.	270
61st Labour Coy.	270
133rd Labour Coy.	50
147th Labour Coy.	50
174th Labour Coy.	70
6th Labour Coy.)	
84th Labour Coy.)	
92nd Labour Coy.)	30
110th Labour Coy.)	
138th Labour Coy.)	
	4,420

2. Busses have been asked for to convey 224th and 229th Field Companies from vicinity of their billets to the line. If these are not available units will have to proceed by march route.

3. An amended schedule, showing the location of troops referred to above, is attached.

4. ACKNOWLEDGE.

                                                    Major,
Issued at 11.59 p.m.   General Staff, 40th Division.

```
Copy No. 1 to G.O.C.
        2    119 Bde
        3    120 Bde
        4    121 Bde
        5    Div. Signal Coy.
        6    O.C. No. 5 Labour Group.
        7    O.C. No. 31 Labour Group.
        8    O.C. No. 26 Labour Group.
        9    O.C. No. 64 Labour Group.
       10    Labour Commandant VIIth Corps.
       11.   C.R.E. 40th Division.
       12.   C.R.E. No.1 Sector.
       13.   C.R.E. 2, 3 & 5 Sect.
       14.   A.D.M.S.
       15.   D.A.D.V.S.
       16.   D.A.D.O.S.
       17.   Div. Train.
       18.   40th Div. M.T.Coy.
       19.   S.S.O.
       20.   A.P.M.
       21.   Camp Commandant.
       22.   Div. Gas Officer.
       23.   VIIth Corps G.
       24.     "       Q.
       25.   XVth Corps G.
       26.     "       Q
       27.   40th Division "Q".
       28.)  War Diary
       29.)
       30    File.
       31    Labour Commandant, G.H.Q. Defence Lines.
```

SCHEDULE TO ACCOMPANY 40th DIVISION ORDER O. 169.

	Unit.	Location.	Labour Group
Southern Section.	120th Infantry Bde.	LEDERZEELE	
	236th A.T.Coy. R.E.	C.9. SERCUS.	
	94th Labour Coy.	C.22.d.6.5.	No.5
	12th Labour Coy.	C.5.d.9.5.	No.5
	3rd Labour Coy.	C.23.b.	No.64
Centre Section.			
	121st Infantry Bde.	H.36.d.2.5.	
	234th Field Coy. R.E.	W.1.b.6.7.	
	224th Field Coy. R.E.	R.33.b.6.5.	
	229th Field Coy. R.E.	R.25.b.5.2.	
	55th Labour Coy.	V.25.a.7.2.	No.5
	13th Labour Coy.	V.13.d.2.2.	No.5
	67th Labour Coy.	U.5.c.8.9.	No.31
	178th Labour Coy.	C.5.b.8.8.	No.5
	4th Labour Coy.	C.4.c.7.6.	No.64
	35th Labour Coy.	C.8.b.central	No. 64
	48th Labour Coy.	C.5.d.5.3.	No.64
	136th Labour Coy.	C.26.b.5.2.	No.64
	173rd Tunnelling Coy. R.E. (3 sections)	BLARINGHEM	
Northern Section	119th Infantry Bde.	NIEURLET	
	231st Field Coy. R.E.	V.15.a.5.1.	
	164th Labour Coy.	ST.MARIE CAPPEL (P.26.d.6.8.)	No.5
	188th Labour Coy.	P.25.b.central	No.31
	111th Labour Coy.	V.15.a.7.3.	No.5
	132nd Labour Coy.	P.36.a.9.2.	No.5
	61st Labour Coy.	V.3.c.8.3.	No.5
	133rd Labour Coy.	U.15.d.1.9.	No.31
	147th Labour Coy.	U.5.c.central.	No.31
	174th Labour Coy.	I.3.a.6.5.	No.64
	6th Labour Coy.	N.35.b.2.6.	No.26
	84th Labour Coy.	S.6.a.5.5.	No.26
	92nd Labour Coy.	T.11.d.6.7.	No.26
	110th Labour Coy.	N.27.c.6.6.	No.26
	136th Labour Coy.	N.35.b.6.3.	No.26.

Ref. maps sheet 27, 36A, and HAZEBROUCK.

16/6/18.

SECRET.   Copy No. 34.
                                                                         17/6/18.
                        40th Division Order No. 170.
Ref. Maps.
Sheet 27.) 1/40,000.
Sheet 36A.)

1. 40th Division Order No. 167 is cancelled and all copies should be destroyed.

2. In the event of an enemy attack on the Second Army front, the 40th Division and attached troops will man the WEST HAZEBROUCK Line from D.25.c. in the South to V.6.d. in the North, a distance of about 13,000 yards.

3. For purposes of defence the Divisional Sector is divided into three Brigade Sections, viz:
   120th Inf. Bde.   Southern Section.   H.Qrs at C.9.d.90.35.
   121st Inf. Bde.   Centre Section.   "   U.25.b.3.5.
   119th Inf. Bde.   Northern Section.   "   P.31.d.50.75.
         Divl. Headquarters will be at RENESCURE, T.21.c.4.5.

4. The boundaries of the Brigade Sections are as follows :-

   Southern Section: Southern Boundary, - a line drawn from D.26.c.4.
                      3., D.25.d.3.5., C.29.d.5.8., to C.26.a.5.7.

                      Northern Boundary, - C.6.d.8.2., C.6.c.0.6.,
                      C.5.d.0.., C.4.d.5.2., C.3.d.2.0., C.2.d.0.7.

   Centre Section: Southern Boundary, - Northern boundary of
                      Southern Section.

                      Northern Boundary, - V.21.b.9.0., V.15.c.5.7.,
                      V.14.b.6.0., U.17.a.0.0., U.13.a.0.0.

   Northern Section: Southern Boundary, - Northern boundary of Centre
                      Section.

                      Northern Boundary, - W.7.b.3.7., V.12.b.50.99.,
                      V.6.c.0.5., V.5.Central, P.34.c.8.5., P.32.b.
                      99.60., O.31.a.9.6.

5. The Brigade Sections will be commanded by the following Brigadiers :-

   Southern Section: Brigadier-General C.J.Hobkirk, C.M.G., D.S.O.
                           Commanding 120th Infantry Bde.

   Centre Section: Brigadier-General W.B.Garnett, D.S.O.,
                           Commanding 121st Infantry Bde.

   Northern Section: Brigadier-General F.P.Crozier, C.M.G., D.S.O.,
                           Commanding 119th Infantry Bde.

6. The troops allotted to the defence of the Sections, and their present location are shown in Appendix "A".

7. The line will be held in accordance with the principle laid down in S.S. 210 "The Division in Defence", so far as troops are available, but in any case Brigades will so dispose their troops that they hold the Observation Line and the Main Line of Resistance.

   It must be clearly impressed on the troops that they are to hold the line in which they are posted, whether it be the Observation Line, Main Line of Resistance, or Reserve Line. No withdrawal of troops will take place even from the Line of Observation until orders are issued from Divisional Headquarters to do so.
                                                                        G.O's.C

-ii-

G.O's.C. Infantry Brigades, C.R.E's and Labour Group Commanders will ensure that the instructions laid down in this paragraph are understood by all ranks.

8. The following troops will be conveyed by bus from billets to their assembly positions, under arrangements which have been made by "Q", 40th Division. A table showing embussing and debussing points has been issued :-

        119th Infantry Bde.
        120th Infantry Bde.
        121st Infantry Bde.
        224th Field Coy. R.E.) in lorries, under arrangements
        229th Field Coy. R.E.) made by Maj-General Kenyon.
        26th Labour Group.
        131st Company, 12th Labour Group (with 26th Labour Gr)
        258th Tunnelling Company.

In the event of busses or lorries not being available, units must be prepared to move by march route.
Brigadiers, C.R.E's and Labour Group Commanders will be responsible for the embussing and debussing of troops under their command.

9. The following Assembly Positions are allotted to Sections :-

    Southern Section   ...   C.17.c. and 23.a.
    Centre Section   ...   U.23.b.& d. and U.29.a.
    Northern Section   ...   U.11.

On the alarm being given, all Field, Tunnelling, Army Troops, Area Employment and Labour Companies will be concentrated by their C.R.E's. and Labour Group Commanders at the assembly positions, and there handed over to Infantry Brigades to whom they are allotted.
At the same time each Brigade will send forward a staff officer to the assembly positions to take over the troops and to issue any necessary orders.

10. 120 rounds of S.A.A. will be carried by each man to the trenches and 2,000 rounds per Lewis Gun.
Brigades will be responsible for the further supply of ammunition to attached troops once they have joined their command.

11. Rations for the day and one Iron Ration per man will be carried on the man. Brigades will be responsible that all attached units receive their rations. The S.S.O. will consult with Bde. Headquarters Staff on this subject. Labour Group Commanders and C.R.E's. will establish a Headquarters in the vicinity of Brigade Headquarters.

12. Medical arrangements are laid down in R.A.M.C. Operation Order No. 74 dated 15/6/18.
The Labour Group Commanders of Nos. 5, 31, and 64 Groups will each detail 100 unarmed men as stretcher bearers. These men will report for duty as follows :-

From 64 Labour Group, for Southern Section at C.2.c.3.9., reporting to Captain W.L. Johnson, R.A.M.C.
From 31 Labour Group, for Centre Section at U.16.b.6.4., reporting to Lieutenant N. McCullough, R.A.M.C.
From 5 Labour Group, for Northern Section at V.1.c.7.2., reporting to Captain Elkington, R.A.M.C.

13. Reconnaissance of the line has been carried out by battalion staffs of 119th and 120th Infantry Bdes. Battalion staffs of 121st Infantry Bde. will carry out the reconnaissance on the day following their arrival in the ST.MARTIN-AU-LAERT area.

-iii-

14. Brigades will prepare a scheme for the occupation of their Section with the troops allotted in Appendix "A".

These schemes should be based on the assumption that Brigades have two battalions of infantry in the line and one battalion in reserve.

All Labour Companies will be affiliated to battalions and will not be grouped separately.

In the event of this order being put into force before the 19th instant, the Reserve Battalions of the 119th and 120th Infantry Brigades will be attached to 121st Infantry Brigade to man the Centre Section.

Copies of schemes to be submitted to Divisional Headquarters.

15. A daily state will be issued to Brigades showing the approximate number of rifles and Lewis Guns at their disposal.

16. Acknowledge by wire.

Major.

Issued at... 9 p.m.

General Staff, 40th Division.

Copy No. 1 to G.O.C.
2. 119 Bde.
3. 120 Bde.
4. 121 Bde.
5. Div. Sig. Coy.
6. No. 5 Labour Group.
7. No. 12 Labour Group.
8. No. 26 Labour Group.
9. No. 31 Labour Group.
10. No. 64 Labour Group.
11. Labour Commdt. VIIth Corps.
12. ,, ,, G.H.Q. Defence Lines.
13. C.R.E., 40th Div.
14. C.R.E., No. 1 Sect.
15. C.R.E., No. 2.3.5. Sect.
16. Lt. Col. Pakenham Walsh R.E. DOORNAERT.
17. Lt. Col. H. Butler, R.E. BLARINGHEM.
18. Lt. Col. E.W. White, R.E. ST. MOMELIN.
19. A.D.M.S.
20. D.A.D.V.S.
21. D.A.D.O.S.
22. Div. Train.
23. 40th Div. M.T. Coy.
24. S.S.O.
25. A.P.M.
26. Camp Comdt.
27. Div. Gas Officer.
28. VIIth Corps G.
29. VIIth Corps Q.
30. XVth Corps G.
31. XVth Corps. Q.
32. 40th Div. "Q".
33. File.
34 - 35. War Diary.

APPENDIX "A".

(To 40th Division Order No. 170.)

Unit.	Location.	Approximate rifle strength.	Employed under the command of
SOUTHERN SECTION.			
Infantry.			
120th Infantry Bde.	LEDERZEELE.	2265	
R.E.			
236 Army Troops Coy.	C.9.SERCUS.	130	Lt.Col.Hoysted. O.25.c.2.7, C.R.E.40th Divn. DOORNAERT.
229 Field Coy.	B.25.b.5.2.	100	
258 Tunnelling Coy. (less 1 Section)	M.29.a.0.0.	170	Lt.Col.White,R.E. ST.HOMELIN.
Labour Coys.			
64th Labour Group consisting of :-	BLARINGHEM.		
No. 3 Labour Coy.	C.23.b.	140	
No. 4 Labour Coy.	C.4.c.7.6.	210	
No.35 Labour Coy.	C.8.central.	380	
No.48 Labour Coy.	C.5.d.5.3.	260.	
No. 136 Labour Coy.	U.26.b.5.2.	250	Labour Commdt. ST. OMER Defences.
No. 174 Labour Coy.	36A/I.3.a.8.5.	140	
26th Labour Group consisting of :-	EBBLINGHEM		
No. 6 Labour Coy.	M.35.b.3.6.	)	
No. 84 Labour Coy.	S.6.a.5.5.	)	
No. 92 Labour Coy.	T.11.d.6.7.	) 30	
No.110 Labour Coy.	N.27.c.6.6.	)	
No.138 Labour Coy.	N.35.b.6.3.	)	
Total No. of Rifles :-		4075.	
CENTRE SECTION.			
Infantry.			
121st Infantry Bde. (H.Q. only).	ST.MARTIN-AU-LAERT.	50	
R.E.			
234 Field Coy.	U.1.b.6.7.	70	Lt.Col.Hoysted. C.R.E. 40th Divn.
224 Field Coy.	H.33.b.6.5.	75.	
173 Tunnelling Coy.	BLARINGHEM.	290	Lt.Col.Butler, BLARINGHEM.
554 Army Troops Coy.	T.11.a.3.8.	130	-do-
Carry forward :-		615	

-ii-

APPENDIX A Continued.

Unit.	Location.	Approximate rifle strength.	Employed under the command of
CENTRE SECTION (Continued).	Bt. Fwd.	615	
Labour Coys.			
5th Labour Group consisting of :-	U.4.d.3.4.		
No. 12 Labour Coy.	C.5.d.9.5.	350	)
No. 13 Labour Coy.	V.13.d.3.3.	350	)
No. 55 Labour Coy.	V.25.a.7.2.	350	)
No. 61 Labour Coy.	V.3.c.8.3.	350	) Labour Comdt.
No. 94 Labour Coy.	C.22.d.6.5.	350	) VIIth Corps.
No.111 Labour Coy.	V.15.a.7.3.	350	)
No.132 Labour Coy.	P.36.a.9.2.	350	)
No.164 Labour Coy.	P.36.d.6.8.	350	)
No.178 Labour Coy.	C.5.b.8.8.	350	)
Total No. of Rifles :-		3765.	

NORTHERN SECTION.

Infantry.

119th Infantry Bde.	MEURIS.	2500	
R.E.			
231 Field Coy.	V.15.a.5.1.	105	C.R.E. 40th Div.
227 Field Coy.	N.12.c.8.1.	80	Lt.Col.Hoysted.
214 Army Troops Coy.	U.13.a.4.8.	115	Lt.Col.Butler.
Labour Coys.			
31st Labour Group consisting of :-	O.36.b.1.8.		)
No. 67 Labour Coy.	U.5.c.8.9.	350	)
No. 93 Labour Coy.	STAPLE.	350	) Labour Comdt.
No.133 Labour Coy.	U.9.b.3.9.	350	) VIIth Corps.
No.147 Labour Coy.	U.10.c.9.1.	350	)
No.188 Labour Coy.	P.25.b.central.	350	)
Total No. of Rifles :-		4550.	

SECRET.   (W)   Copy No. 35   18
                                                           20/2/18.

                        40th DIVISION ORDER NO. 171.
                        ★★★★★★★★★★★★★★★★★★★★★★★★★★★★
Ref. Map
HAZEBROUCK.

In continuation of 40th Division Order No. 170 dated 17/2/18.—

The following routes will be used by busses and troops moving to the assembly positions laid down in para. 9 of the above mentioned order.

1. BUSSES or LORRIES.

		Embussing Point.	Route.	Debussing Point.
(a)	119th Bde.	HAVERSHERQUE FM. Head of column facing E. at M.2.d.1.1.	LEDERZEELE – LEMENEGAT – QUEUE de BAVINCHOVE – LONGUE CROIX – LE BREARDE.	LE BREARDE.
(b)	120th Bde.	LEDERZEELE CROSS Roads. Head of column facing S. of G.27.b.8.0.	ST. OMER – ARQUES – WARDRECQUES – BLARINGHEM.	LA BELLE HOTESS and SERCUS.
(c)	121st Bde.	SCADERBOURG. Head of Column South of R.33.a.5.0.	ST. OMER – ARQUES – EBBLINGHEM WALLON-CAPPEL	LES CINQ RUES.
(d)	26th Lab. Gr. 258th Tunnelling Co.	LE NIEPPE. Head of Col. facing S. at T.11.a.5.7.	RENESCURE – WARDRECQUES – BLARINGHEM.	LE CROQUET.
(e)	224 Field Co. R.E.	BALEMBERG. H.33.b.2.5. Col. facing E.	ZUYTPEENE – QUEUE de BAVINCHOVE	WALLON CAPPEL.
(f)	229 Field CO. R.E.	LES CINQ RUES B.25.c.8.8. facing N.	ANNEKE – WEMARS CAPPEL CASSEL – HONDEGHEM.	HONDEGHEM.

NOTE. 1. The Debussing Points have been fixed provisionally. The actual point at which troops will debuss will depend on enemy action. The Officer Commanding the troops on the spot will order the debussing to take place.

2. UNITS MOVING BY ROAD.

(a) Troops allotted to 120th Brigade.

		Route.
No. 2 Labour Coy.		Road in C.22.d.
3	,,	Cross country.
174	,,	WALLON CAPPEL – THIENNES Road,– Road in C.16.c.& d.
236 A.T.Coy.		Road in C.9.d.,– C.16.a.c.& d.
35 Labour Coy.		Road in C.8.d., SERCUS – C.9.d., C.16.a.c.& d.
4	,,	Road in C.4.c., C.10.a.& c., C.10.c.& d.
136	,,	SERCUS Road, thence C.9.c., C.16.c.& d.
31	,,	Road, U.19.a.& c., C.8.b., C.16.a.& c. C.16.c.& d.
48	,,	BOIS des Huit Rues Road., Road in C.17 a.

-ii-

2. (b) **Troops allotted to 121st Brigade.**

		Route.
No.173 Tunnelling Coy.		THIENNES - WALLON CAPPEL Road.
94 Labour Coy.		,, ,,
554 A. T. Coy.		BOIS DU HUIT RUES - WALLON CAPPEL Road.
12 Labour Coy.		Track in U.29.a,c,& d.
178	,,	,, ,,
111	,,	V.14.13. & U.18.
13	,,	,, ,,
61	,,	V.9. & V.8 central. U.12.b.& c.
132	,,	U.18.c.& d. - LA BRIARDE, LAKREULE, WEKE MOLIN, LES CINQ RUES.
164	,,	P.32.central, HONDEGHEM, V.13.central RYCK-HOUT CASTEEL.
55	,,	HONDEGHEM, RYCK-HOUT CASTEEL.
234 Field Coy.R.E.		LES CINQ RUES , WALLON CAPPEL.

2. (c) **Troops allotted to 119th Brigade.**

		Route.
231 Field Coy.R.E.		V.8.central, V.7.d.& b.& a. , U.12.b.& a.
227	,,	P.26.d.& c. , P.32.& 31. LES CISEAUX
188 Labour Coy.		P.25.central. - P.31.a & c. - LES CISEAUX.
147	,,	)
93	,,	) Cross Country route.
67	,,	)
133	,,	LONGUE CROIX.
214 A.T.Coy.		LE HEIL - U.15.a.& c. U.16.a.& c.

NOTE. 1. 300 yards distance will be maintained between Coys. on the march.
2. In the event of a Block on the roads, troops will march off the road until clear of the obstruction.
3. Should troops of 31st Division be met on the Line of March, they are to have priority of road.
4. In the event of locations of Coys. being altered before amendment is notified, the Group Commander will detail the route to the assembly position.

3. Acknowledge.

Issued at 9.p.m.

General Staff, 40th Division.

Copy No. 1 G.O.C.
2 119 Bde.
3 120 Bde.
4 121 Bde.
5 Div. Signal Coy.
6 No. 5 Lab. Group.
7 No. 12 Lab. Group.
8 No. 26 Lab. Group.
9 No. 31 Lab. Group.
10 No. 64 Lab. Group.
11 Labour Comdt. VIIth Corps.
12 Labour Comdt. G.H.Q. Defence Lines.
13 C.R.E., 40th Div.
14 C.R.E., No. 1 Sector.
15 C.R.E., 2, 3 & 5. Sector.
16 Lt. Col. Butler, R.E. Blaringhem.
17. Lt. Col. E.W. White, ST. MOMELIN.
18 Major-General E.R. Kenyon.
19 A.D.M.S.
20 D.A.D.V.S.
21 D.A.D.O.S.
22 Div. Train.
23 40th Div. M.T. Coy.
24 S.S.O.
25 A.P.M.
26 Camp Commandant.
27 Div. Gas Officer.
28 VIIth Corps   G.
29 VIIth Corps   Q.
30 XVth Corps   G.
31 XVth Corps   Q.
32 Second Army.
33 40th Div. "Q".
34 File.
35-36 War Diary.

Appendix E. 21

SECRET.
****

Copy No. 36.
21/6/18.

40th Division Warning Order NO.172.

The Division will be prepared to move by march route, tomorrow the 22nd instant.

W Cavlin
Major.
General Staff, 40th Division.

Issued at 11.a.m.

To all recipients of 40th Div. Order No. 170. of 17/6/18.

Appendix 9. 22

SECRET   Copy No.....   37

40th DIVISION WARNING ORDER NO.173   21/6/18.

Map
Hazebrouck 1/100,000.
Sheet 27/ 1:40,000.
----

1. The 40th Division (less Artillery) will move on 23rd instant, as follows :-

   (a) Divl. Headquarters to RENESCURE, T.21.c.3.5.

   (b) 119th Inf. Brigade, less Transport, by rail from ST.OMER Rly Station to V.19.c. & d.
       Brigade Headquarters will be established at V.13.c.0.6.
       Units of the Brigade will be accommodated under canvas in U.16, 17, and 18.
       Transport will move by road to the Camp.

   (c) 120th Inf. Brigade (less transport) will move by Busses or Lorries from LEDERZEELE Cross Roads G.28.a.0.3. to LA BELLE HOTESSE.
       Bde Headquarters will be established at C.22.c.4.4.
       Units of the Brigade will be accommodated under canvas in C.14, 21 and 22.
       Transport will move by road to the Camp.

   (d) 121st Inf. Brigade (less transport) will move by Busses or lorries from TILQUES Area to LE NOIR TROU.
       Brigade H.Qrs will be established at C.3.c.3.2.
       Units of the Brigade will be accommodated under canvas at U.26, 27, & 28.

   (e) The 224th and 229th Field Companies will be moved into 121st Brigade and 120th Bde areas respectively, under arrangements to be made by Major General KENYON,C.B. who will also arrange for the transfer of C.R.E. 40th Div. from BALEMBERG and C.R.E. No.1 Section from West Hazebrouck Line.

   (f) Other units not mentioned in this order under arrangements being made by 40th Div. "Q".

ACKNOWLEDGE.

Issued at 10 p.m.   Major,
                                              General Staff, 40th Division.

                                              Distribution over-leaf.

Copy No. 1	to	G.O.C.
2		119 Bde.
3		120 Bde.
4		121 Bde.
5		Div. Signal Coy.
6		No. 5 Labour Group.
7		No. 12 ,,
8		No. 26 ,,
9		No. 31 ,,
10		No. 54 ,,
11		Labour Comdt VIIth Corps
12		Labour Comdt. G.H.Q.Defence Lines
13		C.R.E. 40th Div.
14		C.R.E. No.1 Sect.
15		C.R.E. 2, 3 & 5.
16		C.R.E. ST.OMER Defences.
17		Lt.Col. BUTLER, R.E. BLARINGHEM
18		Lt.Col. WHITE, ST.MOMELIN.
19		Major General KENYON.
20		A.D.M.S.
21		D.A.D.V.S.
22		D.A.D.O.S.
23		Div. Train.
24		40th Div. M.T.Coy.
25		S.S.O.
26		A.P.M.
27		Camp Commandant.
28		Div. Gas Officer.
29		VIIth Corps G.
30		VIIth Corps Q.
31		XV Corps G.
32		XV Corps Q.
33		Second Army.
34		40th Div. Claims Officer.
35		40th Div. Q.
36		File
37 & 38		War Diary.

SECRET.   Copy No. 44

    40th DIVISION ORDER NO. 174.   22/6/18.
    ****

Ref. maps
HAZEBROUCK.
Sheet 27/1/40,000.
Sheet 36A 1/40,000.
----

1. The 40th Division is transferred from VIIth to XVth Corps as from to-day.

2. The 40th Division (less Artillery) will move from VIIth Corps area to XVth Corps area to-morrow, in accordance with attached table.

3. On arrival in the new area the Division will be located as shown in 40th Division Administrative Instructions issued with these orders.

4. An officer from Brigade Headquarters will be detailed by Brigades to supervise entraining and detraining, Embussing and Debussing.

  Troops will arrive at ST.OMER Station 30 minutes before train is due to depart.

5. Major General E.R.KENYON, C.B.,C.M.G. is arranging for the move of the Headquarters and two Field Companies Divl. R.E. to the new area.

6. Move of units not mentioned in this table is being arranged by 40th Div. "Q".

7. All transport will move by road under Brigade arrangements. Any roads may be used.

8. Completion of moves and location of Headquarters will be notified to Divl. Headquarters by telegram.

9. Divl. Headquarters will close at LEDERZEELE at 3.0 p.m. and will re-open at RENESCURE at the same hour.

10. ACKNOWLEDGE.

              W. Carter
                  Major,

Issued at 5 p.m.
          General Staff, 40th Division.

              Distribution over-leaf.

Copy No. 1 to G.O.C.
2. 119 Bde.
3. 120 Bde.
4. 121 Bde.
5. Div. Signal Coy.
6. No. 5 Labour Group.
7. No. 12 ,,
8. No. 26 ,,
9. No. 31 ,,
10. No. 64 ,,
11. Labour Comdt VIIth Corps
12. Labour Comdt. G.H.Q. Defence Lines.
13. C.R.E. 40th Division.
14. C.R.E. No. 1 Sect.
15. C.R.E. 2, 3 & 5.
16. C.R.E. ST. OMER Defences.
17. Lt. Col. BUTLER, R.E. BLARINGHEM.
18. Lt. Col. WHITE, ST. MOMELIN.
19. Major General KENYON.
20. A.D.M.S.
21. D.A.D.V.S.
22. D.A.D.O.S.
23. Div. Train.
24. 40th Div. M.T. Coy.
25. S.S.O.
26. A.P.M.
27. Camp Commandant.
28. Div. Gas Officer.
29. VIIth Corps G.
30. VIIth Corps Q.
31. XV Corps G.
32. XV Corps Q.
33. Second Army
34. Area Commandant LEDERZEELE.
35. ,,, ST. MOMELIN.
36. ,,, ST. MARTIN AU LAERT.
37. ,,, BLARINGHEM.
38. ,,, RENESCURE.
39. 40th Division Reception Camp.
40. 40th Div. Claims Officer.
41. 40th Div. "Q".
42. File
43 & 44. War Diary

Table to accompany 40th Division Order No. 174.

Serial No.	Formation	From	To.	Method of movement	Embussing Point or Entraining Station.	Debussing Pt. or Detraining Station	Remarks
1.	H.Q. 40th Division.	LEDERZEELE	RENESCURE T.21.c.5.5.	Lorries	--	--	
2.	119th Inf. Bde.	ST. MOMELIN AREA	Area S.W. of HONDEGHEM.	Tactical Train	ST. OMER	About V.19.	Two trains each capable of carrying 1900 all ranks. 1st Train leaves 10 a.m. 2nd Train leaves 1 p.m.
3.	120th Inf. Bde.	LEDERZEELE AREA	Area West of BELLE HOTESSE	Bus.	ST.MOMELIN-LEDERZEELE Road. Head of column facing S.W. at G.53.c.	East of BLAR-INGHEM, from B.23.b. to C.13.d.	Embussing to commence about 8 a.m. Route ST.MOMELIN- OWERSTEL- SERQUES-TILQUES X.4 - X.10 - ARQUES-CAMPAGNE- B.28.d.- BLARINGHEM.
4.	121 Inf. Bde.	EPERLECQUES AREA	Area West of WALLON CAPPEL.	Bus	TILQUES-ST.OMER Rd. Head of column about R.26.central.	About U.19 & U.20.	Embussing to commence about 2 pm. Route X.4 - X.10 - ARQUES - EBBLINGHEM.

SECRET.

11th Cam Highrs

S 24

40TH DIVISION.
ORDER OF BATTLE.

Headquarters Staff.	Page 1.
Royal Artillery.	Pages 1 & 2.
Royal Engineers.	Page 2.
119th Infantry Brigade.	Page 3.
120th Infantry Brigade.	Pages 3 & 4.
121st Infantry Brigade.	Page 4.
Divisional Troops.	Page 5.

-------oOo-------

June 25th, 1918.

ORDER OF BATTLE.

4OTH DIVISIONAL HEADQUARTERS.

Commander.	Maj.-Gen.J.Ponsonby,C.B. C.M.G.,D.S.O.
A.D.C.	Capt.M.D.FitzGibbon,Middx.Reg.
A.D.C. & Camp Commandant.	Capt.J.H.C.Graham, R of O. Coldstream Guards.
G.S.O. (1).	Lt.-Col.C.H.G.Black,D.S.O., 12th Lancers.
G.S.O. (2).	Major W.Carter,M.C. The King's Own (R.Lancs.R.).
G.S.O. (3).	Capt.R.McL.Chapman,M.C.,Gen.List (A/Bde.Major 121st Bgde).
A.A. & Q.M.G.	Lt.-Col.C.F.Moores,C.M.G., D.S.O.,A.S.C.
D.A.A.G.	Maj.A.L.Cowtan,M.C.,London Regiment (T.F).
D.A.Q.M.G.	Maj.S.Dawson,M.C., R.A.
A.D.M.S.	Col.L.Humphry.C.M.G.,A.M.S.
D.A.D.M.S.	Major A.G. Jebb, R.A.M.G.
D.A.D.V.S.	Major W.N.Rowston, A.V.C.
A.P.M.	Capt.C.L.B.Powell,Gen.List.
D.A.D.O.S.	Maj.G.Edwardes-Lawrence,M.C. A.O.D.
Div.Intell.Offr.	Capt.E.R.NASON,(acting G.S.O. (3).
Div.Claims.Offr.	Lt.J.W.Bowler, The Buffs.
Div.Gas Officer.	
S.C.F.(C.of E).	Rev.H.Gibson, M.C.,C.F.
S.C.F.(non C.of E).	Rev.E.Mathias, C.F.
Liaison Officer.	M. le. sous Lieut.Desmazes.

DIVISIONAL ARTILLERY.

Commander.	Brig-Genl.C.E.Palmer,C.M.G., D.S.O.,R.A.
Brigade Major.	Maj.F.A.Pile,D.S.O.,M.C.,R.A.
Staff Captain.	Capt.H.J.P.Oakley,MC.RA.(TF).
Staff Lieut.	Lieut.W.D.Key,R.F.A.

DIVISIONAL ARTILLERY (Contd).

178th Bde.R.F.A.   Lt.-Col.T.McGowan, D.S.O.
Adjutant.   Capt.W.D.Pile,

Battery Commdrs.
'A' Battery.   Major K.P.Atkinson.
'B' Battery.   Major H.B.Emerton.
'C' Battery.   Major H.B.Bavister.
'D' Battery.   Major A.L.Wilks,M.C.

181st Bde. R.F.A.   Lt-Co.Hon.H.R.Scarlett,
    D.S.O.,R.F.A.
A/Adjutant.   Lt.L.I.J.Sharkey.

Battery Commdrs.
'A' Battery.   Major E.L.Cook.
'B' Battery.   Major W.J.Deacon.
'C' Battery.   Major W.B.J.Grey,M.C.
'D' Battery.   Major H.P.Nesham,M.C.

40th Div.Ammn.Col.   Lt-Col.R.R.Stewart,(T.F).R.A.
Adjutant.   Capt.W.G.Meacock.

DIVISIONAL ENGINEERS.

Commander.   Lt-Col.W.P.E.Lock-M.Walsh.
    M.C.,R.E.
Adjutant.   Capt.H.R.Ruggles-Brise,
    M.C.,R.E.

R. E. Units.
224th Field Coy.   Major E.L.Martin,M.C.,R.E.
229th Field Coy.   Major F.W.Clark,M.C.,R.E.
231st Field Coy.   Major J.E.Villa,M.C.,R.E.

40th Div.Signal Coy.   Major G.E.Carpenter,M.C.,
    R.E.

119TH INFANTRY BRIGADE.

Commander. Brig.-Genl.F.P.Crozier,
C.M.G.,D.S.O.
Brigade Major. Capt.A.J.Muirhead,M.C.,
Oxford Yeomanry.
Staff Captain. Capt.R.W.May,M.C.,Welsh Regt.

U N I T S.

13th Garr.Bn.R.Innis.Fus.
Commander. Lt-Col.J.F.Plunkett,D.S.O.,
M.C.,D.C.M.
2nd in Command. Maj.T.K.Fardoe,D.S.O.,
Adjutant. Capt.D.P.Fleming.

13th Garr.Bn.E.Lancs.Regt.
Commander. Lt-Col. R.I.B.Johnson D.S.O.
2nd in Command. Major S.Tabor.
Adjutant. Capt. G.W.Stopford.

12th Garr.Bn.N.Staffs.Regt.
Commander.
2nd in Command. Major H.F.Wallis.
A/Adjutant. Capt.A.G.F.Pitts.

120TH INFANTRY BRIGADE.

Commander. Brig-Genl.C.J.Hobkirk,
E.M.G.,D.S.O.
Brigade Major. Capt.H.G.Eady,M.C.,R.E.
Staff Captain. Capt.H.B.Kerr,M.C.,Gen.List.

11th Garr.Bn.Cameron Hldrs.
Commander. Lt-Col.Hon.O.R.Vivian,M.V.O.,D.S.O.
2nd in Command. Maj.J.T.Gracie.
Adjutant. Capt.J.Neilson.

10th Garr.Bn.K.O.S.Bdrs.
Commander. Lt-Col.M.Archer-Shee,D.S.O.
2nd in Command. Major S.Boyle,M.C.

120TH INFANTRY BRIGADE (Contd).

15th Garr.Bn.K.O.Y.L.I.
Commander.   Lt-Col.F.C.McCordick.
2nd in Command.   Major H.J.R.Bock.
Adjutant.   Capt.L.M.Eamdison.

12th Yorks Regt.
Bn.Training Staff.
Commander.   Lt-Col.H.W.Becher,D.S.O.
Adjutant.   Capt.T.K.G.Ridley.

121ST INFANTRY BRIGADE.

Commander.   Brig.Genl.W.B.Garnett,D.S.O.
Brigade Major.   Capt R.C.Matthews,M.C.,
    The King's Own(R.Lancs.R)(Detd)
A/Brigade Major.   Capt.R.McL.Chapman,M.C.Gen.List.
Staff Captain.   Capt.P.H.Lawless,Gen.List.

U N I T S.

2nd Garr.Bn. R.Irish.Regt.
Commander.   Lt-Col.M.A.Tighe.
2nd in Command.   Major T.Carson.
Adjutant.   Capt.T.R.Robinson.

2nd Garr.Bn.Lancs.Fus.
Commander.   Lt-Col.G.Hesketh,D.S.O.
2nd in Command.   Major G.L.Bennett.
Adjutant.   Capt.J.Brown.

23rd Garr.Bn.Cheshire Regt.
Commander.   Lt-Col.A.E.Churcher.
2nd in Command.   Major W.A.H.Vincent.
Adjutant.   Capt.W.A.Garrett.

17th Garr.Bn.Worcester Regt.
Commander.   Lt-Col.T.W.T.Isaac.
2nd in Command.   Major R.J.Ingles.
Adjutant.   Major F.R.O'Neill.

ARMY SERVICE CORPS.

40th Divisional Train A.S.C.

Commander.	Lt.-Col. E.G. Evans, D.S.O., A.S.C.
S.S.O.	Capt. L.E.S. Leese, A.S.C.
Adjutant.	Capt. H.E. Cowan, M.C., A.S.C.
40th Divn. M.T. Coy.	Major J. Gilman, A.S.C.

MEDICAL UNITS.

135th Field Ambulance.	Lt.-Col. R.N. Hunt, D.S.O.
136th Field Ambulance.	Lt.-Col. I.R. Hudleston.
137th Field Ambulance.	Lt.-Col. W. McK.H. McCullagh, D.S.O., M.C.

VETERINARY UNIT.

51st Mob. Vet. Section.	Capt. S. Hunter, A.V.C.

-------oOo-------

SECRET   Copy No......

40th DIVISION ORDER NO. 175.   24/6/18.

Ref. map
HAZEBROUCK 1:100,000.
Sheet 27A) 1:40,000.
Sheet 36A)

1. 40th Division orders Nos. 170 and 171 and Appendix A attached are hereby cancelled and should be destroyed.

2. In the event of an enemy attack on the Second Army front the 40th Division and attached troops will man the West HAZEBROUCK Line from D.25.c. in the South to the road (inclusive) running through V.6.central, a distance of about 13,000 yards.
Divisional Headquarters is at RENESCURE, T.21.a.15.05.

3. For purposes of defence the Divisional Sector will be divided into three Brigade sections, viz:-

   Southern Section, with Headquarters at C.21.d.0.3.
   Centre Section,   ,,   C.3.c.5.3.
   Northern Section,   ,,   V.13.c.0.6. P.31.d.50.75

4. The boundaries of Brigade sections are as follows :-

   Southern Section : Southern boundary - a line drawn from D.26.c.4.5. - D.25.d.3.5. - C.29.d.5.8. to C.26.a.5.7.

   Northern boundary - C.6.d.8.2. - C.6.c.0.6. - C.5.d.0.3. - C.4.d.5.2. - C.3.d.2.0. - C.2.d.0.7.

   Centre Section :- Southern Boundary - Northern boundary of Southern section.

   Northern Boundary - V.21.b.9.0. - V.15.c.5.7. - V.14.b.6.0. - U.17.a.0.0. - U.13.a.0.0.

   Northern section: Southern boundary. Northern boundary of Centre Section.

   Northern boundary - W.7.b.3.7. - V.12.b.50.99. - V.6.c.0.5. - V.5.central - P.34.c.8.5. - P.32.b.99.60. - O.31.a.9.6.

5. The Brigade Sections will be commanded by the following Brigadiers :-

   Southern section - Brigadier General C.J.Hobkirk,C.M.G.,D.S.O. Commanding 120th Infantry Brigade.

   Centre Section - Brigadier General W.B.Garnett,D.S.O. Commanding 121st Infantry Brigade.

   Northern Section - Brigadier General F.P.Crozier, C.M.G.,D.S.O. Commanding 119th Infantry Brigade.

6.....

-ii-

6. The troops allotted to the defence of the Sections, and their present location, are shown in Appendix "A".

7. The line will be held in accordance with the principle laid down in S.S.210 "The Division in Defence". Troops will be so disposed that they hold the Line of Observation, Main Line of Resistance, Reserve Line and Defended Localities.

It must be clearly impressed on the troops that they are to hold the line in which they are posted, whether it be the Observation Line, Main Line of Resistance, or Reserve Line. No withdrawal of troops will take place even from the Line of Observation until orders are issued from Divisional Headquarters to do so.

G.O's.O. Infantry Brigades, C.R.E's and Labour Group Commanders will ensure that the instructions laid down in this paragraph are understood by all ranks.

8. The following troops will be conveyed by bus from billets to their assembly positions, under arrangements which have been made by "Q" 40th Division.

26th Labour Group & ~~131st Labour Coy.~~ } will embus at
258th Tunnelling Coy. }
LE NIEPPE: head of column facing South at T.11.a.5.7
Troops for Southern section will proceed via
RENESCURE, WARDREQUES and BLARINGHEM, debussing at
LE CROQUET. Those for Northern section via STAPLE,
debussing at LONGUE CROIX.

236 A.T.Company) in lorries under arrangements made by
207 Field Coy.) Major General KENYON,C.B.,C.M.G.

In the event of busses or lorries not being available, units must be prepared to move by march route.
C.R.E's and Labour Group Commanders will be responsible for the embussing and debussing of troops under their command.

9. The following assembly positions are allotted to sections :-

Southern section ... C.17.c. and C.23.a.
Centre Section ... U.23.b & d and U.29.a. - U.18.d.
Northern section ... U.11.

Divisional reserve will assemble at U.19.d., U.20.c.

On the alarm being given, all Field, Tunnelling, Army Troops, Area Employment and Labour Companies will be concentrated by their C.R.E's and Labour Group Commanders at the Assembly position and there handed over to Infantry Brigade Commanders. Should these Commanders wish any particular Company to occupy a specified position in the line, instead of assembling at the position, they will issue orders to that effect.

Each Brigade will send a Staff Officer to the assembly positions to take over the troops and to issue the necessary orders.

10. 120 rounds of S.A.A. will be carried by each man to the trenches, and 2,000 Rounds per Lewis Gun. Brigades will be responsible for the further supply of ammunition to attached troops once they come under their command.

Three.....

-iii-

Three reserve Ammunition Dumps will be established in each Brigade area.

11. Rations for the day and one Iron ration per man will be carried on the man. Brigades will be responsible that all attached units receive their rations. The S.S.O. will consult with Brigade Headquarters Staff on this subject. Labour Group Commanders and C.R.E's will establish a Headquarters in the vicinity of Brigade Headquarters. In the case of Labour Groups who have a large number of unarmed personnel who do not proceed to the line, an advanced H.Qrs may be established.

12. Medical arrangements are laid down in R.A.M.C. Operation Order No. 74 dated 15/6/18. 76 dated 27.6.18

The Labour Group Commanders of Nos. 5, 31, and 64 Groups will each detail 100 unarmed men as stretcher bearers. These men will report for duty as follows :-

36A/B.13.c.0.0

From 64 Labour Group, for Southern section at B.18.c.5.6. reporting to Captain W.L.Johnson, R.A.M.C. 135 Field Ambulance.

Northern

From 31 Labour Group, for Centre Section at U.16.b.8.4. T.18.c.8.7 reporting to 1st Lieutenant E.P.NORWOOD, M.O.R.C.,U.S.A.
136 Field Ambulance
Centre

From 5 Labour Group, for Northern Section at V.1.c.7.2., T.22.a.3.4 reporting to Captain ELKINGTON, R.A.M.C. 137 Field Ambulance

13. Brigades will prepare a scheme for the occupation of their section with the troops allotted in Appendix A.

All Labour Companies will be affiliated to Battalions for holding the line, and will not be allotted to sub-sections separately.

14. Copies of schemes will be submitted to Divl. Headquarters.

15. Change in location of all units mentioned in this order will be notified to Divl. Headquarters at once.

A C K N O W L E D G E by wire.

Lieut. Colonel,
General Staff, 40th Division.

*****

Issued at 11.50 p.m.

APPENDIX "A" to 40th DIVISION ORDER No.175.

Unit	Location	Approx. Strength. Rifles L.G's	Employed under
Southern Section.			
120th Inf. Bde.	C.21.d.0.3.	2,111 45	
R.E.Troops.			
258th Tunnelling Coy. less 1 section.	27/M.29.a.0.0.	171 1	Lt.Col.White,RE ST.MOMELIN.
Labour Coys.			
84th Labour Group, consisting of :-	BLARINGHEM.		
No.3 Labour Coy.	C.23.b.	230 1)	
4 ,,	C.4.c.7.6.	232)	
6 ,,	C.22.d.2.0.	386)	
31 ,,	T.18.c.2.7.	205 1)	
35 ,,	C.8.central.	380)	Labour Comdt
48 ,,	C.5.d.5.5.	307 1)	ST.OMER
138 ,,	U.22.b.5.2.	331 1)	Defences.
174 ,,	C.22.d.2.0.	292 1)	
Part of 26th Labour Group, consisting of:-	EBBLINGHEM		
No.84 Labour Coy.	S.6.a.5.5.	364)	
92 ,,	T.11.d.6.7.	372)	
110 ,,	N.27.c.6.6.	332)	
		5,793 51	
Centre Section.			
121st Inf. Bde.	C.3.c.5.3.	3,078 42	
R.E.Troops.			
173 Tunnelling Coy.	I.2.b.8.6.	266 1	Lt.Col.Butler RE BLARINGHEM.
Labour Coys.			
5th Labour Group, consisting of :-	U.4.d.2.4.		
No.12 Labour Coy.	C.6.d.9.5.	226 1)	
13 ,,	V.14.b.7.5.	281 1)	
55 ,,	P.20.central.	309 1)	
61 ,,	V.3.c.8.3. V.4.c.6.9	302 1)	Labour Comdt
94 ,,	C.5.c.8.8. U.23.d.55	351 1)	VII Corps
111 ,,	V.15.a.7.3.	213 1)	
132 ,,	V.5.a.7.8.	227 1)	
164 ,,	P.26.d.6.0.	328 1)	
173 ,,	P.26.c.8.6.	302 1)	
		5,883 52	
		5,272 50	
			Northern ......

Unit	Location	Approx.Strength Rifles L.G's.		Employed under

Northern Section.

| 119th Inf. Bde. | V.13.c.0.6. | 2,590 | 48 | |

R.E.

| 227th Field Coy. RE and reinforcements. | P.27.a.2.7 N.12.c.8.1. | 211 | 1 | |

Labour Coys.

31st Labour Group, O.36.b.1.8. consisting of :-

No.87 Labour Coy.	U.5.c.8.9.	363	1	)
93 ,,	U.5.c.5.3.	438	1	)
133 ,,	U.9.b.2.9.	254	1	) Labour Comdt
147 ,,	U.10.b.9.1.	347	1	) VII Corps
188 55 ,,	P.25.b.central	271	1	)
178 ,,	P.20.central	309	1	)
Part of No.'26	P.26.c.8.0. d.6.7. EBBLINGHEM	302	1	)
Labour Group, consisting of :-				)
No.131 Labour Coy.	N.31.a.8.5.	302	1	)
138 ,,	N.35.b.6.3.	311	1	)
151 ,,	T.11.a.8.7.	188	1	)
		5,886	59	

Divisional Reserve, under the command of Lieut. Col. Pakenham Walsh, C.R.E. 40th Division.

229 Field Coy. R.E.	C.3.d.8.1.	100	1	) under
224 ,,	U.18.d.central	101	1	) C.R.E.
231 ,,	V.15.a.4.1.	113	1	) 40th Div.
236 A.T.Coy.	B.25.b.5.3.	127	1	Lt.Col.Close R.E.
234 Field Coy.R.E.	U.1.b.6.7.	107	1	Lt.Col.Hoysted RE
554 A.T.Coy.	C.21.d.8.5.	116	1	Lt.Col.Butler RE.
214 A.T.Coy.	U.13.a.4.8.	113	1	
207 Field Coy. R.E.	H.33.b.6.7.	100	1	
		877	8	

(17th Bn Worcester R.(P).

******

Distribution :-

Copy No.	Recipient
1 to	D.O.C.
2	119 Bde.
3	120 Bde.
4	121 Bde.
5	Div. Signal Coy.
6	No.5 Labour Group
7	No.12 ,,
8	No.26 ,,
9	No.31 ,,
10	No.64 ,,
11	Labour Comdt VIIth Corps
12	Labour Comdt, G.H.Q. Defence Lines.
13	C.R.E. 40th Div.
14	C.R.E. No.4 Sector.
15	C.R.E. 2,3 & 5 Sectors
16	Lt.Col. Butler, R.E.Blaringhem.
17	Lt.Col. E.W.White, ST.MOMELIN.
18	Major General KENYON.
19	A.D.M.S.
20	D.A.D.V.S.
21	D.A.D.O.S.
22	Div.Train
23	40th Div.M.T.Coy.
24	S.S.O.
25	A.P.M.
26	Camp Commandant
27	Div. Gas Officer
28	C.R.E.St.Omer Defences.
29	VII Corps G
30	,, Q
31	XV Corps G
32	,, Q
33	Second Army
34	Claims Officer
35	40th Div. Q
36	File
37 & 38	War Diary
39	C.O.C. R.A. XV Corps
40	XV Corps Heavy Artillery

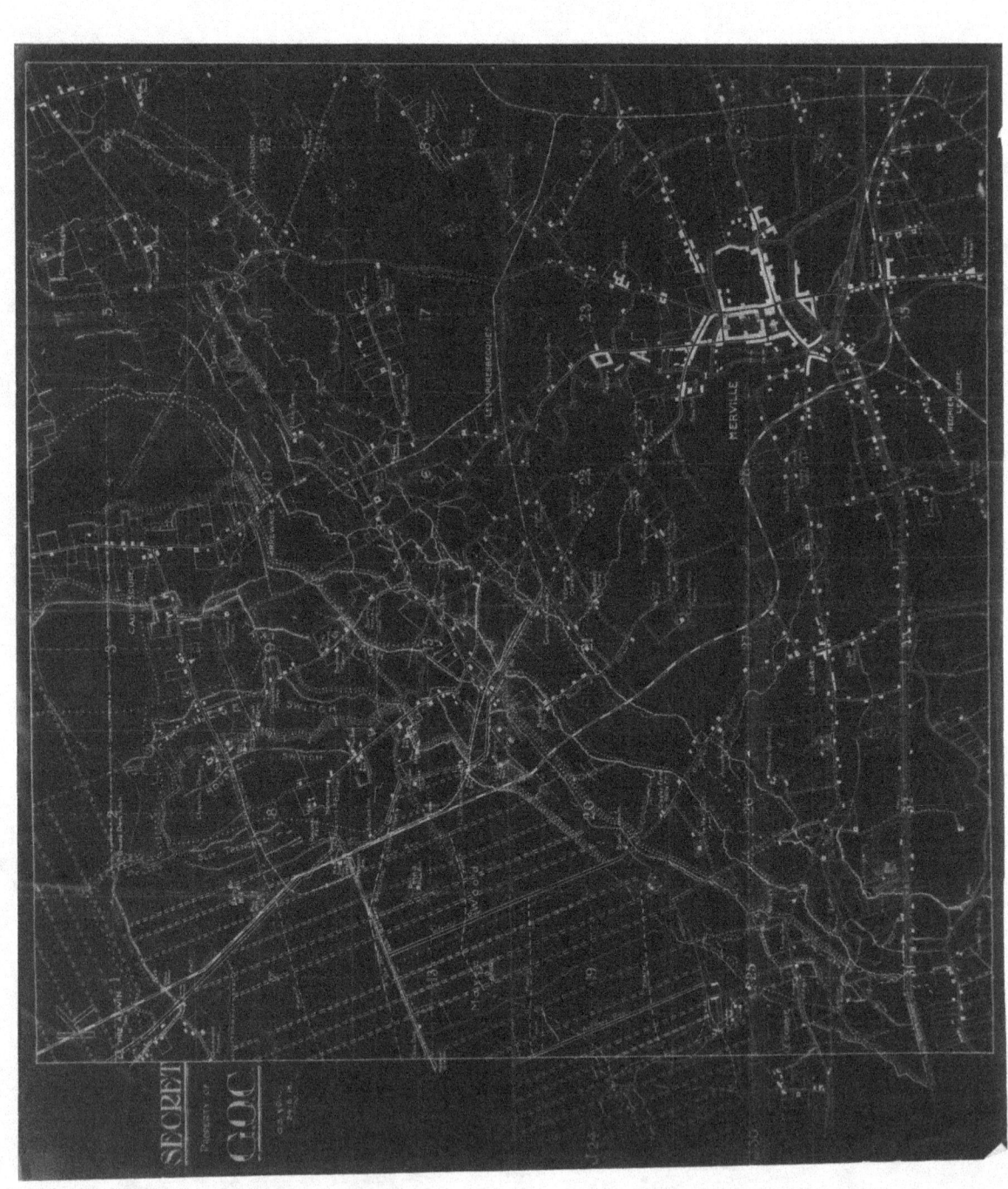

June 18

SECRET   Copy No. 37

40th DIVISION ORDER NO.176.   25/6/18.

1. With reference to 40th Division Order No.175 dated 24/6/18, troops will move to the assembly positions by the following routes :-

   120th Infantry Brigade (Southern Section).

Unit.	Routes
Battalions of Brigade	Routes laid down by Brigadier .
258th Tunnelling Coy.	LE CROQUET LA BELLE HOTESSE Rd.

   64th Labour Group

No.3 Labour Coy.		Cross country Route.
No.4	,,	WALLON CAPPEL - LA BELLE HOTESSE Road - C.16.c & d.
No.6	,,	Track in C.22.d.
No.31	,,	Track in U.19 - ST.LEGER - SERCUS -C.16.c & d.
No.35	,,	SERCUS - C.16.c & d.
No.48	,,	Track in C.11.a. & c & C.17.a.
No.136	,,	WALLON CAPPEL - BELLE HOTESSE Rd - C.16.c & d.
No.174	,,	- do -

   (handwritten: SERCUS - C.16 c & d.)

   26th Labour Group

No.84 Labour Coy.	)	
No.92	,,)	LE CROQUET - LA BELLE HOTESSE Rd.
No.110	,,)	

   121st Infantry Brigade (Centre Section).

Battalions of Brigade.	Routes as laid down by Brigadier .
173rd Tunnelling Coy.	LA BELLE HOTESSE - WALLON CAPPEL Road.

   5th Labour Group.

No.12 Labour Coy.		Track through U.29.a. & d. and C.5.b.
No.13	,,	Track through V.14.a & b - V.13.b & a, U.19.c. & d.
~~No.55~~	~~,,~~	~~HONDEGHEM - V.7.d. - U.18.~~
No.61	,,	V.7 & 8 - V.13 - U.18. *(Hondeghem - V.8 ceuT. U.18.d.)*
No.94	,,	Track in U.29.a & d. *(Camped on assembly position)*
No.111	,,	Track in V.14 - V.13 - U.18.
No.132	,,)	
No.164	,,)	HONDEGHEM-V.7.d.-U.18.
~~No.178~~	)	

                                                          119th.....

-11-

119th Infantry Brigade (Northern Section).

Battalions of Brigade	Routes as laid down by Brigadier.
227th Field Company.	LES TROIS ROIS - QUEUE DE BAVINCHOVE - LONGUE CROIX.

31st Labour Group.

No.67 Labour Coy.
No.93   ,,
No.133   ,,
No.147   ,,
No.188   ,,
No. 55   ,,
No. 178
26 Labour Group
  131 Labour Coy.
  138   ,,
  151   ,,

Track in U.5.d.
Track in U.10.a & d.
Cross Country Route.
P.31.a & c - U.6.b & a - U.5.d.
CAMPAGNE DREVE-CASSEL WALLON CAPPEL Road
P.31.c & d. and U.6.a.
Hondeghem - V.S central - V.18 d.

Track in U.5.d.

Divisional Reserve.

229th Field Coy.	LE NOIR TROU
224th ,,	Track in U.17 & 18 and HAZEBROUCK -EBBLINGHEM Road.
231st ,,	Track in V.14 - U.17 & 18 and HAZEBROUCK - EBBLINGHEM Road.
236 A.T.Company.	Debus at Assembly Position.
234 Field Company	LES SIX RUES - LE HEYL.
554 A.T.Company.	LYNDE - Track in U.25.c.
214 A.T.Company.	U.13 - U.20.
207 Field Company.	Debus at Assembly position.
17th Worcestershire Regt. (P.)	HAZEBROUCK - EBBLINGHEM Road.

NOTE 1. 300 yards distance will be maintained between Companies on the march.
  2. In the event of a Block on the roads, troops will march off the road until clear of the obstruction.
  3. Should troops of 29th Division be met on the Line of March, they are to have priority of road.
  4. In the event of locations of Coys being altered before amendment is notified, the Group Commander will detail the route to the assembly position.
  5. Routes are to be reconnoitred.

ACKNOWLEDGE.

W. Carter Major
for Lieut. Colonel,
General Staff, 40th Division.

***

To all recipients of Order No. 175.

SECRET. Copy No. 23

40th DIVISION ORDER NO. 177.   25/6/18.

1. With reference to 40th Div. Order No. 175, a practice concentration of Labour and R.E. units will be carried out on the 27th instant.

2. Labour Group Commanders and C.R.E's of Sectors will arrange for their units (with the exception of those mentioned in the following paragraph) to be at the Assembly Positions allotted to them at 11 a.m. when they will be met by Staff Officers from Brigades and receive orders regarding their disposition in the line.
   These orders will be actually carried out on the ground so far as is possible.

3. (a)   26th Labour Group & 131st Labour Coy. } will move
         258th Tunnelling Coy.

   as complete units only as far as the Bus Concentration Point at LE NIEPPE, arriving there at 9.30 a.m.
   At this point there will only be one bus each for Northern and Southern Sections to take selected officers and N.C.O's to the Assembly Positions. The remainder will, after inspection, march back to billets.

   (b)   236th A.T.Coy.   } will receive orders from Major
         207th Field Coy.

   General KENYON, C.B., C.M.G.

4. In conjunction with this concentration, Brigadiers may, if they please, carry out another practice manning of the WEST HAZEBROUCK Line.

5. The arrangements for stretcher bearers detailed in para. 12 of 40th Div. Order No.175 will also be practised at the same time.

6. Reports on the concentration will be submitted by Labour Group Commanders and C.R.E's of Sectors through the Brigadiers under whose orders their units come in the event of a hostile attack.

7. ACKNOWLEDGE by wire.

Issued at 11.0 p.m.

H.S.Black.   Lt. Col.
General Staff, 40th Division.

Distribution over-leaf.

```
Copy No.1 to  G.O.C.
     2        119 Bde.
     3        120 Bde.
     4        121 Bde.
     5.       No. 5 Labour Group.
     6.       No. 12      ,,
     7.       No. 26      ,,,
     8.       No. 31      ,,
     9.       No. 64      ,,
    10.       Labour Commandant VIIth Corps
    11.          ,,           G.H.Q.Defence Lines.
    12.       C.R.E. 40th Div.
    13.       C.R.E.No.4 Sector
    14.       C.R.E. 2, 3 & 5 Sectors.
    15.       Lt.Col. BUTLER, R.E. BLARINGHEM.
    16.       Lt.Col  E.W.WHITE, ST.MOMELIN.
    17.       Major General KENYON, C.B.,C.M.G.
    18.       A.D.M.S.
    19.       C.R.E. St. OMER Defences.
    20.       XV Corps G.
    21.       40th Div. "Q".
    22.       War Diary.
    23.          ,,
    24.       File.
```

CONFIDENTIAL.   ORIGINAL.

WAR DIARY

40th DIVISION

GENERAL STAFF, BRANCH.

VOL. XXVI

FROM :- 1st July, 1918.
TO   :- 31st July, 1918.

Brig-General,
Commanding 40th Division.

35807. W16879/M1879 500,000 3/17 R.T. (1074) Forms/W3091/3   Army Form W.3091.

Cover for Documents.

Nature of Enclosures.

Notes, or Letters written.

WAR DIARY

40th DIVISION

GENERAL STAFF BRANCH.

VOL. XXVI

FROM :-   1st JULY, 1918.
TO   :-   31st JULY, 1918.

INDEX

Pages 1 - 3   ... War Diary
       4 - 13   ... Appendices.

Army Form C. 2118

WAR DIARY
or
INTELLIGENCE SUMMARY

(Erase heading not required.)

40th DIVISION.

JULY, 1918.

Instructions regarding War Diaries and Intelligence Summaries are contained in F.S. Regs., Part II. and the Staff Manual respectively. Title Pages will be prepared in manuscript.

Place	Date	Hour	Summary of Events and Information	Remarks and references to Appendices
RENESCURE.	1st		Training of the Division continued.	
,,	2nd		Inspection of Infantry Brigades by Field Marshal H.R.H. The Duke of Connaught.	
,,	3rd		Maj-General Sir W.E.Peyton, K.C.B., K.C.V.O., D.S.O., assumed command of the Division in succession to Maj-General J.Ponsonby, C.B., C.M.G., D.S.O., who left to command the 5th Division.	
,,	3rd		One Battalion from each Brigade occupy the East HAZEBROUCK Line for training purposes for 4 days.	
,,	4th		The 119th Trench Mortar Battery is attached for a tour of duty in the line to the 31st Division.	
,,	5th		Training continued.	
,,	6th		The Divisional Field Companies R.E. are transferred from VIIth to XVth Corps.	
,,	7th		Practice concentration of troops allotted to the Southern Section of the West HAZEBROUCK Line is ordered for 10th instant.	Appendix 1.
,,	7th		The battalions occupying the East HAZEBROUCK Line for training purposes are relieved. Three further battalions, one from each Brigade take their place.	
,,	8th		⎫ Training continued.	
,,	9th		⎭	
,,	10th		Orders issued for a practice concentration of the troops allotted to the Centre Section of the West HAZEBROUCK Line.	Appendix 2.
,,	11th		The 119th Trench Mortar Battery returns to the Division from temporary attachment to the 31st Division.	
,,	12th		The last three battalions, (one from each Bde.) relieve three battalions who are training in the East HAZEBROUCK Line.	

Army Form C. 2118

WAR DIARY
or
INTELLIGENCE SUMMARY

40th DIVISION.

(Erase heading not required.)

JULY, 1918.

Instructions regarding War Diaries and Intelligence Summaries are contained in F.S. Regs., Part II. and the Staff Manual respectively. Title Pages will be prepared in manuscript.

Place	Date	Hour	Summary of Events and Information	Remarks and references to Appendices
RENESCURE	12th		Orders issued for a practice concentration of troops allotted to the Northern Section of the West HAZEBROUCK LINE.	Appendix 3
,,	13th		Training continued.	
,,	13th		Authority received for the elimination of the word "Garrison" from the title of the Division. The title of the 2nd Garrison Battalion Royal Irish Regiment is changed to 8th Royal Irish Regiment.	
,,	14th		Training continued.	
,,	15th		All battalions completed one tour of duty in the East HAZEBROUCK Line, and Brigade arrangements have been made for further tours.	
,,	15th		Practice manning under Division Order No. 180 of the Northern Section of the West HAZEBROUCK Line, by troops allotted thereto.	Appendix 3
,,	16th		Training continued.	
,,	17th		119th Inf. Bde. moves to relieve 87th Inf. Bde. of the 29th Div. and for this purpose becomes attached to the 1st Australian Div. in the Line.	
,,	17th		One Coy. of the 17th (Pion) Bn. Worcestershire Regt. is placed at disposal of 119th Inf. Bde. during the period of such attachment.	
,,	17th		Tours in East HAZEBROUCK Line cease.	
,,	18th		Relief of 87th Inf. Bde. by 119th Inf. Bde. and Coy. of 17th Worc Regt. (P) completed.	
,,	18th		Lieut-Gen. Sir W.E.Peyton, K.C.B.,K.C.V.O.,D.S.O., assumed temporary command of the XVth Corps vice Gen. Sir B. de Lisle, K.C.B. on leave. Brigadier-General C.J. Hobkirk, C.M.G., D.S.O. Commanding 120th Inf. Bde. assumed temporary command of the Division.	
,,	19th		In consequence of the detachment of the 119th Inf. Bde. the scheme for the manning of the West HAZEBROUCK Line is reconstructed. See Div. Order 182.	Appendix 4.
,,	20th		Training continued.	

Army Form C. 2118

WAR DIARY
or
INTELLIGENCE SUMMARY

(Erase heading not required.)

40th DIVISION.

JULY, 1918.

Place	Date	Hour	Summary of Events and Information	Remarks and references to Appendices
RENESCURE	21st to 31st		Training continued.	
,,	31st		do.	
,,	31st		The 121st Inf. Bde. relieved the 119th Inf. Bde. in the front line under 1st Australian Division just South of MERRIS on the night 31st July/1st August. Major-Gen. Sir W.E.Peyton, K.C.B., rejoined the 40th Division from XVth Corps.	

[signature] Lieut-Colonel.
General Staff, 40th Division.

1st August, 1918.

Appendix 1

SECRET.   Copy No. 18

40th DIVISION ORDER NO.178.   7/7/18.

1. With reference to 40th Division Order No.175, a practice manning of the trenches in the Southern Section of the West HAZEBROUCK Line will be carried out by the 120th Infantry Brigade and affiliated Labour and R.E. Companies, on Wednesday the 10th instant.

2. Troops of the 120th Brigade will be in position by 10 a.m. They will be re-inforced by the affiliated Labour and R.E. Companies (with the exceptions mentioned in the following paragraphs), under arrangements to be made between G.O.C. 120th Infantry Brigade and Labour Group and R.E. Company Commanders concerned.

3. One bus only will be available to take selected officers and N.C.O's of the 92nd Labour Company and 258th Tunnelling Company from the Bus concentration point LA NIEPPE to the Assembly places allotted by the 120th Infantry Brigade. The 110th Labour Company need not be represented as it is shortly leaving the area. Bus will be at LA NIEPPE cross roads (T.11.a.5.7) at 8 a.m.

4. All Labour and R.E. units will be at the allotted Assembly Places by 9.30 a.m. where they will be met by Staff Officers from Brigade who will give them orders regarding their disposition in the line. These orders will be carried out on the ground, but the units will not move forward from the Assembly Places into the trench system until 10 a.m.

5. Arrangements for stretcher bearers detailed in paragraph 12 of 40th Division Order No. 175 (as amended) will also be practised at the same time.

6. Men of labour units will, in addition to their weapons and equipment, carry great coats and waterproof sheets.

7. Arrangements will be made by Labour Company Commanders, so far as may be possible, to give their men hot dinners in the trenches. Where this is not possible, haversack rations will be taken.

8. Reports on the practice will be submitted by G.O.C. 120th Brigade, Labour Group and R.E. Coy. Commanders concerned.

9. ACKNOWLEDGE.

                                         H.S.Black.
                                                   Lieut. Colonel,
                                    General Staff, 40th Division.

Distribution over-leaf.

Copy No. 1 to G.O.C.
    2   120th Infantry Brigade.
    3   64th Labour Group.
    4   Labour Commandant VIIth Corps.
    5   Labour Commandant G.H.Q. Defence Lines.
    6   A.D.M.S.
    7   C.E. VIIth Corps.
    8   C.R.E. ST. OMER Defences.
    9   VIIth Corps G
   10   XVth Corps G.
   11.   Div. Signal Coy.
   12.   C.R.E. 40th Division.
   13   "Q" 40th Div.
   14   War Diary
   15   "
   16   File

SECRET

ADDENDUM NO.1 to 40th DIVISION ORDER 178
dated 7th July, 1918.

Owing to changes in location of Nos. 31, 136, and 151 Labour Companies, only representatives of these Companies will be required to carry out the practice scheme for manning of the WEST HAZEBROUCK LINE on Wednesday, and the following arrangements for their conveyance will be made:-

1. 2 Busses will be at LE NIEPPE Cross Roads at 8 a.m. to take representatives from the 31st Labour Company as well as those from 92 Labour Coy and 258 Tunnelling Company.

2. One bus will be at Cross Roads BELLE CROIX, B.13.a., at 8 a.m. on Wednesday to take representatives of Nos. 136 and 151 Labour Companies to Assembly Places.

3. 64th Labour Group Commander will detail the numbers from each Company who are to attend.

H.J. Black.   Lieut. Colonel,
General Staff, 40th Division.

7/7/18.

To:-

    120th Infantry Brigade.
    64th Labour Group.
    C.E.VIIth Corps.
    "Q" 40th Division.

SECRET Copy No.......
  10-7-18.
40th DIVISION ORDER No. 179.

1. With reference to 40th Division Order No. 175, a practice manning of the trenches in the Centre Section of the WEST HAZEBROUCK LINE will be carried out by 121st Brigade and affiliated Labour and R.E. Companies on Friday 12th instant.

2. Troops of the 121st Brigade will be in position by 10 am. They will be reinforced by the affiliated Labour and R.E. Companies under arrangements to be made between G.O.C., 121st Bde. and Labour Group and R.E., Company Commanders concerned.

3. All Labour and R.E., units will be at the allotted Assembly Places at 9-30 am. where they will be met by Staff Officers from Brigade who will give them orders regarding their disposition in the line.
   These orders will be carried out on the ground but units will not move forward from the Assembly Places into the trench system until 10 am.

5. Arrangements for stretcher bearers detailed in paragraph 12 of 40th Division Order No. 175 (as amended) will also be practised at the same time.

6. Men of Labour Units will, in addition to their weapons and equipment, carry great-coats and waterproof sheets.

7. Arrangements will be made by Labour Company Commanders, so far as may be possible, to give their men hot dinners in the trenches. Where this is not possible, haversack rations will be taken.

8. Reports on the practice will be submitted by G.O.C., 121st Brigade, Labour Group and R.E., Company Commanders concerned.

9. ACKNOWLEDGE.

                                Lieut-Colonel,
                           General Staff, 40th Division.

Copy No.1 to G.O.C.,
     2   121 Bde.
     3   5th Lab. Group.
     4   Lt.Col. BUTLER, R.E., BLARINGHEM.
     5   Labour Commandant VIIth Corps.
     6   A.D.M.S.
     7   C.E., VIIth Corps.
     8   VIIth Corps "G"
     9   XVth Corps "G"
    10   Div. Sig. Coy.
    11   C.R.E., 40th Div.
    12   40th Div. "Q"
    13   File
    14   War Diary.
    15   War Diary.

SECRET.   Copy ...15...

      40th DIV. ORDER 180.   13/7/18.

1. With reference to 40th Division Order No.175, a practice manning of the trenches in the Northern Section of the WEST HAZEBROUCK Line will be carried out by the 119th Infantry Brigade and affiliated Labour and R.E. Companies on Monday 15th instant.

2. Troops of the 119th Brigade, (including 12th Gar. Bn: N. Staffs) will be in position by 10 am. They will be reinforced by the affiliated Labour and R.E. Companies (with the exception mentioned in following paragraphs), under arrangements to be made between G.O.C. 119th Infantry Brigade and Labour Group and R.E. Company Commanders concerned.

3. One bus will be available to take selected Officers and N.C.Os of the 133rd and 178th Labour Companies. The embussing point will be at STUYVER, N.18.a.f.f. and the bus will be there at 8 am.
    Debussing point will be at HONDEGHEM V.2.b.2.5.

4. All Labour and R.E. units will be at the allotted Assembly Places by 9.30 am. where they will be met by Staff Officers from Brigade who will give them orders regarding their disposition in the line. These orders will be carried out on the ground, but the units will not move forward from the Assembly Places into the trench system until 10 am.

5. Arrangements for stretcher bearers detailed in paragraph 12 of 40th Division Order No. 175 (as amended) will also be practised at the same time.

6. Men of Labour Units will, in addition, to their weapons and equipment, carry great coats and waterproof sheets.

7. Arrangements will be made by Labour Company Commanders, so far as may be possible, to give their men hot dinners in the trenches. Where this is not possible, haversack rations will be taken.

8. Reports on the practice will be submitted by G.O.C., 119th Brigade Labour Group and R.E. Company Commanders concerned.

9. ACKNOWLEDGE.

                                           Lieut-Colonel,
                           General Staff, 40th Division.

Copy No.1 to G.O.C.
     2   119th Bde.
     3   31st Labour Group.
     4   26th   do.
     5   Labour Commandant, VIIth Corps.
     6.   A.D.M.S.
     7.   C.E., VIIth Corps.
     8.   VIIth Corps G.
     9.   XV Corps G.
    10.   Signals.
    11.   C.R.E.
    12.   40th Div. "Q"
    13.   File.
 14 & 15 War Diary.
    16   Lt.Col. HOYSTED R.E.

SECRET.

Appendix A

40th DIVISION ORDER NO. 182.

COPY NO. 38

17/7/18.

Ref Maps
HAZEBROUCK 1/100,000.
Sheet 27)
Sheet 36A)

1. 40th Division Order No. 175, Appendix "A" and amendments thereto are cancelled.

2. In view of the detachment of the 119th Infantry Bde. to the 1st Australian Division it becomes necessary to make a re-distribution of the troops of the Division together with affiliated Labour and R.E.Companies for the occupation of the WEST HAZEBROUCK Line in case of necessity.

3. The Divisional Sector will now be divided into two Brigade Sections, viz:

Southern Section with Headquarters at C.3.c.5.3.

   and Bn. Headquarters at :-

   10th Bn. K.O.S.Bord.   C.23.a.
   15th Bn. K.O.Y.L.I.   C.18.c.3.9.
   11th Bn. Cameron Hrs.   Camp of 23rd Lanc. Fus. at U.27.b.3.C

Northern Section with Headquarters at U.18.d.9.8.

   and Bn. Headquarters at :-

   8th R.Irish Regt.   Camp of 12th N.Staffs.R.at U.10.c.
   23rd Cheshire Rgt.   Camp of 13th R.Innis.Fus at U.17.c.
   23rd Lanc. Fus.   Camp of 13th E.Lanc.Rgt. at V.13.d.

   Divisional Headquarters   RENESCURE.

   Moves in accordance with the above paragraph will be carried out on the 19th instant, under arrangements to be made by the Brigadiers concerned.

   Instructions regarding tonnage are issued in Appendix "B".

4. The boundaries of Brigade Sections are as follows :-

Southern Section: Southern Boundary - A line drawn from D.25.c.5.8 to C.25.c.0.8.

                   Northern Boundary - WALLON CAPPEL along the grid line to U.30.b.1.9. - U.30.b.8.8. - V.25.a.8.8.

Northern Section: Southern Boundary - Northern boundary of Southern Section.

                   Northern Boundary - A line drawn from V.12.b. 50.95. (excl) to V.6.a.5.7. (excl) V.5.c.5.7. - V.4.d.5.7. - V.3.a.0.4. - V.2.a.0.4. - V.1.a. 0.3. - U.6.a.0.1. - U.9.a.5.9.

5. The 120th Infantry Bde. will have responsibility for the defence of the Southern Section and the 121st Infantry Bde. for that of the Northern Section.

N O T E. Nucleus garrisons for the LE PEUPLIER Line between the road in V.6.central (inclusive) and the WINDMILL W.9.b.0.1. (exclusive) will be found by troops under command of Major BELLAMY D.S.O.,R.E., and will be tactically under the orders of the G.O.C. Left Division.

6. The troops allotted to the defence of the Sections, and their present location, are shown in Appendix "A". The Divisional Reserve will form, under the orders of Lieut-Colonel H.W. BECHER D.S.O., 17th Bn. Worcestershire Regt. (P) and will assemble in U.22.a. and b.

7. The line will be held in accordance with the principles laid down in S.S.210 "The Division in Defence". The degree of resistance in each line of defence will be to the last man and the last round.

G.O.Cs. Infantry Brigades, C.R.E's and Labour Group Commanders will ensure that the instructions laid down in this paragraph are understood by all ranks.

8. With certain exceptions, to be notified hereafter, all troops will proceed by march route to places of assembly.

9. Commanders of Sections will select suitable assembly places and inform Divisional Headquarters and the C.R.E's and Labour Group Commanders concerned of these positions.
On the alarm being given, all Field, Tunnelling, and Labour Companies will be concentrated by their C.R.E's and Labour Group Commanders at the assembly positions and there handed over to the Infantry Brigade Commanders. Should these Commanders wish any particular Company to occupy a specified position in the line, instead of assembling at the position, they will issue orders to that effect.
Each Brigade will send a Staff Officer to the Assembly Positions to meet Labour and R.E.Units.

10. 120 rounds S.A.A. will be carried by each man to the trenches and 2,000 rounds per Lewis Gun. Brigades will be responsible for the further supply of ammunition to attached troops, once they come under their command.

11. Rations for the day and one Iron Ration per man will be carried on the man. Brigades will be responsible that all attached units receive their rations. The S.S.O. will consult with Bde. H.Q. Staffs on this subject. Labour Group Commanders will establish a Headquarters in the vicinity of Brigade Headquarters. In the case of Labour Groups who have a large number of unarmed personnel who do not proceed to the Line, an advanced Hd. Qrs. may be established.

12. Medical Arrangements are laid down in R.A.M.C. Operation Order No. 76 dated 27/6/18.
The Labour Group Commanders of Nos. 5.31. and 64 Groups will each detail 100 unarmed men as stretcher bearers: they will report for duty as follows :-
From 64 Labour Group to 135th Field Ambulance at 37A/B.18.c.0.0.
From 31 Labour Group to 136th Field Ambulance at 27/T.18.c.8.7.
From 5 Labour Group to 137th Field Ambulance at 27/T.22.a.3.4.

13. Brigades will prepare a scheme for the occupation of their section with the troops allotted in Appendix "A".
All Labour Companies will be affiliated to Battalions for holding the line and will not be allotted to sub-sections separately.

iii.

14. Copies of Schemes will be submitted to Divisional Headquarters.

15. Changes of location of all units mentioned in this Order will be notified to Divisional Headquarters at once.

16. ACKNOWLEDGE by wire.

[signature] Lieut-Colonel.
General Staff, 40th Division.

Issued at .....

Copies to :-

No. 1 G.O.C.
    2 119th Bde.
    3 120th Bde.
    4 121st Bde.
    5. Div. Signal Coy.
    6 No. 5 Labour Group.
    7   26 ,,
    8   31 ,,
    9   33 ,,
   10   64 ,,
   11 Labour Comdt. VIIth Corps.
   12 Labour Comdt. G.H.Q.Defence Lines.
   13 C.R.E. 40th Div.
   14 17th Worcester Regt. (P).
   15 Lt. Col. Butler, BLARINGHEM.
   16. A.D.M.S.
   17. D.A.D.V.S.
   18. D.A.D.M.S.
   19. Div. Train.
   20 40th Div. M.T.Coy.
   21 S.S.O.
   22 A.P.M.
   23 Camp Comdt.
   24 Div. Gas Officer.
   25 Div. Claims Officer.
   26 VII Corps. "G"
   27   ,, "Q".
   28 XV Corps "G".
   29   ,, "Q".
   30. C.R.E.XV Corps Troops.
   31 C.E. XV Corps.
   32 Second Army.
   33 G.O.C. R.A. XV Corps.
   34 XV Corps Heavy Artillery.
   35 40th Div. "Q".
   36 File
   37) War Diary.
   38)

APPENDIX "A" to 40th Division Order No. 182.

Unit	Location	Approximate Strength Rifles.	Lewis Guns.	Employed under
SOUTHERN SECTION				
120th Inf. Bde.	36A/C.21.d.0.3.	1,911	48	and 8 L.T.M's.
R.E.Troops.				
173rd Tunnelling Coy.	27/I.2.b.8.6.	266	1	Lt.Col.Butler, BLARINGHEM.
LABOUR COYS.				
Administered by 33rd Labour Group:-	36A/C.13.d.7.2.			
No.3 Labour Coy.	36A/C.23.b.5.9.	230	1	C.R.E.XV Corps Troops.
12 ,,	36A/C.5.d.9.5.	263	1)	
164 ,,	36A/C.11.c.9.2.	416	1)	C.R.E.40th Div.
174 ,,	36A/C.22.d.2.0.	244	1)	
Administered by 64th Labour Group:-	36A/B.23.a.9.4.			
No.4 Labour Coy.	36A/C.4.c.7.6.	289	1)	
35 ,,	36A/C.8.b.central	351	1)	
136 ,,	36A/A.18.c.2.3.	260	1)	
151 ,,	36A/B.19.b.8.4.	250	1)	VII Corps
Administered by 26th Labour Group:-	27/T.12.b.1.4.			
No.31 Labour Coy.	27/T.18.c.2.7.	305	1)	
92 ,,	27/T.11.d.6.8.	327	1)	
138 ,,	27/N.35.b.2.5.	301	1)	
		5,353	60	
NORTHERN SECTION				
121st Infantry Bde.	27/V.13.c.9.6.	2,418	46	and 8 L.T.M's.
Labour Coys.				
Administered by 5th Labour Group:-	27/U.4.d.2.4.			
No.6 Labour Coy.	27/V.15.	350	1	CRE XV Corps Troops
No.13 ,,	27/V.14.b.7.5.	254	1)	
61 ,,	27/V.4.c.5.9.	300	1)	
94 ,,	27/U.23.d.4.5.	328	1)	CRE 40th Div.
111 ,,	27/V.15.a.5.5.	255	1)	
132 ,,	27/V.5.a.7.8.	268	1)	
	Forward ...	4,179	52	

Unit	Location	Approximate Strength		Employed under
		Rifles	Lewis Guns	
	Forward	4,179	58	
Administered by 31st Labour Group:-	27/O.13.d.8.0.			
No.55 Labour Coy.	27/O.21.c.5.8.	309	1)	
67 ,,	27/P.27.d.1.8.	318	1)	
93 ,,	27/O.34.c.2.5.	376	1)	
133 ,,	27/N.18.b.5.8.	302	1)	
147 ,,	27/O.27.d.9.1.	325	1)	VII Corps
* 172 & 750 ,,	27/P.27.d.1.8.	142	1)	
178 Labour Coy.	27/N.24.a.8.8.	302	1)	
188 ,,	27/P.25.b.central	277	1)	
		6,528	60	

* amalgamated.

DIVISIONAL RESERVE : Under the command of O.C. 17th Battalion Worcester Regt. (Pioneers).

Unit	Location	Rifles	Lewis Guns	Employed under
229th Field Coy.RE.	36A/C.3.d.8.1.	100	1	C.R.E.40th Div.
231st ,,	27/V.15.a.4.1.	113	1	,,
554th A.T.Coy. R.E.	36A/C.21.d.8.5.	116	1	Lt.Col.Butler R.E.
17th Bn:Worc.R.(P).	27/U.26.d.4.7.	850	12	
		1179	15	

APPENDIX "B" to 40th Division Order No. 188.

Tents and shelters on charge of units will be disposed of as follows :-

Unit moving	Takes over tents and shelters in Camp site from :-	Tents will be taken on charge of, by :-
H.Q., 121st Inf. Bde.	119th Inf. Bde at the Hd Qrs at V.13.c.	H.Qrs., 121st Inf. Bde.
H.Q., 120th Inf. Bde.	H.Q., 121st Inf. Bde N. of SERCUS.	H.Q. 120th Inf. Bde.
11th Cameron Hrs.	8th Royal Irish Regt at C.3.a.	11th Cameron Highrs (120th Inf. Bde)
8th Bn: Royal Irish Regt.	12th Bn: North Staffs. Regt. at U.10.c.	8th Bn: Royal Irish Regt. (121st Inf. Bde).
23rd Bn: Cheshire Regiment.	13th Bn: Royal Innis. Fus. at U.17.c.	23rd Bn: Cheshire Regt. (121st Inf. Bde).

Tents and shelters vacated by Headquarters 120th Infantry Brigade and 11th Bn: Cameron Highlanders will remain on charge of 120th Infantry Brigade.

Tents and shelters vacated by 23rd Bn: Cheshire Regt. will remain on charge of 121st Infantry Brigade.

Tents and shelters of 13th Bn: E.Lancs Regt. will be taken forward by arrangement of 119th Inf. Brigade on whose charge they will remain.

The Camp site vacated by the 13th Bn: East Lancs Regt. (V.13.d.) will be occupied by 23rd Bn: Lancs Fusiliers whose tentage will be moved from their present camp site to that vacated by the 13th Bn: East Lancs Regt.

All canvas will be moved under Brigade arrangements.

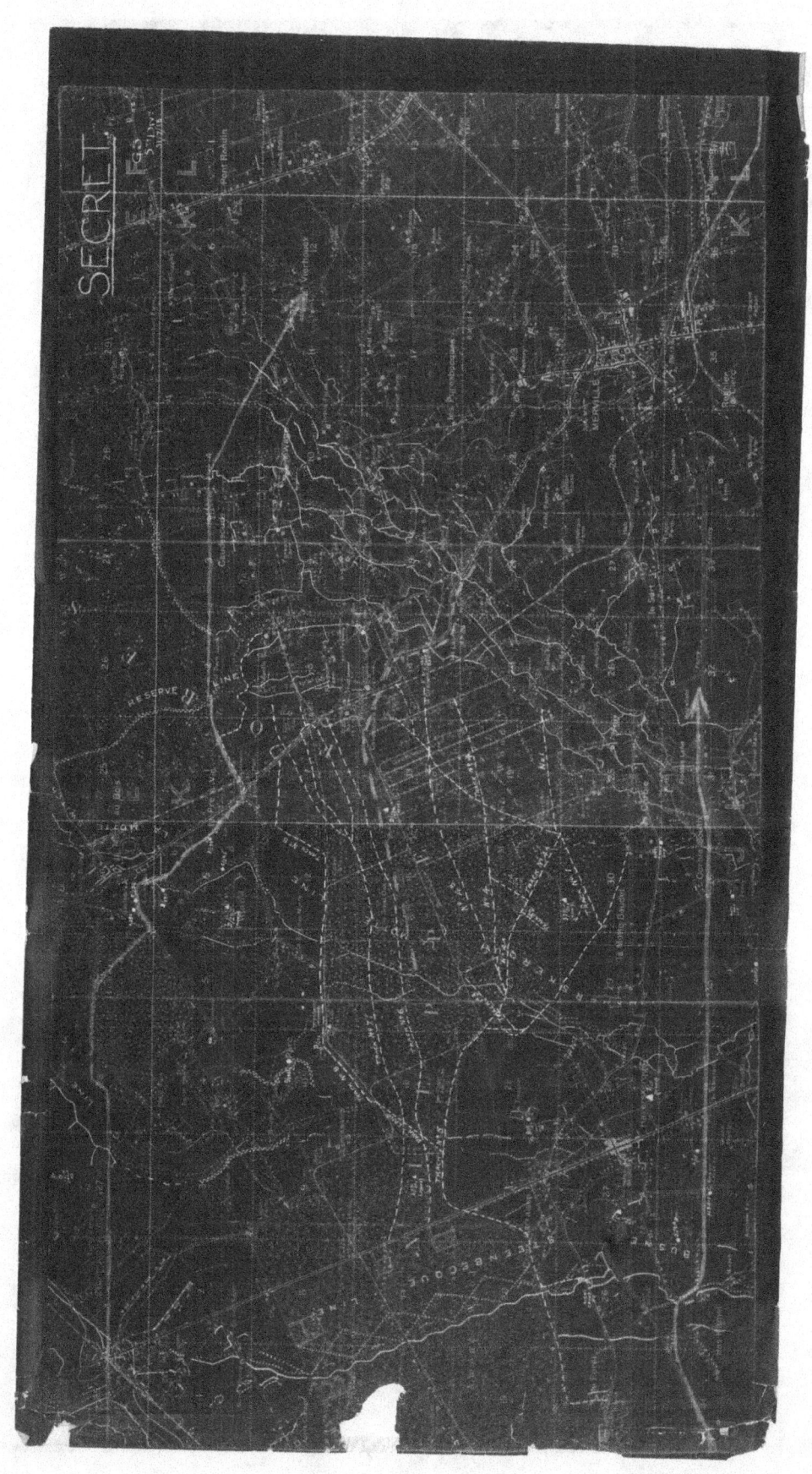

CONFIDENTIAL. ORIGINAL.

WAR DIARY.

40th DIVISION.

GENERAL STAFF BRANCH.

VOLUME XXVII.

FROM :- 1st AUGUST, 1918.

TO 31st AUGUST, 1918.

Major-General,
Commanding 40th Division.

Army Form W.3091.

Cover for Documents.

Nature of Enclosures.

Notes, or Letters written.

CONFIDENTIAL.

WAR DIARY.

40th DIVISION.

GENERAL STAFF BRANCH.

VOLUME. XXVII

FROM :- 1st AUGUST, to 31st AUGUST, 1918.

CONTENTS.

    WAR DIARY. ... ... Page 1 to Page 5.

    APPENDICES. ... ... Page 6 to Page 36.

******

Army Form C. 2118

WAR DIARY
or
~~INTELLIGENCE SUMMARY~~

(Erase heading not required.)

40th DIVISION.   AUGUST, 1918.

Instructions regarding War Diaries and Intelligence Summaries are contained in F. S. Regs., Part II. and the Staff Manual respectively. Title Pages will be prepared in manuscript.

Place	Date	Hour	Summary of Events and Information	Remarks and references to Appendices
RENESCURE.	1st		The Division was disposed as follows :- 119th Inf. Bde. RYCK HOUT CASTEEL; 120th Inf. Bde. SERCUS area; 121st Inf. Bde. in the line under 1st Australian Division.	
,,	2nd		Training continued. 15th K.O.Y.L.I., 120th Inf. Bde. proceeded to Musketry Camp at LUMBRES. 17th Worcester Regt. (P) took over camp of 15th K.O.Y.L.I. at C.14.d.6.2. Major-General Sir W. E. Peyton, K.C.B., K.C.V.O., D.S.O. proceeded on leave and Brig-Gen. F.P. Crozier, C.M.G., D.S.O. assumed command of the Division.	
,,	3rd		Training continued. 40th Div. Order No. 183 issued (move of 121st Inf. Bde.) See Appendix I.	Appendix 1.
,,	4th		121st Inf. Bde. was relieved in 1st Australian Division area by 29th Division and relieved the Right Battalion, Left Brigade, 31st Division. The new Sector, known as Centre Brigade Sector, runs from ANKLE FARM to LA BECQUE FARM, both inclusive. The 121st Inf. Bde. (H.Q. at D.17.a.6.3) came under orders of 31st Division.	
,,	5th to 11th		Training continued.	
,,	7th		10th K.O.S.Borderers went to LUMBRES; 15th K.O.Y.L.I. returned to camp at C.14.d.6.2.	
,,	8th		Divisional Instruction No. 1 (for occupation of Army Second Position issued) See Appendix 2.	Appendix 2.
,,	10th		40th Div. Order No. 184 (relief of 121st Inf. Bde. by 120th Inf. Bde.) See Appendix 3.	Appendix 3.
,,	11th		15th K.O.Y.L.I., 120th Inf. Bde. moved up to relieve 23rd Lancashire Fusrs., 121st Inf. Bde. in Reserve.	
,,	12th		Relief of 121st Inf. Bde. by 120th Inf. Bde. commenced, but was postponed as the Sector to be held was altered. 10th K.O.S.Borderers returned from LUMBRES and 13th E. Lancs. Regt., 119th Inf. Bde. proceeded to LUMBRES.	
,,	13th		120th Inf. Bde. took over Right Battn. front of Right Bde, 31st Div. (H.Q. at D.24.a.8.1). 121st Inf. Bde. was relieved by 92nd Inf. Bde. 31st Div. and moved to C.3.c.5.3.	

Army Form C. 2118.

WAR DIARY
or
INTELLIGENCE SUMMARY

40th DIVISION.   AUGUST, 1918.

(Erase heading not required.)

Place	Date	Hour	Summary of Events and Information	Remarks and references to Appendices
RENESCURE	14th		40th Div. Order No. 186 (move of 121st Inf. Bde. into billets) issued. See Appendix 4.	Appendix 4.
,,	14th 15th		Training continued.	
,,	16th		121st Inf. Bde. moved into billets from camps. Bde.H.Q. moved to C.9.d.7.5. - one Bn. to SHOWS - one Bn. to LYNDE and one Bn. to LA BELLE HOTESSE area.	
,,	17th 18th		Training continued.	
,,	19th		Major-General Sir W.E.Peyton, K.C.B., K.C.V.O., D.S.O., returned from leave. Brig-Gen. F.P. Crozier, C.M.G., D.S.O., returned to 119th Inf. Bde.	
,,	19th		40th Division Horse Show at RENESCURE.	
,,	20th		Instructions received to take over a portion of 31st Div. front on 23rd. 120th Inf. Bde. took over the Right Bn. front of Centre Bde. (92nd I.B.) 31st Div. on night 20th/21st.	
,,	21st		Corps conference took place at 9th Div. H.Q. at 11.30.a.m. and instructions issued for 40th Div. to take over the whole of 31st Div. front by 6.a.m. 23rd inst. The 104th Bn. M.G.C. (Army Troops) allotted this Division as a temporary measure. 40th Div. Order No. 186 issued (Relief of 31st Div) see Appendix 5. The 119th Inf. Bde. moved forward from RYCK HOUT CASTEEL area to camps as follows :- 13th Royal Fanie. Fus. to TIR ANGLAIS; 13th E.Lancs. R. and 12th N.Staffs. R. to D.21.a.0.8.	Appendix 5.
U.30.c.0.7 (WALLON CAPPEL)	22nd	5.p.m.	40th Div. H.Q. closed at RENESCURE at 5.p.m. and reopened at U.30.c.0.7 at the same hour. G.O.C. 40th Div. assumed command of Right Div. front at this hour. 40th Div. Order No. 187 issued (move of 121st Inf. Bde.) See Appendix 6. The line at this time ran roughly as follows :- VIER HOUCK - KEW CROSS - BRACKEN FARM - BLEU - West of CUTLET CORNER. Our patrols pushing forward gradually without meeting with much enemy resistance. 40th Div. Order No. 188 issued (orders for establishing a line from RUE MONTIGNY to CUTLET CORNER). See Appendix 7.	Appendix 6. Appendix 7.

Army Form C. 2118

WAR DIARY
or
INTELLIGENCE SUMMARY

(Erase heading not required.)

40th DIVISION.   **AUGUST, 1918.**

Instructions regarding War Diaries and Intelligence Summaries are contained in F.S. Regs., Part II. and the Staff Manual respectively. Title Pages will be prepared in manuscript.

Place	Date	Hour	Summary of Events and Information	Remarks and references to Appendices
U.30.c.0 7. (Continued.)	22nd (Continued.)		40th Div. Order No. 189 issued (alteration to boundaries) See Appendix 8. During the night 22nd/23rd the 119th Inf. Bde. relieved the 94th Inf. Bde. and part of the 120th Inf. Bde. in the Left Bde. Front. Relief reported completed by 2 a.m. Bde. H.Q. at D.11.d.5.7. Two Battalions (13th R. Innis. Fus. and 13th E.Lancs.R.) in Front Line; one Battn. (12th N. Staffs. R.) in support. The 94th Inf. Bde. moved on relief to the reserve Brigade area. H.Q. at V.27.c.3.2. During the night our line was advanced to the line COCHIN CORNER - KEW CROSS - ROOSTER FARM - BECKET CORNER - CUTLET CORNER. Fairly heavy enemy shelling on forward areas. Bright moonlight night.	Appendix 8.
,,	23rd		The 94th Inf. Bde. 31st Div. moved from Bde. Reserve to 31st Div. Area. The 120th Inf. Bde. attempted to advance their line of posts from the line KEW CROSS - COCHIN CORNER to BECKET CORNER - BISHOPS CORNER at 4. p.m. The attempt was not completely successful as the patrols came under heavy machine gun fire from the enclosures and houses about L.2. c. and d. The left flank advanced to ROOSTER FARM. In the centre patrols got to DENVER, but were unable to get further forward. On the right, the advance in conjunction with the 61st Div. was unable to make headway against the fire from BOWERT COTTAGES. The enemy counter-attacked between ROOSTER FARM and DENVER but was driven off. The enemy shelled the line of the road about PONT RONDIN, beginning at 4.15. p.m. The enemy appears to hold the line of the LAUDICK between L.2.c.1.1. and RUE MONTIGNY fairly strongly. He has erected wire on the West side of the stream. The 121st Inf. Bde. moved from SERCUS area to Bde. Reserve Area. H.Q. at V.27.c.3.2. The 119th Inf. Bde. moved its H.Q. forward to MOLIGHEM FARM, E.10.c.3.6. There was fairly heavy shelling during the night on forward areas. The enemy fired about 25 rounds (probably 5.9. H.V.Gun) into HAZEBROUCK during the night. No infantry action during the night.	Appendix 9.
,,	24th		Forward areas were lightly shelled during the day. 40th Div. Order 190 issued (move of 104th Bn. M.G.C.) See Appendix 9. 104th Bn. M.G.C. moved from RACQUINGHEM to U.24.c.3.4. Transport for this Bn. is being found by S.A.A.Section of 40th D.A.C. 40th Div. Order No. 191 issued (Relief of 31st Bn. M.G.C. by 104th Bn. M.G.C.) See Appendix 10. The night was quiet.	Appendix 10

Army Form C. 2118

WAR DIARY
~~INTELLIGENCE SUMMARY~~
(Erase heading not required.)

40th DIVISION. AUGUST, 1918.

Instructions regarding War Diaries and Intelligence Summaries are contained in F. S. Regs., Part II. and the Staff Manual respectively. Title Pages will be prepared in manuscript.

Place	Date	Hour	Summary of Events and Information	Remarks and references to Appendices
U.30.c.0.7 (Continued)	25th.		On the Left Brigade front our line runs from ROOSTER Farm, through BECKET Corner, through road junction F.21.c.5.0. to OUTLET Corner. The enemy's artillery fire was normal. HULLEBERT Farm, VIEUX BERQUIN, KEW CROSS being the main centres of activity. Our artillery maintained the normal harassing fire. Hostile artillery fire was below normal at night. Our patrols were out to an average depth of 450 yards without meeting any enemy. (Order for attack on BISHOPS CORNER), See Appendix 11. 40th Division Order No. 192 issued.	Appendix 11.
,,	26th.		The 119th Infantry Bde. captured a wounded prisoner of 140th Regt. 4th Saxon Div. at F.21.c. early in the morning (normal.) 40th Div. No. 174/1 (G) issued (additions to D.O.No.192) See Appendix 12. The night was quiet. Troops took up their assembly positions for the attack next morning.	Appendix 12.
,,	27th		At 10.a.m. the 13th R.Innis. Fus., 119th Inf. Bde., attacked astride the BECKET Corner - BISHOPS Corner Road. The account of the operations is attached (See Appendix 13). Our line was consolidated during the night.	Appendix 13.
,,	28th		The 23rd Cheshire Regt., 121st Inf. Bde., was placed at the disposal of the 119th Inf. Bde. and was in position in the "Z" Line by 8.a.m. 40th Div. Order No. 193 issued (orders for attack on RUE PROVOST and BOWERY Cottages. (See App. 14.) 40th Div. Order No. 194 issued (orders for relief of 119th Inf. Bde. by 121st Inf. Bde. to be completed by 31st August) See Appendix 15. During the night patrols of 120th Inf. Bde. endeavoured to seize RUE PROVOST and BOWERY Cottages. These two localities had been shelled all day by Field and Heavy Artillery. Patrols succeeded in reaching BOWERY Cottages but the enclosures on the east of it were strongly held by the enemy and the patrols withdrew. Patrols were unable to reach RUE PROVOST owing to heavy hostile artillery and machine gun fire.	Appendix 14. Appendix 15.
,,	29th		At 1.30.p.m. the 11th Cameron Hrs. 120th Inf. Bde. attacked RUE PROVOST and BOWERY Cottages. All objectives were taken. An account of the operation is attached (See Appendix 16.) Later in the day the 61st Division advanced to RUE MONTIGNY and connected with us at RUE PROVOST. During the night the 23rd Cheshire Regt. relieved the 13th E.Lancs. Rgt. in Right front line. The 61st Div. took over the front from 120th Inf. Bde. as far North as K.4.central - L.5.central	Appendix 16.

1375 Wt. W593/826 1,000,000 4/15 J.B.C. & A. A.D.S.S./Forms/C. 2118.

Army Form C. 2118

WAR DIARY
or
~~INTELLIGENCE SUMMARY~~
(Erase heading not required.)

40th DIVISION.   AUGUST, 1918.

Instructions regarding War Diaries and Intelligence Summaries are contained in F. S. Regs., Part II. and the Staff Manual respectively. Title Pages will be prepared in manuscript.

Place	Date	Hour	Summary of Events and Information	Remarks and references to Appendices
V.30.c.0.7 (Continued)	29th		Troops of the 120th Inf. Bde. withdrew to the BOIS D'AVAL. The 23rd Lancs. Fus. (121st Inf. Bde.) moved forward to GRAND SEC BOIS area. Reports received from Division on our right indicated that the enemy was withdrawing. The 119th Inf. Bde. was ordered to push out patrols and ascertain the position of the enemy.	
"	30th		By 9.a.m. our patrols were reported 500 yards in advance of our old line moving East. On our Right the 61st Div. had advanced to REGAL Lodge. On our left the 29th Div. had taken DROMANA and TROIS TILLEULS. 40th Div. Order No. 195 issued (121st Inf. Bde. to take over the front and form an Advanced Guard). See Appendix 17. During the day our line advanced to the general line GAUL Farm - F.23.d.0.3. - ACTON CROSS. The 61st Div. line runs through L.10. and 29th Div. runs through from GAUL Farm - CORIN - NOOTE BOOM. The Advanced Guard under command of Brig-Gen. W.B.Garnett, D.S.O. consists of 121st Inf.Bde. 2 batteries 18. pdrs, 28th A.F.A.Bde., 1 Sec. Hows., 1 Coy. 104th Bn. M.G.C. and 1 Coy. XVth Corps Cyclists. The Advanced Guard took over command of the front at 10. 30. p.m. The 120th Inf. Bde. moved back during the afternoon to WALLON CAPPEL area. Bde. H.Q. at WALLON CAPPEL. The enemy's shelling during the day was confined to the front line and consisted mainly of 77.mm. at long range, and one 4.2" battery. 40th Div. Order No. 196 issued (orders for 31st Aug). See Appendix 18.	Appendix 17 Appendix 18
"	31st		During the day our patrols worked forward to the line AILERON Farm - PONT WEMEAU - CORIN. Considerable machine gun fire was met with from the direction of POM Cottage (L.6.c.4.0.) The Divisional Boundaries were altered in accordance with Div. Order No. 196. The 119th Inf. Bde. withdrew to the Support Area. Bde. H.Q. V.27.c.3.2. 1 battalion in the "Z" line, - 1 battalion to TIR ANGLAIS and one battalion D.21.a.0.8. The 119th Inf. Bde. was responsible for the defence of the "Z" Line on the whole Divisional Front. The Advanced Guard was ordered to capture DOULIEU and LE VERRIER on the 1st September. A map is attached showing the progress on each day and the alteration in boundaries. See Appendix 19.	Appendix 19

[signature] Lieut-Colonel.
General Staff, 40th Division.

Appendix. I.

SECRET.   Copy No. 17
             40th DIVISION ORDER NO. 185.
                                                                 3/8/18.

1.   The 121st Infantry Bde. are being relieved on the night of
4/5th August on the right of the STRAZEELE Sector, by troops
of the 29th Division.

2.   The 121st Infantry Bde. on relief will take over the right
sub-section of the Left Brigade, LA MOTTE Sector, and will come
under the tactical command of the G.O.C., 31st Division.

3.   Arrangements for the above reliefs have been made by 29th and
31st Divisions.

                                            J. H. Stafford
                                              Maj.
                                            for Lieut-Colonel.
                                    General Staff, 40th Division.

Issued at 3/hr

Copies to :-

    No. 1,   G.O.C.,
       2,   119th Inf. Bde.
       3,   120th Inf. Bde.
       4,   121st Inf. Bde.
       5,   17th Worc. R. (P).
       6,   C.R.E.,
       7,   Signals.
       8,   Train.
       9,   S.S.O.
      10,   29th Division.
      11,   31st Division.
      12,   XV Corps G.
      13,   XV Corps Q.
      14,   XV Corps H.A.
      15,   XV Corps R.A.
      16,   "Q" 40th Division.
      17,   War Diary.
      18,   War Diary.
      19,   File.

40th Div. No. 183 G.　　　　　　　　S E C R E T.

40th DIVISION INSTRUCTION NO. 1,
for the occupation of the Army "Second Position"
(WEST HAZEBROUCK Lines).
****

Ref. maps
HAZEBROUCK
　Sheet 27
　Sheet 36A.
----

1. The instructions embody Div. Order No.182 and all amendments and addenda issued subsequently.

2. In the event of an enemy attack on the Second Army front, the 40th Division and attached troops will be prepared to man the Army "Second Position" (i.e. WEST HAZEBROUCK Lines) from the XVth Corps Southern boundary to the road (exclusive) running through V.6.central.

3. For purposes of defence the Divisional Sector will be divided into two Brigade sections.

4. The Boundaries are as follows :-

SOUTH DIVISIONAL BOUNDARY.

　D.25.d.0.8 - D.25.c.5.8 - C.30.d.0.8 - C.28.d.0.2 - C.27.d.6.2 - C.27.c.6.7 - C.25.central.

NORTH DIVISIONAL BOUNDARY.

　W.7.a.1.1 - V.12.b.50.95 - along road (exclusive) to P.35.b.5.0 - P.35.c.6.1 - P.34.d.2.3 - P.33.d.6.0 - P.27.c.2.0 - P.32.b.4.7 - P.26.d.2.0 - P.32.a.5.8 - P.32.a.7.1 - along road inclusive to U.6.a.4.7.

INTER BRIGADE BOUNDARY.

　V.26.central - V.26.a.0.8 - V.25.a.8.5 - U.30.b.8.6 - U.24.d.0.0 - U.23.c.0.0.

5. Disposition of Troops in case of attack.

　　　Advanced Div. Headquarters ... U.25.b.2.4.

　　　Divl. Headquarters　　　　　... RENESCURE.

SOUTHERN SECTOR.

　'A' Infantry Brigade (billetted in area about SERCUS and LYNDE) and attached troops. (see Appendix A).

　Brigade Headquarters　　　...　　C.3.c.5.3.

　Right Battalion　　　　　...　　D.23.d.8.7.

　Centre Battalion　　　　　...　　D.17.d.2.8.

　Left Battalion　　　　　...　　U.29.d.9.5.

NORTHERN SECTOR

　'B' Infantry Brigade (camped in area round RYCK HOUT CASTEEL) and attached troops (see Appendix A).

　Brigade Headquarters　　　...　　V.13.c.0.6.

　　　　　　　　　　　　　　　　　　Right.....

-ii-

    Right Battalion ... U.18.d.4.3.

    Centre Battalion ... V.10.c.8.2.

    Left Battalion ... V.5.c.7.4.

Divisional Reserve.

'C' Infantry Brigade now in the line, under orders of Right Division.

17th Worc. Regt. (Pioneers) and XV Corps Reinforcement Battalion.

    Brigade Headquarters ... U.15.a.6.9.

    One Battalion ... U.10.c.0.4.

    One Battalion ... U.15.b.6.0.

    One Battalion ... U.9.d.1.2.

    L.T.M.Battery ... U.15.a.b.d.

    17th Worc. Regt (Pioneers)) U.15.d.4.7.
    XV Corps Reinforcement Bn:)

The Defence of the LE PEUPLIER Line, North of the 40th Division is being undertaken by nucleus garrisons under command of Major BELLAMY, D.S.O.,R.E.

This sector is tactically under the command of G.O.C. Left Division. Extracts from the Defence Instructions of the Corps on our right are given in App.'B' (to Bdes and Signals only)

6. The line will be held in accordance with the principles laid down in S.S.210 "The Division in Defence". Only the minimum number of troops will be maintained in the outpost positions. They must however be sufficient to act as "break-waters" if the enemy attacks. (S.S.210, Section 11 (a) (iv).). The degree of resistance in each line of defence will be to the last man and the last round.

Commanders of Formations and Units will ensure that the instructions laid down in this paragraph are understood by all ranks.

7. Machine Guns.

"D" and "F" Machine Gun Battalions are allotted to XV Corps for the defence of the Army line.

Sections are allotted as follows :-

    'D' Battalion M.G.C.

from D.25. to the road U.30.b.8.6 - V.25.a.8.8. inclusive.

    'F' Battalion M.G.C.

from the road U.30.b.8.6 - V.25.a.8.8 - exclusive to V.6.central.

NOTE   For the present only 'D' Battalion M.G.C. is available. This Battalion will temporarily be prepared to occupy the whole Divisional Sector.

8....

- iii -

8. Assembly Positions.

On the alarm being given, all attached troops will concentrate in the assembly areas already notified and will come under the orders of Brigade Section Commanders. Brigades will arrange for the above troops to be met at the assembly positions and guided to their positions in the line.

9. All troops will proceed by march route to their assembly positions with the exception of the following, for whom bus arrangements have been made by "Q" 40th Division.

No. 178 Labour Company will embus at the Cross Roads 27/N.12.d.4.1., head of column facing East. Convoy will proceed via ZUYTPEENE, HULSE HOUCK to main road at STAPLE, thence Eastwards.
Debussing point - Cross roads 27/V.2.c.4.2.

10. 120 rounds S.A.A. will be carried by each man to the trenches and 2,000 rounds per Lewis Gun.

Brigades will be responsible for the further supply of ammunition to attached troops, once they come under their command.

11. Orders for the occupation of the WEST HAZEBROUCK defences will be issued by 40th Division to the following :-

(a) To 'A' and 'B' Infantry Brigades, C.R.E. and XV Corps Reinforcement Battalion.

(b) To Lieut. Colonel HOYSTED, D.S.O., R.E. for 234 Field Company R.E.

(c) To 5th, 26th, 31st, 33rd and 64th Labour Group H.Q. for the Labour Companies which they administer.

The above Formations and Units will be responsible for issuing orders without delay to the units they control.

The orders for 'C' Infantry Brigade will be issued by the Division in the line under whose orders they are.

12. Medical arrangements are laid down in R.A.M.C. Order No.76 dated 27/6/18.

The Group Commanders of 5th, 31st and 33rd Labour Groups will each detail 100 unarmed men as stretcher bearers. They will report for duty as follows :-

33rd Labour Group to 135th Field Ambulance at 36A/B.18.c.0.0.
31st   ,,   to 136th   ,,   at 27/T.18.c.8.7.
5th   ,,   to 137th   ,,   at 27/T.22.a.3.4.

13. Brigades will prepare a scheme for the occupation of their section with the troops allotted in Appendix A. Copies of these schemes will be sent to Divisional Headquarters.
All Labour Companies will be affiliated to Battalions for holding the line and will not be allotted to sub-sections separately.

14. Changes of location of all units mentioned in these instructions will be notified to Divisional Headquarters at once.

15. ACKNOWLEDGE.

H E Black. Lieut. Colonel,

2/8/18. General Staff, 40th Division.

DISTRIBUTION :-

Copy No. 1 to G.O.C.
    2   119th Infantry Brigade.
    3   120th Infantry Brigade.
    4   121st Infantry Brigade.
    5   C.R.E. 40th Division.
    6   17th Worc. Regt. (P).
    7   Div. Signal Company.
    8   40th Div. Train.
    9   40th Div. M.T. Company.
   10   "Q"
   11   A.D.M.S.
   12   D.A.D.V.S.
   13   D.A.D.O.S.
   14   A.P.M.
   15   S.S.O.
   16   Camp Commandant.
   17   D.G.O.
   18   XV Corps "G".
   19   ,,   "Q".
   20   VII Corps G.
   21   9th Division.
   22   29th Division.
   23   31st Division.
   24   G.O.C. R.A. XV Corps.
   25   C.E. XV Corps.
   26   D Battalion M.G.C.
   27   F Battalion M.G.C.
   28   Lt. Col. HOYSTED D.S.O., R.E.
   29   No. 5 Labour Group.
   ~~30~~   ~~26~~ ,,
   31   31 ,,
   32   33 ,,
   33   64 ,,
   34   Labour Comdt. VII Corps.
   35   War Diary.
   36   ,,
   37   File

APPENDIX "A".

Unit	Present location.	Employed under
SOUTHERN SECTION.		
'A' Infantry Brigade	36A/C.3.c.5.3.	
Attached		
R.E.Troops.		
229th Field Coy. R.E.	36A/C.3.d.8.1.	C.R.E.40th Div.
234th " "	27/U.28.c.1.8.	Lt.Col.HOYSTED, D.S.O.,R.E. (H.Q.MAISON BLANCHE).
Labour Coys.		
64th Labour Group.	27/O.13.d.2.0.	
92nd Labour Coy.	27/T.11.d.6.8.	VII Corps
5th Labour Group.	27/U.4.d.2.4.	
4th Labour Coy.	36A/C.4.c.7.6.	XV Corps
35th "	36A/C.8.b.central	XV Corps
31st Labour Group.	27/O.13.d.2.0.	
147th Labour Coy.	36A/C.5.d.5.1.	
33rd Labour Group.	36A/C.13.b.7.2.	
3rd Labour Coy.	36A/C.23.b.5.9.	⎫
12th "	36A/C.5.d.9.5.	⎬ XV Corps
68th "	36A/B.3.a.4.1.	⎬
164th "	36A/C.11.c.9.2.	⎭
NORTHERN SECTION		
'B' Infantry Brigade.	27/V.13.c.0.6.	
Attached		
R.E.Troops		
231st Field Coy. R.E.	27/V.15.a.4.1.	C.R.E.40th Div.
Labour Coys.		
5th Labour Group.	27/U.4.d.2.4.	
5th Labour Coy.	27/V.15.	⎫
13th "	27/V.14.b.7.5.	⎬ XV Corps
132nd "	27/V.15.a.5.5.	⎭
31st Labour Group	27/O.13.d.2.0.	
55th Labour Coy.	27/O.21.c.5.2.	⎫
67th "	27/P.27.d.1.8.	⎬
93rd "	27/U.28.b.6.8.	⎬
133rd "	27/N.18.b.5.2.	⎬ VIIth Corps
172nd "	27/P.27.d.1.8.	⎬
178th "	27/N.24.a.8.8.	⎬
188th "	27/P.25.b.central	⎭

Divisional Reserve.......

APPENDIX "A" (Continued).

Unit	Present location.	Employed under
Divisional Reserve		
'O' Infantry Brigade		Under orders of G.O.C. 31st Div.
attached.		
17th Worcester Regt. (Pioneers).	27/U.26.d.4.7.	C.R.E.40th Div.
Corps Reinforcement Battalion.	36A/D.2.c.9.1.	C.E.XV Corps.

****

APPENDIX 'B'.

Extracts from Defence Instructions of XI Corps.

1. The Division of XI Corps located in area MAZINGHEM - LIETTRES - ST.HILAIRE, is in G.H.Q. Reserve, but will be prepared to act as XI Corps Reserve in event of attack.

2. Three Brigade concentration areas have been selected into which one or more Infantry Brigades of the Reserve Division will move in case of necessity. The area of concentration of the Brigade on the left will be :-

    Area "L" = STEENBECQUE - BOESEGHEM - THIENNES.

3. The "LINGHEM" Brigade (located at LINGHEM and LIETTRES) and one Machine Gun Company will probably move by lorry to area "L". The Brigade report Centre will be at I.8.b.6.1.
    Nucleus garrisons of one company infantry and two Machine guns from this Brigade will be sent forward to garrison the localities of "DENISE FARM" (J.2.c.) and "DELEGATE FARM" (J.1.b.), and will relieve the nucleus garrison of Cyclists and Corps Cavalry (King Edward's Horse) already occupying these localities.
    In event of attack on XV Corps front, the Reserve Division will be prepared :-

    (i) To extend the left of the XI Corps along the LITTLE BOURRE River from GRAND DAM LOCK, or

    (ii) Extend the left flank of the Corps from LA MOTTE-AU-BOIS along the canal running through D.18 and D.11., or

    (iii) To counter-attack North-east to drive the enemy across the canal in D.18 and D.11.

4. The Divisional Artillery of the Reserve Division will accompany the Division. In event of attack on XV Corps front, the preliminary concentration will take place in an area about BOESEGHEM.

5. XI Corps Mounted Troops, consisting of Headquarters and One Squadron of 1st King Edward's Horse and XI Corps Cyclist Battalion, are located at LES OISEAUX and BOESEGHEM, under command of Officer Commanding 1st King Edward's Horse.
    On receipt of orders to "MAN BATTLE POSTS", Officer Commanding King Edward's Horse will at once occupy "DENISE FARM" and "DELEGATE FARM" localities, and obtain touch with nucleus garrison of XV Corps about the level crossing in D.25.d.
    One platoon of Cyclists will be placed at the point where light railway passes through BUSNES - STEENBECQUE Line in J.14.c.
    On relief by nucleus garrison of Brigade (vide paragraph 3) the XI Corps Mounted Troops (less platoon at J.14.c.) will be withdrawn into XI Corps Reserve about PLAINEHAUTE.

Appendix 3.

SECRET.   Copy No. 21

40th DIVISION ORDER NO. 184.   10/8/18.

1. The 120th Infantry Brigade will relieve the 121st Infantry Brigade in the line under the 31st Division on the 11th and night 12/13th August.

2. Orders for relief are being issued by 31st Division.

3. The 17th Worc. Regt. (Pioneers) will remain in their present camp and one battalion 121st Infantry Brigade will move on relief to the camp previously occupied by 17th Worc. Regt. (P) at LE NOIR TROU.

4. The 121st Inf. Brigade will take over the scheme for occupation of the Army 'Second Position' from 120th Infantry Brigade.

5. ACKNOWLEDGE.

J. H. Stafford.
Major G.S.
for. Lieut. Colonel,
General Staff, 40th Division.

Issued at... 2.0 pm.

Copy No. 1 to G.O.C.
    2   119th Inf. Brigade.
    3   120th   ,,
    4   121st   ,,
    5   C.R.E.
    6   17th Worc. Regt. (Pioneers).
    7   Signals
    8   Train
    9   40th Div. M.T.Coy.
   10   "Q" 40th Div.
   11   A.D.M.S.
   12   D.A.D.V.S.
   13   D.A.D.O.S.
   14   A.P.M.
   15   S.S.O.
   16   D.G.O.
   17   XV Corps G.
   18   ,,   Q.
   19   31st Division.
   20   G.O.C.R.A. XV Corps
   21   War Diary
   22   ,,
   23   File

SECRET Copy No. 20

40th DIVISION ORDER NO. 185. 14/8/18.

1. 121st Infantry Brigade will move into billets in the LYNDE-SERCUS area on 16th August.
   The area will be allotted by the Area Commandant BLARINGHEM as follows :-

Brigade Headquarters	SERCUS
One Battalion	SERCUS
One Battalion	LYNDE
One Battalion	Area in squares C.20., 21, 22, 23, 26, 27, 28, 29.

2. All particulars of area to be obtained from Area Commandant BLARINGHEM by Headquarters 121st Infantry Brigade.

3. All tents and shelters on charge of 121st Infantry Brigade are to be handed in to Area Commandant, BLARINGHEM and receipts obtained. Total numbers handed in to be reported to Divl. Headquarters.

4. All drainage and protection trenches dug in present Camp sites and latrines etc., are to be filled in before the camps are vacated and camping grounds are to be left in a clean and sanitary state.

5. Demand for additional transport for the move will be forwarded to 40th Division 'Q' as early as possible.

J.H. Stafford, Major GS.
for Lieut. Colonel,
General Staff, 40th Division.

Issued at 6 p.m.

Copy No. 1 to G.O.C.
  2   119th Inf. Bde.
  3   120th   ,,
  4   121st   ,,
  5   C.R.E. 40th Division.
  6   17th Worc. Regt. (Pioneers).
  7   Div. Signal Company.
  8   40th Div. Train.
  9   40th Div. M.T. Coy.
 10   "Q" 40th Div.
 11   A.D.M.S.
 12   D.A.D.V.S.
 13   D.A.D.O.S.
 14   A.P.M.
 15   S.S.O.
 16   Div. Gas Officer.
 17   XV Corps "G".
 18   ,,   "Q"
 19   Area Commandant, BLARINGHEM.
 20   War Diary
 21   ,,
 22   File

Appendix 5

13.

SECRET.   Copy No. 28

40th DIVISION ORDER NO.186.   21/8/18.

1. The 40th Division will take over the front now held by 31st Division.

2. The front to be taken over will be from the Corps Southern boundary to the PLATE BECQUE RAU at F.14.c.3.5. The Divisional and inter-brigade boundaries are shown on attached map.

3. The 120th Infantry Brigade now under the tactical control of G.O.C.31st Division took over the front now held by the right battalion 92nd Infantry Brigade (R.2.subsector) on night 20/21st. The 120th Infantry Brigade is extending its front to-night to the North and will take over the left battalion front 92nd Infantry Brigade (R.3.sub-sector) to-night 21/22nd.

4. 119th Infantry Brigade will move forward to staging area as follows :-

Bde H.Qrs.	...	V.13.c.0.6. (as at present).
1 Battalion	...	TIR ANGLAIS
1 Battalion	...	D.21.a.0.8.
1 Battalion	...	D.14.d.
T.M.Battery	...	D.21.a.0.8.

5. On 22nd and night 22/23rd the 119th Infantry Brigade will take over the front now held by 94th Infantry Brigade and R.3. sub-sector from 120th Infantry Brigade. Relief will be carried out in accordance with attached table. The 121st Infantry Bde will remain in its present area.

6. Details of relief will be arranged between Brigades concerned. Command of Brigade sections will pass at a time to be settled by Brigadiers concerned.

7. The Field Coys R.E. and 17th Worc. Regt. (Pioneers) will cease work on the Army Second position and will take over from the Field Coys and Pioneer Bn: of the 31st Division under arrangements to be made between C.R.E's concerned.

8. The relief of Field Ambulances will be arranged between A.D.M.S. and A.D.M.S.31st Division.

9. Infantry Brigades in the line will forward to D.H.Q. a map showing their disposition 48 hours after completion of relief.

10. Units will take over Defence Schemes, schemes of work, air-photos etc., from units they relieve.

- ii -

11. Completion of reliefs will be notified to Divl. Headquarters.

12. Divl. Headquarters will close at RENESCURE at 5 p.m. 22nd., and will re-open at U.30.c.0.7. at the same hour.

G.O.C. 40th Division will take over command of right Division sector at the same hour.

13. ACKNOWLEDGE.

Issued at 8.30/pm

Lieut. Colonel,
General Staff, 40th Division.

Copy No. 1 to G.O.C.
2   119th Inf. Bde.
3   120th ,,
4   121st ,,
5   C.R.E.
6   17th Worc. R. (P).
7   104 M.G.Bn:
8   Div. Signal Coy.
9   40th Div. Train.
10   40th Div. M.T.Coy. *
11   40th Div. "Q".
12   A.D.M.S.
13   D.A.D.V.S. *
14   D.A.D.O.S. *
15   A.P.M.
16   S.S.O. *
17   Div. Gas Officer. *
18   Div. Claims Officer. *
19   Camp Commandant. *
20   29th Division. *
21   31st ,, *
22   31st Divl. Artillery.
23   61st Division. *
24   XV Corps "G".
25   XV Corps "Q". *
26.   XV Corps R.A. *
27   XV Corps H.A. *
28   War Diary
29   ,,
30   File.

* = Map not issued.

TABLE TO ACCOMPANY 40th DIVISION ORDER NO.186 dated 21/8/18.

Date	Unit	From	To	In relief of	Remarks
Night 22/23rd.	119th I.Bde H.Q.	V.13.a.0.6.	SEDIMENT HOUSE	94th Inf. Bde H.Q.	
"	A Bn: 119th I.B.	TIR ANGLAIS	Front Line, Left Sector (R.3.)	120th Inf. Bde.	Troops of 120th I.Bde relieved will move back to their own areas.
"	B Bn: 119th I.B.	MORBECQUE	Front Line, Left Sector (R.4).	1 Battalion, 94th Infantry Bde.	
"	C Bn: 119th I.B.	MORBECQUE	Support Left Sector (E.7.b.7.8)	1 Bn: 94th Inf. Bde.	

Appendix 6.

SECRET   Copy No. 28

40th DIV. ORDER NO. 187.   22/8/18.

1. The 121st Infantry Brigade will move into the Reserve Brigade area of the Right Division on the afternoon of 23rd August taking over from 94th Infantry Brigade, 31st Division.

2. Locations will be as follows :-

Brigade H.Q.	...	V.27.c.3.2.
1 Battalion	...	D.9.a.5.8.
1 Battalion	...	D.21.a.0.8.
1 Battalion	...	D.19.a.5.6.

3. The 94th Infantry Brigade will be clear of this area by 4 p.m. and will move in accordance with orders issued by 31st Division.

4. Completion of move of 121st Infantry Brigade will be reported to Div. H.Qrs.

5. ACKNOWLEDGE.

I. H. Stafford.
Major G.
for Lieut. Colonel,
Issued at 12.30 p.m.   General Staff, 40th Division.

1. G.O.C.
2. 119th Inf. Bde.
3. 120th Inf. Bde.
4. 121st Inf. Bde.
5. C.R.E. 40th Div.
6. 17th Worc. R. (Pioneers).
7. Div. Signal Coy.
8. 40th Div. Train.
9. 40th Div. M.T.Coy.
10. 40th Div. "Q".
11. A.D.M.S.
12. D.A.D.V.S.
13. D.A.D.O.S.
14. D.A.P.M.
15. S.S.O.
16. D.G.O.
17. D.Claims Off.
18. 104 M.G.Bn:
19. 94th Inf. Bde.
20. 29th Div.
21. 31st Div.
22. 61st Div.
23. XV Corps G.
24. ,, Q
25. ,, R.A.
26. ,, H.A.
27. War Diary
28. ,,
29. File
30. 31st Div. Arty.
31. 31st M.G.Bn:

War Diary Appendix 7

16.

SECRET.   Copy No. 21

40TH DIVISION ORDER NO. 182.   22/8/17.

1. The 61st Division Outpost Line now runs in the neighbourhood of RUE MONTIGNY. It is proposed to straighten out the re-entrant between this point and OUTLET CORNER previous to handing over a portion of this area to the 61st Division.

2. With this object the 120th Infantry Bde. and the 119th Infantry Bde. on their left will advance to-morrow afternoon 23rd August to the objective shown on attached map. The right flank of the 120th Inf. Bde will be the road COCHIN Corner, - RUE PROVOST - Cross roads L.3.c. inclusive. The left of the 120th Inf. Bde will be the road ROOSTER FARM - BECKET CORNER exclusive.

The 119th Inf. Bde will co-operate with the 120th Inf. Bde and will form junctions with them at ROOSTER FARM and BECKET Corner as the advance progresses.

3. The 61st Division on our right is co-operating from the COCHIN CORNER - NEUF BERQUIN Road in a North Easterly direction towards BISHOPS CORNER.

4. One Group of artillery is placed at the disposal of each Brigadier and all arrangements for artillery support will be made direct between Brigadiers and O.C.Groups.

5. Zero hour will be notified to all concerned by G.O.C. 120th Infantry Brigade.

6. During the night 23rd/24th the area South of the line K.4.central - L.5.central will be handed over to 61st Division under arrangements to be made between Brigadiers concerned.

7. ACKNOWLEDGE.

                                    W.S.Leach   Lieut. Colonel,
Issued at 9.15 pm   General Staff, 40th Division.

Copy No. 1 to G.O.C.   *******
      x 2   119 I.Bde.   x 18   XV Corps "G"
      x 3   120th I.Bde.   19 to XV Corps "Q".
      x 4   121st I.Bde.   x 20   XV Corps R.A.
        5   C.R.E.   x 21   XV Corps H.A.
        6   17th Worc. R. (P).   x 22   War Diary
        7   104th M.G.Bn.   23   War Diary
        8   Div. Signal Coy.   24   File
        9   40th Div. "Q".
       10   A.D.M.S.
       11   D.A.P.M.
      x 12   29th Div.
       13   31st Div.
      x 14   31st Div. Artillery.
      x 15   31st M.G.Bn:
      x 16   61st Div.
      x 17   1st Brigade, Heavy Arty.
      x 17a. 64th   ,,

1:20000 TRENCHES CORRECTED FROM INFORMATION RECEIVED UP TO 19-7-18. LA COURONNE — Part of Sheet 36ᴬ N.E.

Situation up to 4 p.m. 9-8-18

T.S. 265
Corps Topo Section
9/8/18

Trenches from information received other than Photographs

Appendix 8
18.

SECRET   Copy No. 16

        40th DIVISION ORDER NO. 189.   22/8/18.

1.   The map showing boundaries, referred to in para. 2 of Div. Order No. 186 of 21/8/18 will be amended as follows :-

(a) SOUTHERN CORPS BOUNDARY. From K.4.a.5.0. to run K.4.central - L.5.central - G.11.a.0.0.

(b) INTER-DIVISIONAL BOUNDARY between 29th and 40th Divisions. From F.20.b.9.4. to run just South of road passing West to East through F.21.a. and b. to F.16.c.7.0. - thence East along grid line.

                            J.H. Stafford
                            Major g/s Lieut. Colonel,
Issued at 11.59 p.m.   General Staff, 40th Division.

Copy No. 1 to G.O.C.
      2   119th I.Bde.
      3   120th I.Bde.
      4   121st I.Bde.
      5   C.R.E.
      6   17th Worc. R. (P).
      7   104 M.G.Bn:
      8   Div. Signal Coy.
      9   Div. Train.
     10.   40th Div. "Q".
     11.   A.D.M.S.
     12.   D.A.P.M.
     13.   31st Div. Artillery.
     14.   61st Div.
     15.   XV Corps "G".
 16 & 17.   War Diary.
     18.   File.

War Diary   Appendix 9.

SECRET.   Copy No. 23
                                               24/3/18.
            40th DIVISION ORDER NO.190.
            ****

Ref. map Sheet 27.
----

1. The 104th Bn: M.G.C. will move from present camp in
    RACQUINGHEM to tented camp at U.24.c.3.4. this afternoon, to
    be clear of present camp by 6 p.m.

2. Motor transport will park at U.21.b. as previously
    arranged by 40th Division "A".

        Horse transport from S.A.A.Section, 40th D.A.C., will
    join 104th Bn: M.G.C. at U.27.c.3.4. by 6 p.m. to-day.

3. Tented camp at U.24.c.3.4. will remain on charge of
    Reserve Brigade whose guard will remain.

4. Completion of move will be reported to Div. H.Qrs.

5. ACKNOWLEDGE.
                                        J. H. Stafford
                                          Major G.
                                          Lieut. Col.
                                    General Staff, 40th Division.

Issued at 1.30 p.m.

Copy No. 1 to G.O.C.
         2   119th I.B.
         3   120th I.B.
         4   121st I.B.
         5   C.R.E.
         6   17th Worc. R. (P).
         7   Signals
         8   Train
         9   40th Div. M.T. Coy.
        10   40th Div. "Q".
        11   A.D.M.S.
        12   D.A.D.V.S.
        13   D.A.D.O.S.
        14   D.A.P.M.
        15   S.S.O.
        16   D.G.O.
        17   104th M.G.Bn:
        18   31st Div. Arty.
        19   31st M.G.Bn:
        20   S.A.A.Sect. D.A.C.
        21   XV Corps "G".
        22   "   "Q"
        23   War Diary
        24   "
        25   File.

SECRET.   Copy No. 31

40th DIVISION ORDER NO.191.   24/8/1918.

1. The 104th Battalion M.G.C. will relieve the 31st Bn: M.G.C. in the Right Division Section.

2. Relief will be carried out one company at a time and will commence on the 25th instant.

3. The H.Q. 104th Battalion M.G.C. will take over from H.Q. 31st Battalion M.G.C. at 3 p.m. on the 27th at V.25.d.6.1.

4. Completion of the relief will be reported to Div. H.Q.

5. ACKNOWLEDGE.

Issued at 6.30 pm.   [signature]. Lieut. Colonel,
                                   General Staff, 40th Division.

Copy No. 1 to G.O.C.
       2   119th Inf. Bde.
       3   120th   ,,
       4   121st   ,,
       5   C.R.E.
       6   17th Worc. R. (P).
       7   S.A.A. Section 40th D.A.C.
       8   104th M.G. Battalion.
       9   Div. Signal Coy.
      10   'L' Special Coy. R.E.
      11   40th Div. "Q"
      12   A.D.M.S.
      13   D.A.D.V.S.
      14   D.A.D.O.S.
      15   D.A.P.M.
      16   Div. Gas Officer.
      17   Div. Claims Officer.
      18   1st Bde R.G.A.
      19   64th   ,,
      20   Div. Train.
      21   S.S.O.
      22   29th Division.
      23   31st   ,,
      24   31st Div. Arty.
      25   31st M.G.Bn:
      26   61st Division.
      27   XV Corps "C".
      28   ,,   "Q"
      29   ,,   R.A.
      30   ,,   H.A.
    31 & 32   War Diary.
      33   File

SECRET.

XV Corps No. 636/27 G.
24th August, 1918.

40th Division.
————————

The following remarks made by the Corps Commander on your proposals for minor operation are forwarded for information :-

1. Withdraw troops leaving only standing patrols to hold the front East of PONT RONDIN.

2. ~~To let~~ ample supply of Stokes and Rifle Grenades in vicinity of BECKETT CORNER to go forward with the troops and assist their advance towards BISHOPS CORNER.

3. Strength of mopping up parties to be at least equal to probable garrison, i.e., about 2 to 3 companies.

4. Have a party ready to work down line of LAUDICK from the North when our barrage lifts off.

5. Plan is approved with above suggestions.

Action will be taken with regard to making the artillery you ask for available.

It is hoped to be able to furnish you with Maps shewing latest details of enemy wire and trenches to-morrow forenoon.

Please submit orders or plan in detail when made and inform me what assistance is required in the way of duplicating barrage Maps, etc., any extra photographs required will, if it is possible, be made available.
The same applies to special equipment, such as, wire-cutters, bill kooks, any special "S.O.S." signals, other light signals, aeroplane flares, etc.
Will you kindly say what help you require from aircraft in order that arrangements may be made, also how you would like the Heavy Artillery to act.

Brigadier-General,
General Staff.

XV Corps.
24/8/1918.

Appendix II.

SECRET.   Copy No......

        40th DIVISION ORDER NO. 192.   25/8/18.

INFORMATION. 1. The enemy is holding the line of the LAUDICK from L.2.o.1.1. through BOWERY COTTAGES to RUE MONTIGNY.
    It is proposed to turn this position from the North.

INTENTION. 2. On a date and at an hour to be notified later the 119th Infantry Brigade will attack from BECKET CORNER on both sides of the BLEU - BISHOP'S CORNER Road.

OBJECTIVE. 3. The objective will be from BECKET CORNER through BISHOP'S CORNER to RUE PROVOST. The 61st Division are extending this from RUE PROVOST through L.14.b.7.7. to L.14.d.8.2.
    The objective and the Southern boundary are shown on map attached.

METHOD OF ATTACK 4. The attack will be carried out by two companies. These companies will make good the line of the road as far South as BISHOP'S CORNER inclusive.
    The attacking companies will be followed by two companies for mopping-up.
    These companies will turn westwards as soon as the line of the road is established and mop up the area between the road and the LAUDICK including the BISHOP'S CORNER - DENVER Road.
    In addition, a special party will be told off to capture BOWERY Cottages from the North.

ARTILLERY. 5. The attack will be carried out under a creeping barrage of fifty four 18-pdrs which will extend from about GILLIE Farm to the LAUDICK. The barrage will be thickest on the left.

(a) The creeping barrage will come down on a line 300 yards in advance of the ROOSTER FARM - BECKET Corner Road and will move forward at the approximate rate of 100 yards in 3 minutes to the line BOWERY Cottages - RUE PROVOST - PRINCE Farm, where it will remain as a protective barrage till zero plus 75 when it creeps forward again to a line about 300 yards South of the above road, to allow the moppers-up to enter BOWERY Cottages.
    At zero plus 90 this protective barrage will begin to roll up from West to East. As the guns lift off they will switch on to the line PRINCE FARM - REGAL Farm.

(b) In addition to the creeping barrage there will be a standing barrage mixed with smoke on the LAUDICK from L.1.b. 65.25. to L.14.b.7.7. The barrage will remain on this line until zero plus 72 when it will stop.

(c) The Heavy Artillery will put down a standing barrage mixed with smoke on the line GILLIE FARM - PRINCE FARM, searching 400 yards Eastwards, to protect the left flank of the attack. This barrage will cease at zero plus 110.

                                           (d).....

-11-

    (d) A Heavy Artillery standing barrage will be put down on the line of the road BISHOP'S CORNER to L.2.c.15.15.
    At zero plus 21 lifts on to line BOWERY Cottages - RUE PROVOST - L.9.a.8.8. - ACTON Cross. This barrage will roll off at following times :-

Zero plus 65	off	BOWERY Cottages.
Zero plus 90	off	RUE PROVOST.
Zero plus 100	off	L.9.a.8.8.
Zero plus 106	off	REGAL Lodge.
Zero plus 130	off	YATTON Farm and ACTON Cross.

M.G's.   6.   Will be notified later.

TROOPS HOLDING THE LINE.   7.   The troops holding the line from ROOSTER FARM to DENVER will be withdrawn prior to zero hour, to about the red dotted line

ACTION OF 120th I.B.   8.   At zero plus 90 troops of 120th Infantry Brigade will advance from the direction of DENVER and will take over the line BOWERY Cottages - RUE PROVOST - BISHOP'S CORNER, making good any part of this line that the moppers-up have been unable to seize.

ACTION OF 61st DIVISION.   9.   Troops of the 61st Division are to advance in conjunction with the 120th Infantry Brigade.

CONTACT AEROPLANES.   10.   Will be notified later.

SIGNALS.   11.   The signal that the various objectives have been reached will be three white Very lights fired in quick succession.

  12.   After zero plus 130 the S.O.S. line for the artillery will be about 200 yards in advance of the objective shown on the map.

SYNCHRON-IZATION OF WATCHES.   13.   Watches will be synchronized on Y day as follows :-

A Staff Officer from Div. H.Q. will be at 119th Infantry Brigade H.Q. at 6 p.m. on Y day and will proceed afterwards to 120th Inf. Bde H.Qrs to be there at 6.30 p.m.
The 31st Div. Artillery H.Q. will synchronize with Div. H.Q. about 5 p.m. and will arrange to give the time to all artillery taking part.

  14.   If the objective is reached and the situation permits, the area South of the line K.4.central - L.5.central will be handed over to 61st Division on Z/Z plus 1 night, under arrangements which will be notified later.

  15.   ACKNOWLEDGE.

                      H.E. Black. Lieut. Colonel,
                    General Staff, 40th Division.

Issued at 8.45 pm

-iii-

DISTRIBUTION OF ORDER NO. 192.

	Copy No. 1	to	G.O.C.
**	2	119th Inf. Bdo.
**	3	120th "
**	4	121st "
	5	C.R.E.
	6	17th Worc. R. (Pioneers).
**	7	104th Bn: M.G.C.
	8	Div. Signal Coy.
	9	40th Div. "Q".
	10	A.D.M.S.
	11	D.A.D.V.S.
	12	D.A.D.O.S.
	13	D.A.P.M.
**	14	1st Bde R.G.A.
**	15	64th Bde R.G.A.
	16	Div. Train.
	17	S.S.O.
**	18	29th Division.
**	19)	
**	20)	31st Div. Artillery.
**	21)	
**	22	31st Bn: M.G.C.
**	23	61st Division.
	24	XV Corps "G".
	25	XV Corps "Q".
**	26	XV Corps R.A.
**	27	XV Corps H.A.
	28	War Diary.
**	29	
	30	File.

Maps issued to those marked **

SECRET.

XV Corps No. 636/27/1.0.
26th August 1918.

G.O.C.R.A.	A.D.A.S.	G.S.O.2.(T).
C.E.	D.D.M.S.	G.S.O.2.(I).
"Q".	Topo.	G.S.O.3.
"A".	A.P.M.	No.6 Balloon Coy.
C.A.	C.M.G.O.	

A minor operation will be carried out by 40th Division tomorrow morning, 27th August; zero hour will be 10 a.m.

Brigadier-General,
General Staff.

XV Corps,
26/8/1918.

Despatched

S E C R E T.

XV Corps No. 636/27/2.G.
28th August 1918.

G.O.C.R.A.	A.D.A.S.	G.S.O.2.(T).
C.E.	D.D.M.S.	G.S.O.2.(I).
"Q".	A.P.M.	C.M.G.O.
"A".	Topo.	C.A.

40th Division are carrying out a small operation at 7 p.m. tonight to mop up area in Square L.8.

XV Corps,
28/8/1918.

Brigadier-General,
General Staff.

40th Div. No. 174/1 G.   S E C R E T.

In continuation of 40th Div. Order No. 192.

1. **MACHINE GUNS**

   Three batteries of machine guns will fire on the line GILLIE FARM - PRINCE FARM from zero hour.
   This fire will be intense to start with and will die down about + 50, when the infantry will have reached BISHOP'S CORNER.
   They will fire bursts on this line till + 120 opening up to intense in the case of a counter-attack.

2. **AIRCRAFT.**

   A contact aeroplane will call for flares over the objective any time after Zero + 2 hours.
   The contact 'plane will be marked by two black panels on the back edge of the lower plane.

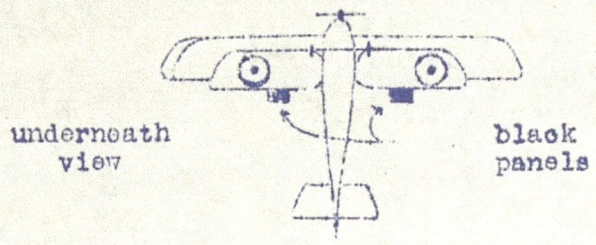

underneath view   black panels

   Flares will be lit by the troops when the aeroplane calls for them with Klaxon Horn or light signal.

3. Care will be taken that troops do not expose themselves prior to zero hour.

                                    I.H. Stafford.
                                    Major g.s.
                                    for. Lieut. Col.
26/8/18.   General Staff, 40th Division.

Issued to all recipients of Order No.192.& 4th Squadron R.A.F.

Appendix 13.

ACCOUNT OF ATTACK ON BISHOPS CORNER, BY 119th INFANTRY BRIGADE AND 120th INFANTRY BRIGADE, ON 27th AUGUST, 1918.

****

1. The troops detailed for the attack were :-

    13th R. Inniskilling Fus., with one   ) of 119th Inf.Bde.
    Company, 12th N. Staffs. Rgt. attached)
    under command of Lieut-Colonel J.F.Plunkett, D.S.O., M.C.
    and
    15th K. O. Y. L. I. of 120th Inf. Bde.
    under command of Lieut-Colonel T.W.T.Isaac.

2. The objective of the attack is shown on map attached to Division Order No. 192. The Barrage Map issued by the Artillery is attached - Appendix "A".

3. At 10. a.m. the artillery barrage opened and the 119th Inf. Bde. advanced from their assembly positions. The advance proceeded well, and by 10.20.a.m. the line was about 350 yards South of BECKET Corner.
    The first enemy machine gun posts were encountered 600 yards North of BISHOPS Corner. The enemy machine gunners put up a stout resistance but their positions were turned by troops on the flanks. A line of rifle posts was encountered about 300 yards from BISHOPS Corner and sharp fighting took place before the posts were overcome. At one post 18 dead Germans were found after the battle.
    The enemy held out at BISHOPS Corner until rushed from three sides. A machine gun and four unwounded prisoners were taken at this corner.
    The situation at 10.50.a.m. was as follows :- We were in possession of the whole of the BECKET Corner - BISHOPS Corner Road and posts were established along the Eastern edges of the enclosures.
    The Right Company reached the BISHOPS Corner - DENVER Road as far West as L.3.d.5.8. and sent one platoon to work down towards BOWERY Cottages. This party worked up to about 300 yards from the cottages. They were unable to advance further in the face of 5 machine guns which were engaging them from BOWERY Cottages and RUE PROVOST

4. The 121st Infantry Bde. in conjunction with the 61st Division on our right, advanced from the line DENVER - COCHIN Corner at 11. 30. a.m.
    They at once came under heavy machine gun fire from BOWERY Cottages, RUE PROVOST and RUE MONTIGNY.
    The Right Company reached the wire on the Western side of the LAUDICK in front of BOWERY Cottages but were unable to make further progress. It was not expected that the battalion would be able to cross the LAUDICK unless the 119th Infantry Bde. had been able to capture BOWERY Cottages from the East.
    This Company eventually swung back to connect with the 61st Division at COCHIN Corner.
    The left company succeeded in turning a hostile machine gun which was on the road at L.2.c.3.2., capturing the gun and killing the crew. They continued to work east up the road to connect with the 119th Infantry Bde. Junction was finally effected at 7. p.m. at L.2.d.9.9.

5.

ii.

5. The 119th Infantry Bde. when they were unable to seize BOWERY Cottages withdrew the right flank to a line L.3.c.7.9. - L.3.c.4.8. - L.2.d.9.9.

6. The line which was consolidated during the night was from F.26.d.9.9. to L.3.c.7.9. - L.2.d.9.9. - L.1.d.85.10. - COCHIN Corner.

7. Our artillery barrage was good and the 119th Infantry Bde. was able to keep up with it, as far as BISHOPS Corner.

8. The enemy's artillery put down a barrage 100 yards East of the line of the LAUDICK at 10. 10. a.m. under the impression we were attacking from the West instead of from the North. Hostile aeroplanes were over about midday locating our posts, which were then heavily shelled.

9. The known enemy casualties were :-

      50 killed (counted on the ground)
      26 unwounded prisoners.
      6 wounded prisoners.

The captured material was :-

      2 Heavy Machine Guns.
      7 Light Machine Guns.
      3 Lewis Guns.

10. Our casualties were :-

	Officers.		Other Ranks.	
	Killed.	Wounded.	Killed.	Wounded.
13th R. Innis.Fus.	2	9	15	60
15th K.O.Y.L.I.	-	-	3	12.
Total :-	2	9	18	72.

40th Div. No. 174. (G).

XV Corps

Proposals for Minor Operation, to take place on

August 27th.

1. It is the intention to make good the line between NEUF BERQUIN and CUTLET CORNER.
   As the enemy appears to hold the line of the LAUDICK from L.2.c.1.1. through BOWERY COTTAGES to RUE MONTIGNY in some strength with wire in front of the ditch, it is proposed to turn the position from the North.

2. A standing barrage (including smoke) will be put down on the LAUDICK and back through RUE PROVOST, PRINCE Farm and GILLIE Farm. Meanwhile a strong party will push out under a creeping barrage up the line of the road from BECKET Corner to BISHOP'S Corner making good this line on their way. Having made good this line, moppers up will turn Westwards and mop up the area between this line and the line between ROOSTER Farm and DENVER including the road from BISHOP'S Corner to DENVER.
   The Artillery programme will be arranged to lift off this area to allow the moppers-up to operate.

3. Our line will then run COCHIN Corner - DENVER - BISHOP'S Corner - F.27.a.1.8.

4. It is expected that the enemy's resistance in BOWERY COTTAGES will be so weakened by this operation that there should be no difficulty in connecting up the line from BISHOP'S Corner through RUE PROVOST to join with the left Brigade, 61st Division in NEUF BERQUIN.
   This will be done subsequently.

5. When both operations are complete the area South of the line K.4. - L.5. will be handed over to the 61st Division.

6. If this scheme of operations as outlined above is approved, the details including the Artillery programme will be notified later.
   The loan of two Brigades of Artillery, one each from the Divisions on either flank, involving a probable change of position for some batteries would be required.

W.E. Peyton

Major-General,

Commanding 40th Division.

24/8/18.

To :- XVth Corps.

copies to :-
119th Inf. Bde.
120th Inf. Bde.
31st Div. Arty.
61st Division.

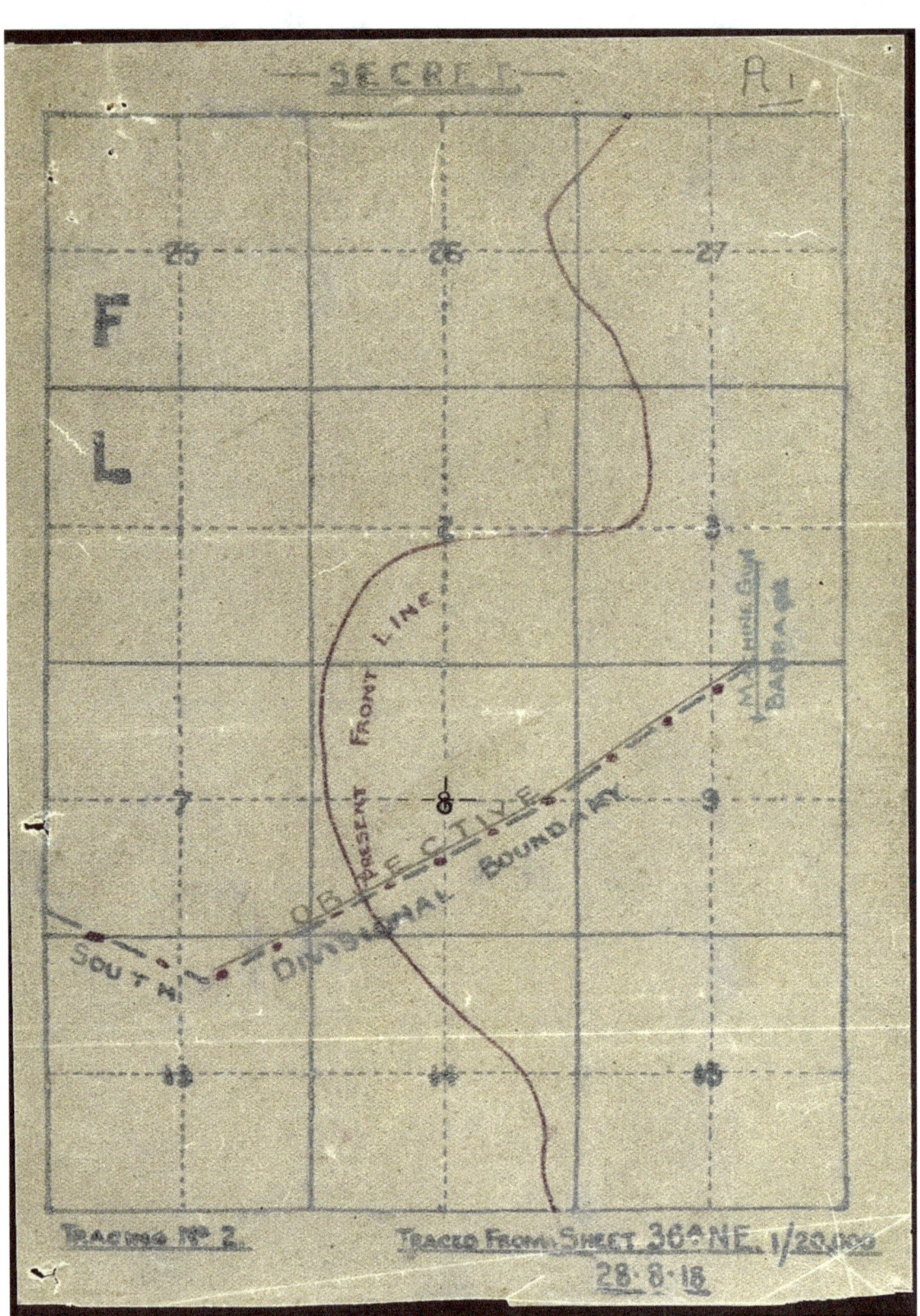

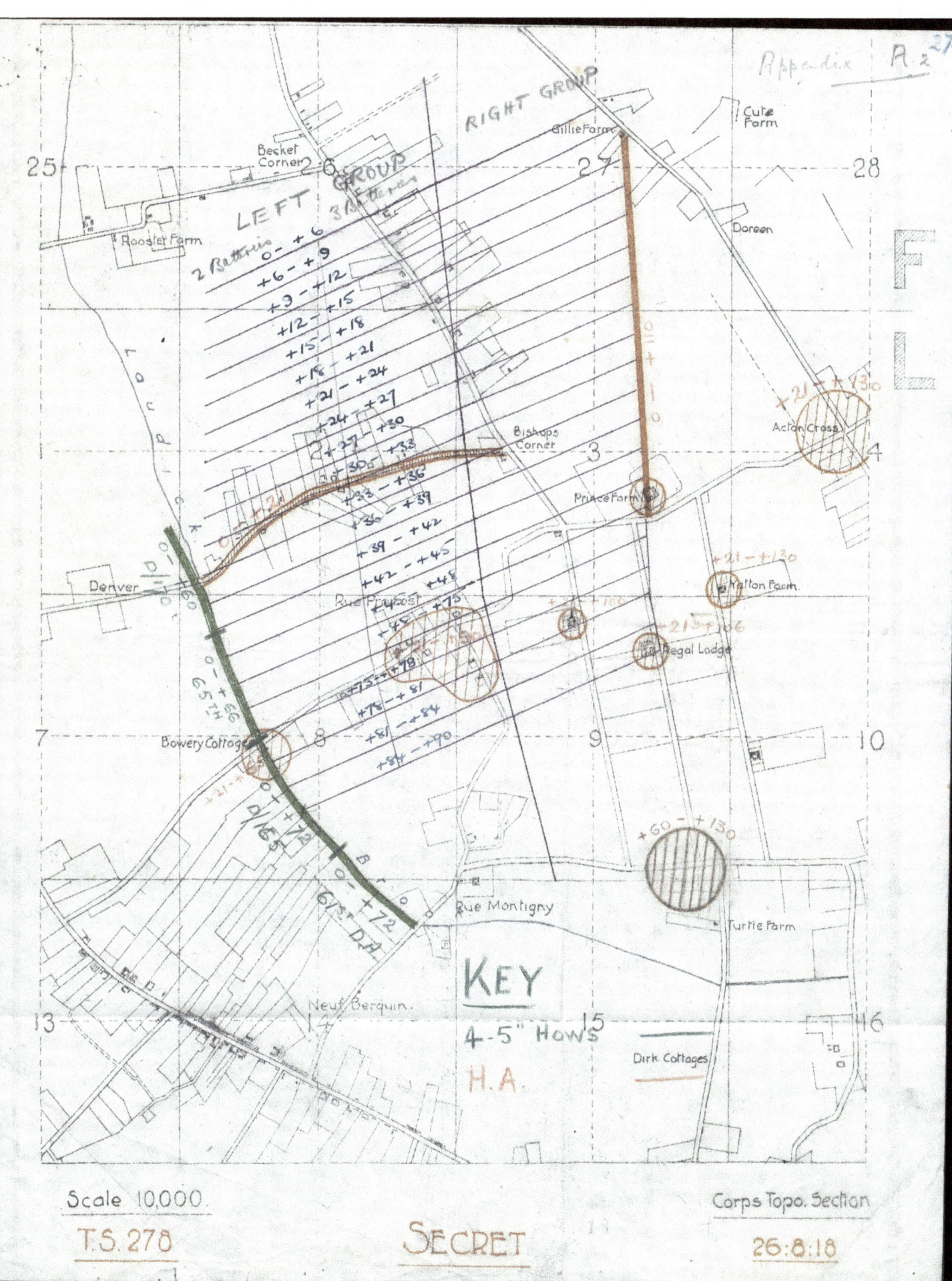

Appendix 14

40th DIVISION ORDER NO. 193.

1. Our new line now runs from the neighbourhood of DENVER along the road to BISHOP'S CORNER, thence to CUTLET CORNER.

2. It is proposed to continue the attack to capture the line BOWERY COTTAGES - RUE PROVOST, on the 29th August at 1.30.p.m.
   This attack will be carried out by 120th Inf. Bde. from the line DENVER - BISHOP'S CORNER.
   The forming up line will be roughly between L.2.d.0.7. and L.2.d.9.9.

3. The first objective will be RUE PROVOST. When this has been taken, a party will work down the Road and take BOWERY COTTAGES in reverse.

4. The Artillery programme will be :-

   (a) A creeping barrage extending from BISHOP'S CORNER to 300 yards West of the LAUDICK, will come down 200 yards in advance of the BISHOP'S CORNER - DENVER ROAD and will move forward at the rate of 100 yards in 3 minutes to Zero + 27 when it will remain as a protective barrage till Zero + 90.

   (b) The 4.5" Hows. will put down a barrage on the RUE PROVOST - BOWERY Cottages Road till + 6 and will then creep forward at the same rate as the 18-pdr barrage till + 20 when it will lift off on to RUE MONTIGNY, REGAL LODGE and PRINCE FARM.

   (c) The Heavy Artillery will fire on following targets :-

   RUE PROVOST   till + 3
   Farm L.9.a.8.8. till + 3
   REGAL Lodge   till + 9
   BOWERY Cottages till +60
   YATTON Lodge   till +90
   RUE MONTIGNY   till +90
   Road from L.3.d.8.7 } till +90.
   to L.10.c.2.7.

5. A battery of 104th Bn: M.G.Corps will be emplaced to thicken the barrage on the East flank of the attack. This M.G.barrage will extend from PRINCE FARM to REGAL Lodge.

6. Troops West of the LAUDICK will be west of the line of the tramway from before zero until after the capture of the objective.

7. A contact 'plane will be over the line and call for flares at 4 p.m. on Z day.

8. The signal announcing the capture of BOWERY Cottages will be three white Very Lights.

9. Watches will be synchronised by the artillery with 120th Infantry Brigade, under arrangements to be made by the C.R.A.

10. Should the patrols which are going out to-night 28th/29th August succeed in capturing RUE PROVOST and not BOWERY Cottages, the second part of above scheme of attack will be carried out, the Artillery and Machine Gun barrages commencing at tasks laid down for zero + 30 and carrying on to zero + 90.

11. ACKNOWLEDGE.

CH² Black

Lieut. Colonel,
General Staff, 40th Division.

P.T.O.

Issued at 7.50. p.m.

```
Copy No. 1  to  G.O.C.
*        2       119th Inf. Bde.
*        3       120th      ,,
         4       121st      ,,
         5       C.R.E.
         6       17th Worc. R. (P).
*        7       104th Bn: M.G.C.
         8       Div. Signal Coy.
         9       40th Div. "Q".
        10       A.D.M.S.
        11       D.A.P.M.
*       12       1st Bde R.G.A.
*       13       64th      ,,
        14       29th Div.
*       15       61st Div.
*       16       31st Div. Arty.
*       17       4th Squadron R.A.F.
        18       XV Corps "G".
        19       XV Corps "Q"
        20       XV Corps R.A.
        21       XV Corps H.A.
        22       War Diary
        23          ,,
        24       File
```

Barrage maps issued to those marked *

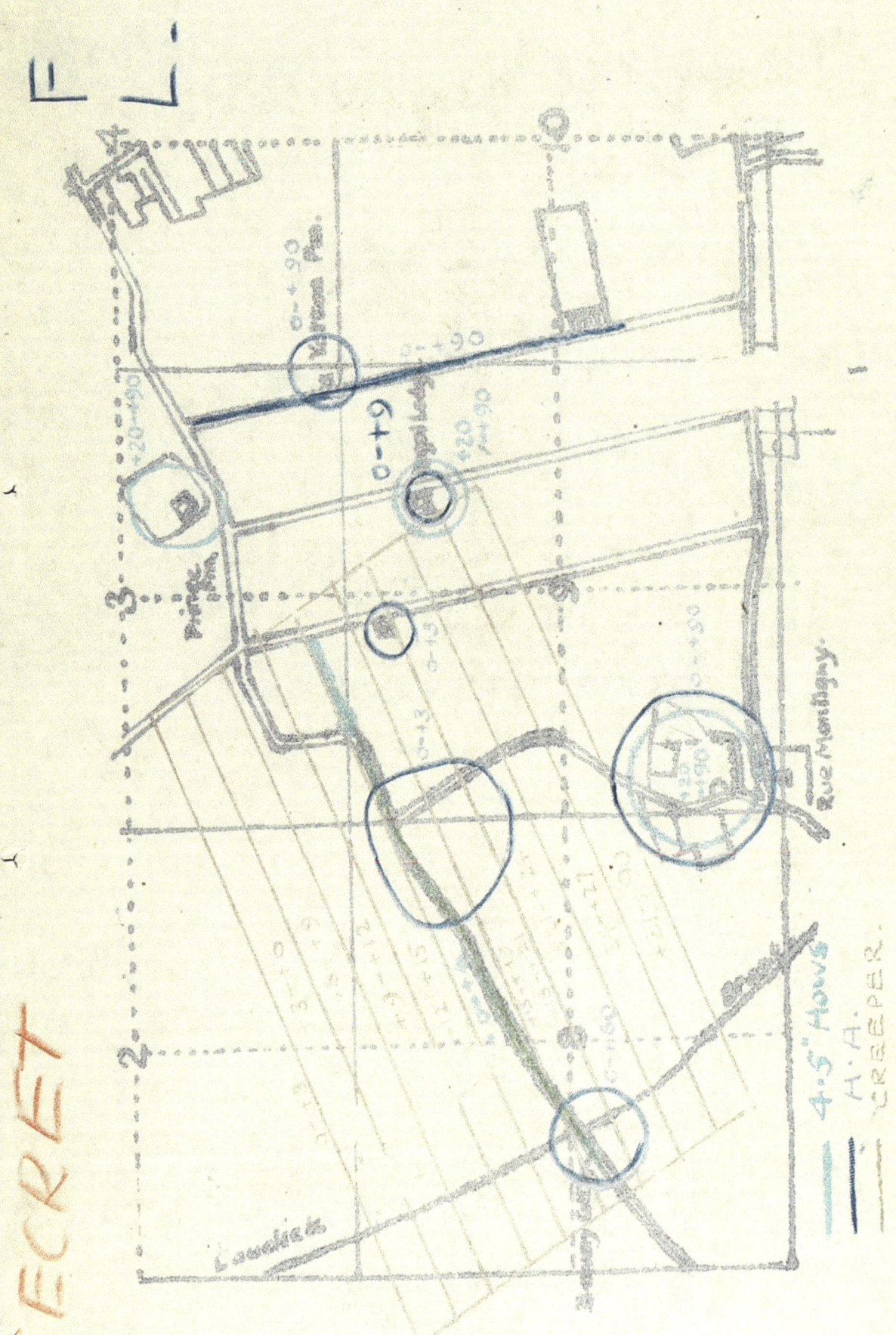

SECRET

Appendix 15

40th DIVISION ORDER NO. 194.

Copy No. 28
28/8/18.

1. The 121st Infantry Bde. will relieve the 119th Infantry Bde. in the line between the dates 29th and 31st August.

2. Moves in relief will be carried out as follows :-

On the 29th.
    A Bn: 121st Inf. Bde. (23rd Cheshire Regt) to line in relief of 13th E. Lancs. Regt.

    B Bn: 121st Inf. Bde. to "Z" Line in place of 23rd Cheshire Regt.

    13th R. Innis. Fus. to camp in Reserve Brigade area.

On the 30th.
    B Bn: 121st Inf. Bde. to line in relief of 12th N.Staffs.Regt.

    C Bn: 121st Inf. Bde. to "Z" Line in place of B.Bn: 121st Inf. Bde.

    13th East Lancs. Regt. to camp in Reserve Bde. area.

On the 31st.
    12th N. Staffs. Regt. to camp in Reserve Bde. area.

3. Command of sub-sector will pass to G.O.C. 121st Infantry Bde. at 10. a.m. 31st.

4. All details, including relief of T.M.Batteries, will be arranged between Brigadiers concerned.
    G.O.C. 121st Inf. Bde. will, at a date to be notified later, be prepared to extend his left up to the HAZEBROUCK - BAILLEUL Railway.

5. As soon as the 61st Division take over the portion of our front South of the grid line K.4.central - L.5.central, the 120th Infantry Bde. will be withdrawn to the neighbourhood of WALLON CAPPEL.

6. The 121st Inf. Bde. will then be responsible for the defence of the whole divisional sector as far back as the "Z" Line (exclusive.) The 119th Inf. Bde. will be responsible for the defence of the "Z" Line maintaining one battalion in this line at all times as a nucleus garrison.

7. ACKNOWLEDGE.

Issued at 9.50 p.m.

(W.I.Black.) Lieut-Colonel.
General Staff, 40th Division.

Copy No.				
1	to G.O.C.	16	to	Div. Gas Officer.
2	119th Inf. Bde.	17		Div. Claims Officer.
3	120th ,,	18		1st Bde R.G.A.
4	121st ,,	19		64th Bde R.G.A.
5	C.R.E.	20		31st Div. Arty.
6	17th Worc. R. (P).	21		29th Div.
7	104 Bn: M.G.C.	22		61st Div.
8	40th Div. Signal Coy.	23		4th Squadron R.A.F.
9	40th Div. "Q".	24		XV Corps G.
10	A.D.M.S.	25		,, Q
11	D.A.D.V.S.	26		,, R.A.
12	D.A.D.O.S.	27		,, H.A.
13	D.A.P.M.	28		War Diary
14	Div. Train.	29		,,
15	S.S.O.	30		File.

Appendix 16.

ACCOUNT OF OPERATIONS OF 29th AUGUST, BY 120th INFANTRY BDE.

****

1. After the operations of 27th which resulted in the capture of BISHOPS Corner it was decided to continue the operation to capture RUE PROVOST and BOWERY Cottages.

2. The Barrage Scheme and Artillery Programme are shown on attached Map "A".

3. The patrols were unable to seize RUE PROVOST and BOWERY Cottages during the night 28th/29th August; arrangements were made to attack this position from the North.

4. The 11th Cameron Highlanders were formed up on the line of the BISHOPS Corner - DENVER Road. At 1.30.p.m. the Artillery Barrage opened and one Company advanced towards RUE PROVOST. This was captured without difficulty. Another Company then passed through the first Company at RUE PROVOST and attacked BOWERY Cottages from the North. The capture of BOWERY Cottages was reported complete at 2.45.p.m.
   About 50 of the enemy were observed to run from RUE PROVOST when our barrage opened. Except for this party there were no enemy met with.

5. The enemy's artillery opened shortly after our barrage came down but did not cause many losses. Our advance was enfiladed by machine guns from the direction of ACTON CROSS.

5. Our casualties were 29 Other Ranks wounded.

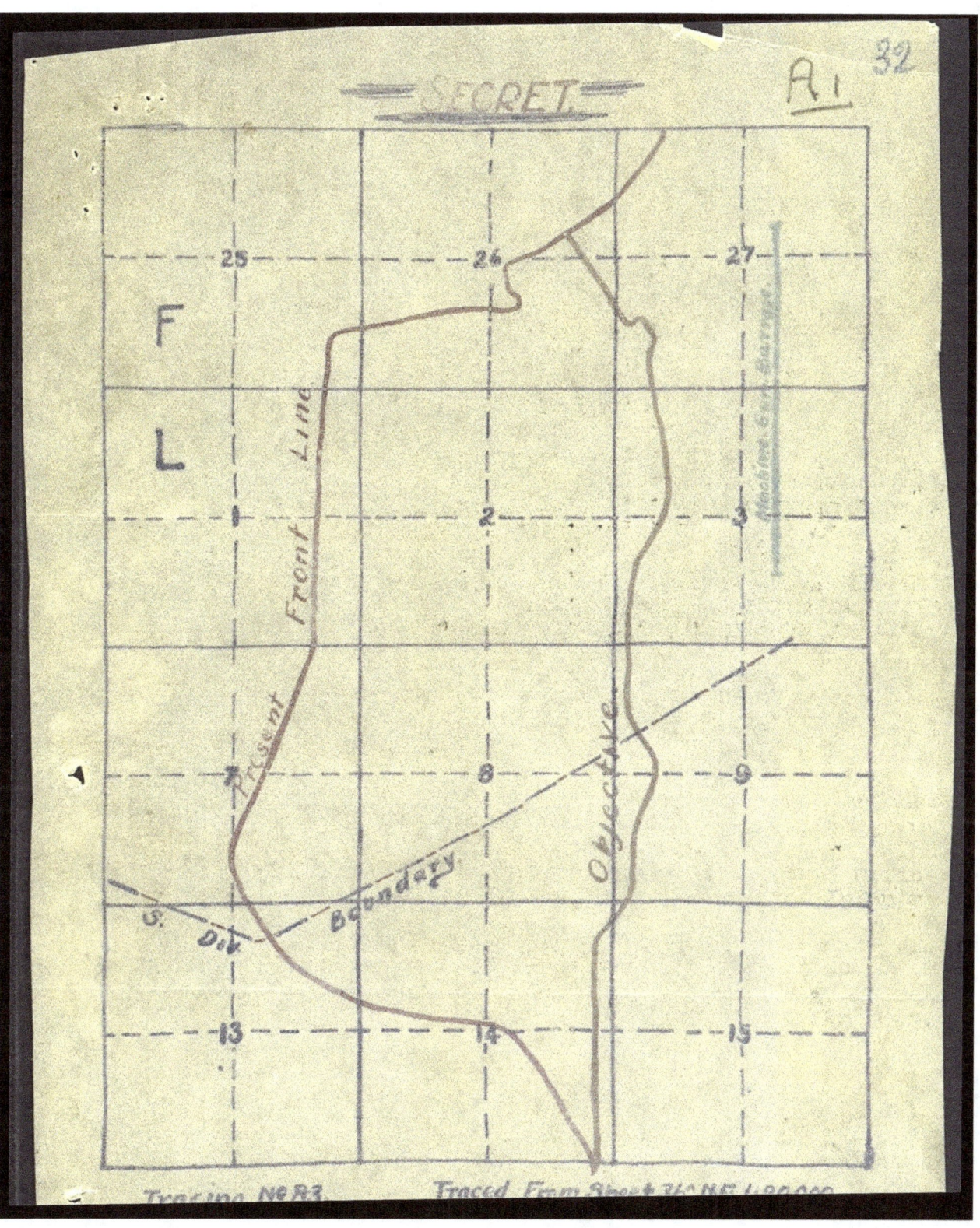

SECRET   A2

Right Group   Left Group
3 Batteries | 1 Bty | 4 Batteries 2 | 1 Bty 3 | 4 Acton Cross
Bishops Corner
Prince Farm
Rue Provost
Kolton Farm
Regal Lodge
+3
+3 +6
+6 +9
+9 +12
+12 +15
+15 +18
+18 +21
+21 +24
+24 +27
+27 +90

Bowry Cottages
Rue Montigny

14   15   16

Sheet 36a N.E.

KEY.
H.A.
4.5" Hows
18 Pdrs.

SECRET.

Copy No. 32.

40th DIVISION ORDER NO. 195.
****

30/8/18.

1. All indications point to the enemy being in retreat in front of us.
   An Advanced Guard to the Division will be formed consisting of the following troops :-

   Advanced Guard Commander - Brig-Gen. W.B.Garnett, D.S.O.

       121st Inf. Bde.
       2 Batteries, 31st Div. Arty.
       1 Coy. 104th Bn. M.G.C.
       1 Coy. XVth Corps Cyclists.

2. Lt. Col. PAYNTER, D.S.O. 28th Army Bde. R.F.A. will be in command of the batteries of the Advanced Guard and will make his Head Qrs. with the Advanced Guard Commander.

3. First bound will be to the line CORIN (F.17.c.2.9) - Cross Roads F.23.c.85.20. - Copse in F.29.a.8.0. - AILERON Farm in L.5.a. Touch will be maintained with 29th Division at CORIN Farm and with 61st Division at LA BRIELLE Farm or on the road from L.5.a.0.0. - PUXTON CROSS.

4. The Northern Boundary of the Division will now run :- Old Boundary from the West as far as F.13.a.45.15. - F.13.central - F.18.a.0.0., thence East along the grid line.
   Southern Boundary as old boundary from the West - K.4.central - L.5.central - G.11.a.0.0.

5. The front of the Division will be covered by one battalion (23rd Cheshire Regt.) The Supporting battalion (23rd Lancs. Fus.) will be brought up to the line OUTLET CORNER - BISHOPS CORNER. The Reserve battalion (8th R. Irish Regt.) will move to the neighbourhood of VIEUX BERQUIN.
   All troops of 121st Inf. Bde. now under orders of 119th Inf. Bde. revert to the command of G.O.C., 121st Inf. Bde.
   The Advanced Guard Commander will establish his Head Qrs. at GRENADE Farm, E.20.b.7.0. as early as possible.

6. As soon as dispositions of the Advanced Guard are complete, the 119th Inf. Bde. will be withdrawn to the following area:-
       Bde. Hd. Qrs.   ..   V.27.c.3.2.
       1 Battalion   ..   in the "Z" Line.
       1 Battalion   ..   TIR ANGLAIS.
       1 Battalion   ..   D.9.a.

   The 119th Inf. Bde. will be responsible for the defence of the "Z" Line along the whole divisional front and will maintain one battalion in this line at all times as a nucleus garrison.
   Liaison posts with Divisions on either flank will be established in this line.
   120th Inf. Bde. will withdraw this afternoon to camps about WALLON CAPPEL as previously ordered.

7. ACKNOWLEDGE.

                               Lieut-Colonel.
                     General Staff, 40th Division.

Issued at 11.15 a.m.

                                     P.T.O.

```
Copy No. 1   to  G.O.C.
        2        119th Inf. Bde.
        3        120th    ,,
        4        121st    ,,
        5        C.R.E.
        6        17th Worc. R. (P).
        7        104th Bn: M.G.C.
        8        Div. Signal Coy.
        9        40th Div. "Q".
       10        A.D.M.S.
       11        D.A.D.V.S.
       12        D.A.D.O.S.
       13        D.A.P.M.
       14        Div. Train.
       15        S.S.O.
       16        40th Div. M.T. Coy.
       17        Div. Gas Off.
       18        Div. Claims Off.
       19        Div. Reception Camp
       20        Area Commandant, WALLON CAPPEL.
       21.       1st Bde R.G.A.
       22        64th    ,,
       23        31st Div. Arty.
       24        29th Div.
       25        61st Div.
       26        4th Squadron R.A.F.
       27        XV Corps G.
       28           ,,    Q
       29           ,,    R.A.
       30           ,,    H.A.
       31        War Diary
       32           ,,
       33        File
       34.       28th Army Brigade R.F.A.
```

SECRET.
　　　　　　　　　　　　　　　　　　　　　　　　　　　　Copy No. 31
　　　　　　　　　　　　　　　　　　　　　　　　　　　　30/8/18.
　　　　　　　　40th DIVISION ORDER NO. 196.

1. The 40th Division will continue its advance tomorrow and maintain touch with the enemy. The Advanced Guard troops will attack the enemy where and when located.

2. The line to be established tomorrow will be :- DU BOIS FARM - LE VERRIER - DOULIEU. The 29th Division is advancing to the line A. 14.c. - A.4.b.

3. The boundaries have been slightly altered and will be as follows :-

   Southern Divisional Boundary - As before to L.5.central, thence to L.6.a.0.0. to G.10.central.

   Northern Divisional Boundary - As before to F.18.central A.13.b.0.0. - A.30.d.0.0.

4. A party of 3 Officers and 50 other ranks of the 3rd Canadian Tunnelling Company has been attached to this Division for the purpose of searching the area for enemy mines etc. This party will work in conjunction with the C.R.E., 40th Division, keeping in touch with the Advanced Guard Commander.

5. ACKNOWLEDGE.

　　　　　　　　　　　　　　　　　　　　J. H. Stafford.
　　　　　　　　　　　　　　　　　　　　　　Major G.S.
　　　　　　　　　　　　　　　　　　　　　for. Lieut-Colonel.
　　　　　　　　　　　　　　　　　General Staff, 40th Division.

Issued at 11.15. p.m.

　　　　　　　　　　　　　　Distribution :-
　　　　　　　　　　　　　　　　　　　　　　　　P. T. O.

```
Copy No. 1  to  G.O.C.
         2      119th Inf. Bde.
         3      120th      ,,
         4      121st      ,,
         5      C.R.E.
         6      17th Worc. R. (P).
         7      104th Bn: M.G.C.
         8      Div. Signal Coy.
         9      40th Div. "Q".
        10      A.D.M.S.
        11      D.A.D.V.S.
        12      D.A.D.O.S.
        13      D.A.P.M.
        14      Div. Train.
        15      S.S.O.
        16      40th Div.M.T.Coy.
        17      Div. Gas Off.
        18      Div. Claims Off.
        19      Div. Reception Camp
        20      Area Commandant, WALLON CAPPEL.
        21.     1st Bde R.G.A.
        22      64th      ,,
        23      31st Div. Arty.
        24      29th Div.
        25      61st Div.
        26      4th Squadron R.A.F.
        27      XV Corps G.
        28         ,,     Q
        29         ,,     R.A.
        30         ,,     H.A.
        31      War Diary
        32         ,,
        33      File
        34.     28th Army Brigade R.F.A.
```

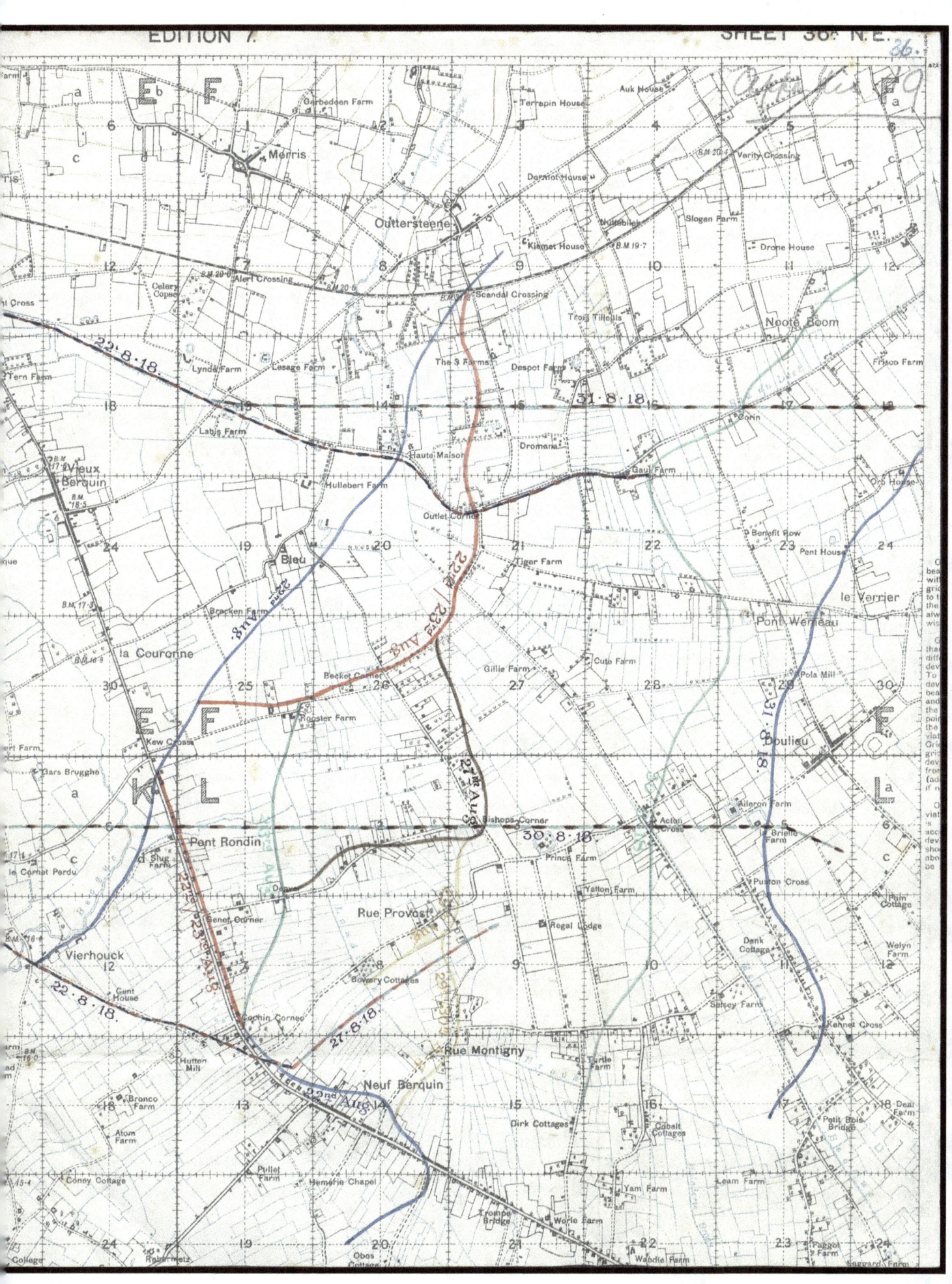

CONFIDENTIAL.   ORIGINAL

WAR DIARY.

40th DIVISION

GENERAL STAFF BRANCH.

VOL. XXVIII

FROM :-   1st September, 1918.
TO   :-   30th September, 1918.

                                                    Major General,
                                        Commanding 40th Division.

35807. W16879/M1879 500,000 3/17 R.T. (1074) Forms W3091/3   Army Form W.3091.

Cover for Documents.

Nature of Enclosures.

Notes, or Letters written.

WAR DIARY

40th DIVISION.

GENERAL STAFF BRANCH.
****

VOL. XXVIII

FROM :- 1st September, 1918.

TO :- 30th September, 1918.

INDEX

```
Pages 1 - 9    ***   ***   ***   *** War Diary.
"     10 - 34  ***   ***   ***   *** Appendices.
"     35 - 67  ***   ***   ***   *** Intell? Summaries.
```

****

Army Form C. 2118.

WAR DIARY
or
INTELLIGENCE SUMMARY.

(Erase heading not required.)

40th DIVISION. SEPTEMBER, 1918.

Place	Date	Hour	Summary of Events and Information	Remarks and references to Appendices
	1st		Early on the morning of 1st Sept. the 121st Infantry Bde. captured DOULIEU and LE VERRIER and by the morning of the 2nd had reached the line of the STEENBECQUE. They were in touch with the 29th Division on the left who held STEENWERCK. The 61st Division on our right was some 1500 yards behind our right flank.	
	2nd		The 40th Division took over from the 29th Division as far North as the line A.18.central - B.15.central. The 121st Inf. Bde. took over this front with one battalion, making two battalions in the Front line and one in Support. After taking over, the 121st Inf. Bde. pushed forward, and by the morning of 3rd Sept. was on the line CROIX DE BAC (inclusive) - A.30.a.& d. - A.24.d. - MURDER FARM (exclusive). On our left we were in touch with the 29th Division whose line ran thence to DE SEULE. On our right the 61st Division was still behind, from G.10. central - G.16.c.0.0.	
LA MOTTE.			40th Div. H. Qrs. closed at U.30.c.0.7. at 4.p.m. and opened at LA MOTTE at the same hour. The 119th Inf. Bde. moved forward. - Bde. H.Qrs. E.20.b.7.0. (GRENADE FARM) one battalion PONT WEMEAU Area, one Battalion VIEUX BERQUIN Area. One officer and 2. O.R. (all wounded) of 140th I.R. (4th Div.) were taken by the 121st Inf. Bde. in CROIX DU BAC. The 51st Div. Artillery which had been covering the 40th Division was withdrawn and returned to 51st Division, the 40th Division front being covered by the 28th Army Field Arty. Bde.	
"	3rd		The 121st Inf. Bde. continued their advance and by the morning of the 4th had reached the line CROIX-DU-BAC - JESUS FARM - WATERLANDS - TOUQUET PARMENTIER. On our right, the 61st Div. line ran from G.12.a.4.0. to SAILLY Station (G.29.b). On our left the 31st Division (who had relieved the 29th Division) line ran from NIEPPE due North. Hostile Artillery fire had increased, all the guns firing from East of the LYS. Hostile Machine Guns East of the LYS were also active.	
"	4th		40th Div. Order No. 197 issued (relief of the 121st Inf. Bde. by 119th Inf. Bde. on 6th Sept) see Appendix 1. Enemy Artillery continued to shell CROIX DU BAC and roads behind our line. During the morning our patrols encountered considerable machine gun fire in attempting to advance. Little headway could be made, but by the morning of the 5th, our line ran from JESUS FARM - Cross Roads (B.27.c.2.6.) - WATERLANDS - MILNER LODGE - B.22.a.2.2. - LE GIBET. On our left the 51st Division line still ran in front of NIEPPE. On our right the 61st Div.	Appendix 1.

Army Form C. 2118.

WAR DIARY
or
INTELLIGENCE SUMMARY.

40th DIVISION. (Erase heading not required.) SEPTEMBER, 1918.

Instructions regarding War Diaries and Intelligence Summaries are contained in F. S. Regs., Part II. and the Staff Manual respectively. Title pages will be prepared in manuscript.

Place	Date	Hour	Summary of Events and Information	Remarks and references to Appendices
LA MOTTE	4th (Continued)		line ran in front of MAC ST. MAUR Southwards. Battalions of the 119th Inf. Bde. moved forward to LE PETIT MORTIER - LE GRAND BEAUMAL and PONT WEMEAU Areas.	
" "	5th		Our patrols advanced and occupied TAFFY FARM and L'EPINETTE. By the morning of the 6th, our line ran - JESUS FARM - PETIT MOULIN - H.3.d.9.9. - B.28.d.2.7. - B.22.d.7.5. One Company of 8th Royal Irish Regt. was sent up from the direction of L'EPINETTE to work across to the left flank. Reports show that this Company proceeded up the road leading to PONT DE NIEPPE, through PONT DE NIEPPE, to a position at B.17.d.6.4. A report was received from this Company during the afternoon of 5th giving their position. No touch was obtained with this Company after this, and it is to be presumed that they were surrounded and captured by the enemy. There was no change in the situation of the troops on our flanks. 119th Inf. Bde. H.Qrs. moved forward to A.20.b.3.3. with 121st Inf. Bde.	
" "	6th		The 121st Inf. Bde. pushed out patrols towards PONT DE NIEPPE to endeavour to get touch with the Company of the 8th R. Irish Regt. which was missing. Posts were established at B.23.b.2.0. B.23.b.6.1. and B.17.d.0.4. These posts were not in touch with each other and were ordered to withdraw on the night 6/7th. They had found no trace of the Company, 8th R. Irish Regt. The 119th Inf. Bde. were to relieve 121st Inf. Bde. during the day. Owing to the resistance of the enemy, 119th Inf. Bde. was not able to pass through 121st Inf. Bde. and orders were issued for 119th Inf. Bde. to take over at night on the line JESUS FARM - PETIT MOULIN - MANCHESTER KEEP, thence back to NIEPPE System. Bde. Hd. Qrs. 119th Inf. Bde. were established at A.24.c.7.7.	
" "	7th		Arrangements were made between 119th Inf. Bde. and 92nd Inf. Bde. (31st Division) to attack PONT DE NIEPPE and the line of the LYS to B.18.d.0.7. The 31st Division to carry on to LE BIZET and Northwards along PLOEGSTEERT Road. The attack was supported by four Brigades of Artillery. The attack started at 10. a.m. under a creeping barrage. One Company succeeded in working its way through PONT DE NIEPPE and established a line on the North bank of the River LYS from B.24.c.0.8. to B.24.a.6.8. Right of this Company prolonged by a second Coy. back to the NIEPPE System at about B.23.b.9.5. The Bde. on the left were held up on line of the WARNAVE River, and during the afternoon our exposed left flank was counter-attacked from the North and driven in, and the whole Divisional line was withdrawn into the NIEPPE System. Div. Order No. 198 issued (Arrival of 66th Div. Arty). See Appendix 2.	Appendix 2.

Army Form C. 2118.

WAR DIARY
or
INTELLIGENCE SUMMARY.

40th DIVISION. *(Erase heading not required.)* SEPTEMBER, 1918.

Instructions regarding War Diaries and Intelligence Summaries are contained in F. S. Regs., Part II. and the Staff Manual respectively. Title pages will be prepared in manuscript.

Place	Date	Hour	Summary of Events and Information	Remarks and references to Appendices
LA MOTTE	8th		A deserter from the 88th I.R. (56th Division) came into our lines at B.22.b.9.9. in the early morning. This was a normal identification. A quiet day: usual patrolling activity, while a post was established at MANCHESTER KEEP	
"	9th		A quiet day: Patrols entered PONT DE NIEPPE in the late evening and saw small party of enemy, which was presumed to be a German patrol.	
"	10th		40th Div. Order No. 199 issued (relief of 121st Inf.Bde. in Div. Support by 120th Inf.Bde.	Appendix 3.
			40th Div. Order No. 200 issued (relief of 104th Bn. M.G.C. by 39th Bn. M.G.C.	Appendix 4.
			40th Div. Order No. 201 issued (relief of 119th Inf.Bde. in outpost line by 120th Inf.de.	Appendix 5.
			Operations confined to active patrolling on the Div. Front: PONT DE NIEPPE was thoroughly reconnoitred and no signs of enemy occupation found. A bridgehead of 1 platoon was established at dusk at B.23.d.9.8. East of PONT DE NIEPPE and posts were also established at bridgehead H.4.c.85.55 and H.4.c.1.5. Enemy activity on the whole below normal.	
"	11th		A quiet day: During the night 11/12th our line was advanced without opposition; the new line running Railway Crossing B.23.b.8.5. - MANCHESTER KEEP - B.23.b.8.5. - along trench to B.17.c. 7.5. to B.17.a.4.0.: touch was gained with Bde. on our left. A patrol pushed across the bridge B.23.d.95.75. but was withdrawn. Enemy artillery was more active in the evening, B.13.c receiving 200 rounds 15.cm. How. and about 20 gas shells on our Support line during the night. 40th Div. Order No. 202 issued(Relief of 104th Bn. M.G.C. by 39th Bn. M.G.C. postponed 1 day)	Appendix 6.
			40th Div. Order No. 203 issued (330th Bde. R.F.A. to be tactically under orders of 31st Div. otherwise under 66th Div. Artillery).	Appendix 7.
"	12th		In the early morning one of our patrols encountered the enemy at about B.17.d.2.6. and inflicted a few casualties on him and sustaining a few themselves: a shoulder strap bearing No. 77 was obtained from the body of a German killed in this encounter: this may either be the 77th I.R., 2nd Guards Reserve Division or 77th Res. Inf. Rgt. 20th Division, in either case, a new Divn. in this Sector. Attempt to gain road in B.18.a. did not succeed. During the night the farm at B.17.d.05.80. was occupied and a post established at B.17.d.0 .9. without opposition. Enemy artillery activity normal. NIEPPE System, PONT DE NIEPPE and STEENWERCKE being lightly shelled at intervals and the main roads kept under harassing fire at night. 120th Inf. Bde. relieved the 121st Inf. Bde. in Support, the latter moving back into the SEC BOIS area with Bde. H.Q. at FETTLE FARM and becoming the Reserve Bde. Bde. H.Q. actually moved	

Army Form C. 2118

WAR DIARY
or
INTELLIGENCE SUMMARY
(Erase heading not required.)

40th DIVISION. SEPTEMBER, 1918.

Instructions regarding War Diaries and Intelligence Summaries are contained in F.S. Regs., Part II. and the Staff Manual respectively. Title Pages will be prepared in manuscript.

Place	Date	Hour	Summary of Events and Information	Remarks and references to Appendices
LA MOTTE (Continued)	12th		into HAZEBROUCK, vide 40th Div. Order No. 204. 40th Div. Order No. 204 issued (Res. Bde. to Move from SEC BOIS area to billets in HAZEBROUCK. Bde. H.Q. V.27.c.3.8.)	Appendix 8.
,,	13th		Fighting patrols from 119th Inf. Bde. attempted, during the night, to cross the R. LYS, at the following points - H.4.c.1.5., B.23.d.90.75., and B.29.c.60.95. The former was detected by the enemy and the river being much swollen and the bridge practically demolished, no crossing was possible: in the other two cases the bridges were either demolished or submerged and consequently crossings were not effected. Hostile artillery was unusually quiet until 4.p.m. when it resumed its normal state. Enemy M.G's were active throughout the day on our posts firing from buildings on the outskirts of PONT DE NIEPPE, those on the N.E. of this place now appear to be re-occupied.	
,,	14th		During the night 13/14th, the 120th Inf. Bde. relieved the 119th Inf. Bde. in the Div. Outpost line with 10th K.O.S.B's in the line, 15th K.O.Y.L.I. in Support and 11th Camerons in Reserve. Bde. Hd. Qrs. changed over at 10. a.m. Our patrols were active during the night: an observation post was established in Laundry at B.29.c.5.9. River LYS was still much swollen. Hostile artillery was slightly more active than yesterday about NIEPPE and PONT DE NIEPPE and our battery zones. A prolonged intermittent bombardment by all natures of guns on the area immediately North of PONT DE NIEPPE and between the WARNAVE and the R. LYS, was commenced in the evening of the 14th. H.Q. 39th Bn. M.G.Corps took over from H. Q. 104th Bn. M.G.Corps during the day, the latter withdrawing to MORBECQUE.	
,,	15th		Operations confined to patrolling: a liaison post with the Division on our Right was established at H.3.c.3.7. and continuous touch ensured. The bombardment commenced yesterday evening in the area North of PONT DE NIEPPE was continued throughout the the day and night. Slight increase in hostile artillery and aircraft activity: a hostile balloon and 1 hostile aeroplane were brought down by our aeroplanes on the Divisional front. POSTON Farm, a battalion H.Q. of the Outpost Bde., was heavily shelled with 5.9" guns in the afternoon.	
,,	16th		The bombardment of the area North of PONT DE NIEPPE was continued throughout the day till 7.p.m. when it finished: patrols were pushed out in the area which was found to be still held by the enemy: posts being located at B.18.c.1.9., B.17.d.5.4. in the former of which there appeared to be about 40 of the enemy.	

1875 W: W593/826 1,000,000 4/15 J.B.C. & A. A.D.S.S./Forms/C. 2118.

Army Form C. 2118.

WAR DIARY
or
INTELLIGENCE SUMMARY.

40th DIVISION (Erase heading not required.) SEPTEMBER, 1918.

Place	Date	Hour	Summary of Events and Information	Remarks and references to Appendices
LA MOTTE (Continued)	16th (Cont'd)		Enemy aeroplane (Fokker) - Pilot Lieut Kresse, from near LILLE, 7th Squadron) brought down by A.A. fire near POSTON FARM, B.20.central, about 8.30.a.m. Very much increased activity in the air by both our own aircraft and E.A., hostile artillery also more active on the whole forward area. During night 16/17th, 15th K.O.Y.L.I. relieved 10th K.O.S.B. in the line. 40th Div. Instruction No. 2. issued (Defensive arrangements of Div. Front. (STEENWERCK SECTOR)).	Appendix 9.
"	17th		40th Div. Instruction No. 3. issued (Dispositions of and arrangements of Supporting Troops). Brigadier-General G.C.Stubbs, D.S.O. (Suffolk Regt.) took over command of 121st Infantry Bde. from Brigadier-General W.B. Garnett, D.S.O. (to England) Quiet day: infantry operations confined to usual patrolling. Two 18.pdrs. and 1 How.Batty. from 66th Div. Artillery, were lent to the 31st Division on our left to assist in a minor operation carried out at 5.30.am. on the 17th, for the capture of SOYER Farm and other objectives, all of which were captured with 60 prisoners. These batteries fired a standing barrage along line of WARNAVE from B.12.central to B.18.a.1.9. Our trench mortars fired 34 rounds on suspected T.M. and M.G. emplacements during the day. Our aircraft very active. Hostile artillery normal, their artillery becoming slightly more active during the evening.	Appendix 10.
"	18th		40th Div. Order No. 205 issued (Relief of 119th Inf. Bde. by 121st Inf. Bde. in support, and 120th Inf. Bde. by 121st Inf. Bde. in Line). Quiet day: Nothing to report. Enemy artillery somewhat active on area between LOWER FARM (Bde. H.Q.) and POSTON Farms (Squares B. 20. 19. and 25. 500 rounds of Yellow Cross being put into B.20.a.& c. In the early hours of the night) Usual patrolling carried out.	Appendix 11.
"	19th		Quiet day. Operations confined to usual patrolling. Activity normal;during night 19/20th 11th Cameron Highlanders relieved the 15th K.O.Y.L.I. in front line and 10th K.O.S.B. relieved 11th Cameron Highlanders in Support.	
"	20th		Patrol went out along trench to road at B.23.b.8.3. - the trench was clear of enemy. A second patrol reconnoitred our line of wire from B.23.d.7.7. to B.29.a.05.75. and found it a good belt, with occasional gaps. A quiet day and no infantry operations. Artillery normal. TAFFY FARM somewhat heavily shelled with 77 mm. in the evening and areas B.15.b., B.16.a., B.17.b., B.22. received particular attention during the night with a few gas shells intermingled. A	

Army Form C. 2118.

WAR DIARY
or
INTELLIGENCE SUMMARY.

(Erase heading not required.)

40th DIVISION. **SEPTEMBER, 1918.**

Instructions regarding War Diaries and Intelligence Summaries are contained in F. S. Regs., Part II. and the Staff Manual respectively. Title pages will be prepared in manuscript.

Place	Date	Hour	Summary of Events and Information	Remarks and references to Appendices
LA MOTTE	20th (Continued)		A heavy concentration put down on CROIX DU BAC at 9.15.p.m. Brig-Gen. F.P.Crozier, C.M.G., D.S.O., assumed temporary command of the Division in the absence of Major-General Sir W. E. Peyton, K.C.B., K.C.V.O., D.S.O.	
"	21st		40th Div. Order No. 206 issued (Warning Order for extension Northwards of Divisional Front and move up of 119th Inf. Bde. etc. Divisional Commander attended a Corps Conference at 3.pm. in HAZEBROUCK at which pending operations and readjustments of Corps area, and dispositions necessitated thereby were discussed. Plans for a minor operation North of PONT DE NIEPPE and between the R. LYS and R. WARNAVE, were also submitted. There were no infantry operations on the Divisional front and hostile artillery activity was normal: the only heavy shelling reported, beyond slightly increased harassing fire on battery areas at night, being 100 rounds of 5.9 in the vicinity of HOLLEBECQUE Farm, B.20.c., the H.Q. of the 10th K.O.S.B. between 3.15.pm. and 4.45.pm; this vicinity was again shelled with 5.9's at 7.15. pm. Slightly increased enemy aerial activity in the evening, while ours was considerable throughout the day. An escaped Portuguese prisoner of war, a Corporal of the 4th Infantry Regt. who was captured at NEUVECHAPELLE on April 9th, was found in Divisional area on the railway in B.28.b. 121st Inf. Bde. relieved 119th Inf. Bde. in Divisional Support, the 119th Inf. Bde. withdrawing into Divisional Reserve in HAZEBROUCK.	Appendix 12.
"	22nd		A quiet day: activity normal. During the night 22/23rd, 121st Inf. Bde. relieved the 120th Inf. Bde. in the Front Line, with 23rd Cheshire Regt. in the front line, 8th R. Irish Regt. in Support and 23rd Lancashire Fus. in reserve, the 120th Inf. Bde. withdrawing into Divisional Support. 40th Div. Order No. 207 issued (Continuation of Warning Order No. 206 (Appendix 12) move of 119th Inf. Bde. into line.) 40th Div. Order No. 208 issued (Orders for a minor operation to be carried out by 121st Inf. Bde. N. and N. E. of PONT DE NIEPPE on morning of 24th Sept.)	Appendix 13. Appendix 14.
"	23rd.		Major-General Sir W. E. Peyton, K.C.B., K.C.V.O., D.S.O., returned and reassumed command of the Division.	

Army Form C. 2118.

WAR DIARY
or
INTELLIGENCE SUMMARY
(Erase heading not required.) SEPTEMBER, 1918.

Instructions regarding War Diaries and Intelligence Summaries are contained in F. S. Regs. Part II. and the Staff Manual respectively. Title pages will be prepared in manuscript.

40th DIVISION

Place	Date	Hour	Summary of Events and Information	Remarks and references to Appendices
LA MOTTE (continued).	23rd		119th Inf. Brigade commenced moving up in accordance with 40th Div. order No.207, the 13th R.Innis. Fus and 13th E.Lancs Regt. proceeded by train to BAILLEUL at 9 a.m., the remainder to go at 11.30 a.m. At 9.45 a.m. telephonic orders received from H.Q. XV Corps that the move not necessary and was left to the discretion of Divl. Commander who cancelled all moves and all units returned to their billets in HAZEBROUCK as soon as orders to that effect could be got to them. With a few small exceptions, advanced parties, advanced transport etc., all were back in billets by 12noon. 40th Div. Order No.209 issued (postponement of moves ordered in Div. Order No.207). Divl. Commander attended a Conference of the Corps Commanders/ at H.Q. 31st Division at 12 noon, where it was decided that the minor operation (vide 40th Div. Order No.208 of 22/9/18) should be postponed 48 hours. Infantry patrols active. Enemy posts at B.24.a.1.1., B.24.a.0.5., B.17.d.6.4. found to be still occupied. Our artillery was active during the night carrying out special harassing fire. Enemy activity normal except his A.A. fire which was particularly active. A German aeroplane brought down in flames opposite the 61st Div. front South of the River LYS about 5.30 p.m.	App.15
,,	24th.		Div. Order No.210 issued (relief of 31st Bn: M.G.C. by 39th Bn: M.G.C. on night 25/26th). During the day the enemy fired several concentrated shoots on our battery positions, particularly about B.14.c., B.20.b. and B.21.a. During the night our patrols established posts at B.24.a.1.1., B.23.b.8.2., B.17.d.6.4. and B.17.d.1.9. The first two posts were established without opposition but considerable M.G. fire was directed at the patrols which established the last two posts. One M.G. was captured at B.17.d.6.4.	App.16
,,	25th.		Normal activity on both sides during the day. During the night further posts were established at B.24.a.0.5. and along road from B.17.d.1.9. to B.17.d.6.4. which had been occupied by the enemy the previous night. Div. Order 211 issued (119th I.B. to take over from 92nd I.Bde on 26/27th Sept.). Div. Order 212 issued (attack by 121 I.Bde to take place morning of 27th Sept.) 40th Div. Instructions No.4 issued (Policy of defence when new front taken over). One company 39th Bn: M.G.C. relieved one company 31st Bn:M.G.C. in new sector during the night 25/26th Sept.	App.17 App.18 App.19
,,	26th.		The 119th Inf. Bde moved by train from HAZEBROUCK to BAILLEUL in the morning.	

Army Form C. 2118.

WAR DIARY
or
INTELLIGENCE SUMMARY.
(Erase heading not required.) SEPTEMBER, 1918.

40th DIVISION.

Instructions regarding War Diaries and Intelligence Summaries are contained in F. S. Regs., Part II. and the Staff Manual respectively. Title pages will be prepared in manuscript.

Place	Date	Hour	Summary of Events and Information	Remarks and references to Appendices
LA MOTTE (continued)	26th.		During the night the 119th Inf. Bde relieved the right battalion 92nd I.B. as far North as C.1.d.2.9. 119th Inf. Bde H.Qrs established at B.8.a.4.2. There was normal activity during the night. Our artillery specially harassed the area B.17.d., B.18.a. c. and d. and B.24.a.	
"	27th.		At 5.45 a.m. the 23rd Lan. Fus. attacked under a creeping barrage from the Northern outskirts of PONT DE NIEPPE, with a view to gaining the line of the LYS as far North as B.18.d.2.8., thence along the road to connect with 119th I.Bde about B.12.c.2.0. A smoke barrage was put down partly by 121st L.T.M.Battery and partly by 4.5" Hows., from B.24.c.1.4. to B.18.d.8.8. The attack met with considerable opposition in the centre. Progress was made on the left flank but our troops were eventually forced back to the original line. Enemy M.G's were particularly active from the LAUNDRY in B.18.c., BRICKWORKS in B.24.a. and CUSTOM HOUSE in B.18.a. Twenty prisoners of 186th I.R. and 88th I.R. (56th Division) were captured. Five prisoners of 186 I.R. surrendered to the right post of 119th I.Bde at 6 a.m. The G.O.C. 40th Division established an Advanced H.Q. at A.21.b.3.8. for the day. One Battalion 120th Inf. Bde moved from PONT WEMEAU to A.11. 40th Div. Order No.213 issued (attack by 2nd Army and action of 40th Division).	App.20
"	28th.		At 5.30 a.m. the attack by Second Army was launched. In conjunction with this attack a smoke screen was put up from the NIEPPE System from B.22.d.4.4. to B.16.d.9.6. at following times, by "L" Special Coy. R.E. with a party of 10th K.O.S.B. attached :- 5.25 a.m. to 7.30 a.m; wind S.S.W. Weak discharge owing to direction of the wind. 9.30 a.m. to 11.30 a.m. wind S.W. Full discharge, good cloud. Again at 2 p.m. to 5 p.m. wind S.W.,full discharge, good cloud, to screen the forming up of 31st Div. on our left for their attack at 3 p.m. Subsequent to the 31st Div. attack our patrols were active to ascertain if the enemy was withdrawing opposite our front. The 119th Infantry Brigade (Left Bde) made bridges during the night over the WARNAVE at B.17.b.8.6., B.12.c.4.8., B.12.c.8.8. The enemy were encountered at B.18.a.3.7., B.18.a.1.9., B.12.b.4.5. and along the road to B.6.d.8.0. (Defence arrangements). 40th Div. Instructions No.5 issued	App.21
"	29th.		We continued to drive in the enemy's covering screen and established the following line.....	

… Army Form C. 2118.

WAR DIARY
or
INTELLIGENCE SUMMARY.

40th DIVISION.   SEPTEMBER, 1918.

(Erase heading not required.)

Instructions regarding War Diaries and Intelligence Summaries are contained in F. S. Regs., Part II. and the Staff Manual respectively. Title pages will be prepared in manuscript.

Place	Date	Hour	Summary of Events and Information	Remarks and references to Appendices
LA MOTTE (Continued)	29th		line :- C.1.c.15.60. - C.1.c.10.23. - C.1.c.05.10. - C.7.a.2.9. - C.7.a.40.55. - B.12.B.90.15. - B.12.d.2.5. - B.18.a.95.60. - B.18.b.05.20. - along West bank of LYS to PONT DE NIEPPE.	
36/A.21.b.3. (near STEENWERCK)	30th		40th Div. Orders No.214 (Move of 1st Echelon D.H.Q.) and 215 (relief of 121 I.B. by 120 I.B.) issued. We continued to follow up the enemy and at nightfall the following line had been established by Left Brigade - B.12.d.8.6. - B.12.b.95.05. - C.7.a.6.8. - C.1.d.4.1. Patrols pushed forward by 3 a.m. (1st) to the following line - C.13.c.4.7. - C.13.a.3.4. - C.13.a.2.9 - C.7.c.3.4. - C.7.c.8.6. - C.7.d.1.9. - C.7.b.6.2. - C.7.b.9.4. with a defensive flank from B.18.central to C.13.c.4.7. Posts were established by Right Brigade at B.18.d.1.8., LAUNDRY (B.18.c) and B.24.a.3.9. A map is attached showing the progress on each day and the alterations to the boundaries.	Apps. 22 & 23 App. 24.

[signature]

Lieut. Colonel,
General Staff, 40th Division.

****

W 5 App. 1

SECRET Copy No. 31

40th DIVISION ORDER NO. 197. 4/9/18.

1. The 119th Infantry Brigade will relieve the 121st Infantry Brigade in the Advanced Guard on 6th instant.

2. Lt. Col. R.I.B.JOHNSON, D.S.O., will take over the command of the Advanced Guard from Brig. General W.B. GARNETT, D.S.O., at 10 a.m. on that date.

3. Details of the relief will be arranged by the Brigade Commanders concerned.

4. Preparatory to this relief, the 119th Inf. Brigade will move forward to-day as follows:-

   A Bn: to LE PETIT MORTIER Area.

   B Bn: to LE GRAND BEAUMAL Area (A.21).

   C Bn: to PONT WEMEAU Area.

   Brigade Headquarters will open at WINK COTTAGES, A.20.b.3.3. at midday 5th instant.

5. The working party of the North Staffs will rejoin its battalion after work to-morrow.

6. ACKNOWLEDGE.

(signed) Lieut. Col.
General Staff, 40th Division.

Issued at 12.30 pm

Copy No.			
1 to G.O.C.		19	Div. Reception Camp
2	119 I.B.	20	1st Bde R.G.A.
3	120 I.B.	21	64th Bde R.G.A.
4	121 I.B.	22	28th A.F.A. Brigade.
5	C.R.E.	23	29th Div.
6	17th Worc. R. (P).	24	61st Div.
7	104 Bn: M.G.C.	25	4th Squadron R.A.F.
8	Div. Signal Coy.	26	Major BELLAMY.
9	40th Div. "C".	27	XV Corps G.
10.	A.D.M.S.	28	XV Corps Q.
11	D.A.D.V.S.	29	XV Corps R.A.
12	D.A.D.O.S.	30	XV Corps H.A.
13	D.A.P.M.	31	War Diary.
14	Div. Train.	32	,,
15	S.S.O.	33	File
16	40th Div. M.T. Coy.	34	31st Div.
17	Div. Gas Officer.		
18	Div. Claims Off.		

SECRET. Copy No. 32

40th DIVISION ORDER NO 198.   7/9/18.

1. The 66th Divisional Artillery have been allotted to 40th Division and will come under the orders of G.O.C. 40th Division.

2. The 66th Divl. Artillery are at present located in the vicinity of CAESTRE (H.Q. P.36.c.1.6).

3. They will move to-morrow 8th instant to areas as under :-

    66th Div. Arty. H.Qrs. to LA MOTTE.

    A Brigade   A.25.a. and c.

    B Brigade.

        2 Batteries   F.30.a.
        1 Battery   F.29.b.
        1 Battery   F.24.c.

    D.A.C.   F.23.a. and c.

    No.1 Coy. 66th Div. Train. F.23.a.

4. Special attention will be paid to Traffic Regulations as laid down in S.S.724, particularly with reference to an interval between every six vehicles.

5. Route - STRAZEELE- VIEUX BERQUIN- F.13. - PONT WEMEAU.

6. G.O.C. 66th Divl. Artillery will move one Artillery Brigade into action with the Advanced Guard on the evening of the 9th September.
    The other Brigade of artillery will be in Reserve and will be in readiness to come into action to cover the STEENWERCK Switch Line (Corps Battle Line).

7. ACKNOWLEDGE.

                                    C.H. Black.   Lieut. Col.
Issued at 8.30 pm   General Staff, 40th Division.

Copy No.1 to G.O.C.   18 Div. Gas Off.
     2   119th Inf. Bde.   19. Div. Claims Off.
     3   120th   ,,   20. Div. Reception Camp.
     4   121st   ,,   21. 1st Bde. R.G.A.
     5   C.R.E.   22. 64th   ,,
     6   17th Worc. R. (Pioneers).   23. 28th A.F.A.Bde.
     7. 66th Divl. Artillery.   24. 31st Div.
     8. 104 Bn: M.G.Corps.   25. 61st Div.
     9. Div. Signal Coy.   26. 4th Squad. R.A.F.
    10. 40th Div. "Q".   27. Maj. BELLAMY.
    11. A.D.M.S.   28. XV Corps G.
    12. D.A.D.V.S.   29.   ,,   Q.
    13. D.A.D.O.S.   30.   ,,   R.A.
    14. D.A.P.M.   31.   ,,   H.A.
    15. Div. Train.   32 War Diary.
    16. S.S.O.   33   ,,
    17. 40th Div. M.T.Coy.   34 File.
                                       35. S.A.A.Sect.D.A.C.

SECRET   Copy No. 32

        40th DIVISION ORDER NO. 199.   10/9/18.

1. The 120th Infantry Brigade will relieve the 121st Infantry Brigade in Brigade Support on the 11th and 12th September.

2. 23 lorries have been placed at the disposal of 40th Division to move the 120th Infantry Brigade. These lorries will arrive in WALLON CAPPEL on the evening of the 10th and will be available on the 11th and 12th September, doing two journeys each day.

3. The 121st Infantry Brigade will move back by march route to the SEC BOIS area.
   Brigade Headquarters will be at FETTLE FARM.

4. Moves will be in accordance with attached table. Details will be arranged between Brigadiers concerned.

5. Brigade Headquarters of both Brigades will move on the 12th instant.

6. Completion of move will be notified to Divisional H.Qrs.

7. ACKNOWLEDGE.

                                    J. H. Stafford

                                        Major,
                          General Staff, 40th Division.

Issued at 10-30 a.m.

Copy No. 1 to G.O.C.
     2   119th Inf. Bde.   20. Div. Reception Camp.
     3   120th   ,,   21. 1st Bde. R.G.A.
     4   121st   ,,   22. 64th ,,
     5   C.R.E.   23. 31st Division.
     6   17th Worc. R. (P).   24. 61st Division.
     7   66th Div. Artillery. 25. 28th A.F.A. Brigade.
     8   104 Bn. M.G.C.   26. S.A.A. Section D.A.C.
     9   Div. Signal Coy.   27. XV Corps G.
    10   40th Div. "Q".   28. ,,   Q.
    11   A.D.M.S.   29. ,,   R.A.
    12   D.A.D.V.S.   30. ,,   H.A.
    13   D.A.D.O.S.   31. War Diary
    14   D.A.P.M.   32. ,,
    15   Div. Train.   33. File.
    16   S.S.O.
    17   40th Div. M.T. Coy.
    18   Div. Gas Off.
    19   Div. Claims Off.

Table to accompany 40th Division Order No. 199.

Date	Unit.	From.	To	
11th.	1 Battalion 120th Inf. Bde.	WALLON CAPPEL.	A.16.c.	⎱ By lorry from WALLON CAPPEL
	1 Battalion 120th Inf. Bde.	WALLON CAPPEL.	A.27.b.	⎰
	1 Battalion 121st Inf. Bde.	A.16.c.	GRAND SEC BOIS Area.	⎱ By march route.
	1 Battalion 121st Inf. Bde.	A.27.b.		⎰
12th.	120th Inf. Bde.H.Q. and T.M.B.	WALLON CAPPEL	WINK Cottage	By lorry from WALLON CAPPEL
	121st Inf. Bde H.Q. and T.M.B.	WINK Cottage	FETTLE Farm	By march route.
	1 Battalion 120th Inf. Bde.	WALLON CAPPEL.	F.22.d.	By lorry from WALLON CAPPEL
	1 Battalion 121st Inf. Bde.	F.22.d.	GRAND SEC BOIS Area	By march route

SECRET.   Copy No. 31

         40th DIVISION ORDER NO. 200.   10/9/18.

1.   The 39th Battalion M.G. Corps has been allotted to 40th Division and will arrive at MORBECQUE on the 11th September from LIERES.

2.   The 39th Battalion M.G.C. will relieve the 104th Bn: M.G.C. and 104th Bn: M.G.C. will withdraw to MORBECQUE. Relief will be complete by the morning of the 15th September.

3.   One company 39th Bn: M.G.C. will move forward on the 12th September to LE VERRIER and will relieve the Reserve Company of 104th Bn: M.G.C.
        On the 13th/14th September this company will relieve the advanced guard company 104th Bn: M.G.C. which will withdraw to reserve.

4.   On the 13th September 2 companies 39th Bn: M.G.C. will move forward and take over from the two companies 104th Bn: M.G.C. covering the STEENWERCK Switch. The two companies 104th Bn: M.G.C. will withdraw to MORBECQUE.

5.   On the 14th September 1 company 39th Bn: M.G.C. will move forward and take over from the Reserve Company 104th Bn: M.G.C. which will withdraw to MORBECQUE.

6.   To assist the 39th Bn: M.G.C. in moving forward, 104th Bn: M.G.C. will detail lorries to bring forward personnel as far as LABIS FARM (36A/F.13.a.7.2).
        These lorries will report as follows :-
            Six lorries on 12th for one company 39th Bn: M.G.C.
            Twelve   "   " 13th "   two companies 39th Bn: M.G.C.

        They will be at MORBECQUE Chateau (36A/D.14.c.6.0.) at 9 a.m.
        The personnel will march from LABIS FARM and O.C. 104th Bn: M.G.C. will arrange to have guides here at 10.30 a.m.
        Guns and ammunition will be brought forward on the Limbers and not in these lorries.

7.   104th Bn: M.G.C. will hand over all maps, air photos etc., to 39th Bn: M.G.C.

8.   39th Bn: M.G.C. H.Q. will take over from 104th Bn: M.G.C. H.Q. at 3 p.m. on 14th September at 36A/F.24.a.1.7.

9.   Details of relief will be arranged between Battalion Commanders.
        Completion of relief will be notified to Divl. H.Qrs.

10.   Orders for the move of 104th Bn: M.G.C. from MORBECQUE will be issued later.

11.   ACKNOWLEDGE.

                                              J. H. Stafford.

                                                      Major,
                                      General Staff, 40th Division.

                                    ******

                                                    Distribution.....

Issued at... 4.30/pm

```
Copy No. 1 to  G.O.C.
         2     119th Inf. Brigade.
         3     120th        ,,
         4     121st        ,,
         5     C.R.E.
         6     17th Worc. R. (Pioneers).
         7     26th Divl. Artillery.
         8     39th Bn: M.G.Corps.
         9     104th        ,,
        10     Div. Signal Coy.
        11     S.A.A. Section D.A.C.
        12     40th Div. "Q".
        13     A.D.M.S.
        14     D.A.D.V.S.
        15     D.A.D.O.S.
        16     D.A.P.M.
        17     Train.
        18     S.S.O.
        19     40th Div. M.T. Coy.
        20     Div. Gas Officer.
        21     Div. Claims Officer.
        22     Div. Reception Camp.
        23     64th Bde R.G.A.
        24     31st Division.
        25     81st        ,,
        26     XV Corps G.
        27     XV Corps Q.
        28.    XV Corps R.A.
        29.    XV Corps H.A.
        30     War Diary.
        31         ,,
        32     File
```

BELGIUM AND PART OF FRANCE — EDITION 9.A. — TRENCHES CORRECTED TO 26-6-18. — SHEET 36 N.W.

GLOSSARY.

...ye, Abb⁰	Abbey.
...oir, Abr	Watering place.
...de douanes	Custom-shelter.
...	Steel works.
...illes	Pointe (Rly.)
...	Alley, Narrow road
...es - ne, Anc⁰⁰	Old.
...edic	Aqueduct.
...re	Tree.
...ventail	fan-shaped.
...décharne	barn.
...fourchu	forked.
...isolé	isolated.
...penché	leaning.
...rineau	Small tree.
...ediie	Arch.
...oisière, Ard⁰⁰	Slate quarry.
...s	Salt.
...re	Asylum.
... des aliénés	Lunatic asylum.
...de charité	
...des pauvres	Asylum.
...de refuge	
...erge, Aub⁰⁰	Inn.
...	Alder-tree.
...à traille	Ferry.
...	Baths.
...s aux bains	Bathing place.
...	Buoy, Beacon.
...de sable	Sand-bank.
... vase	Mud-bank.
...aque	Hut.
...rage	Dam.
...itre	Gate, Stile.
...alance à bascule	Weigh-bridge.
...	Pool, Pond.
... d'échouage	Tidal dock.

Bassin de radoub	Dry dock.
Bateau phare	Light-ship.
Blanchisserie	Laundry.
B.M. (borne millière)	Mile stone.
B⁰ (borne kilométrique)	
Boukinserie	
Fabⁿ de boulons	Bolt Factory.
Bouée	Buoy.
Brasserie, Brass⁰⁰	Brewery.
Briqueterie, Briq⁰⁰	Brickfield.
Brise-lames	Breakwater.
Bureau de poste	Post office.
... de douane	Custom house.
Butte	Bott, Mound.
Cabane	Hut.
Cabaret, Cab⁰	Inn.
Câble sous-marin	Submarine cable
Caisaire, Cals⁰⁰	Calvary.
Canal de dessèchement	Drainage canal.
Canal d'irrigation	Irrigation canal.
Fabⁿ de caoutchouc	Rubber factory.
Carrière, Carr⁰⁰	Quarry.
... de gravier	Gravel-pit.
Caserne	Barracks.
Champ de courses	Race course.
... manoeuvres	Drill-ground.
... tir	Rifle range.
Chantier	Building yard.
	Ship yard.
	Dock yard.
Chantier de construction	Slip-way.
Chapelle, Ch⁰⁰	Chapel.
Charbonnage	Colliery.
Château d'eau	Water tower.
Chaussée	Causeway, Highway.
Chemin de fer	Railway.
Cheminée, Chⁿⁿ	Chimney.
Chêne	Oak tree.
Cimetière, Cim⁰⁰	Cemetery.
Clocher	Belfry.
Clouterie	Nail factory.
Colombier	Dove-cot.

Coron	Workmen's dwellings.
Cour des marchandises	Goods yard.
Couvent	Convent.
Crassier	Slag heap.
Croix	Cross.
Darse	Inner dock.
Démoli - e, Dét⁰⁰	Destroyed.
Déversoir	Weir.
Digue	Dyke, causeway
Distillerie, Distⁿ	Distillery.
Douane	Custom-house.
Bureau de douane	
Entrepôt de douane	Custom warehouse.
Dynamitière, Dynam⁰⁰	Dynamite magazine.
Dynamiterie	Dynamite factory.
Ecluse	Sluice, Lock.
Ecluzette, Ecl⁰⁰	Sluice.
Ecole	School.
Ecurie	Stable.
Eglise	Church.
Emaillerie	Enamel works.
Embarcadère, Emb⁰⁰	Landing-place.
Examinet, Estam⁰	Inn.
Etang	Pond.
Fabrique, Fabⁿ	Factory.
Fabⁿ de produits chimiques	Chemical works.
Fabⁿ de faïence	Pottery.
Faïencerie	
Ferme, Fⁿ	Farm.
Filature, Filⁿⁿ	Spinning mill.
Fonderie, Fondⁿⁿ	Foundry.
Fontaine, Fontⁿ	Spring, Fountain.
Forêt	Forest.
Forme de radoub	Dry dock.
Forge	Smithy.
Fosse	Mine, Pit.
Fossé	Moat, Ditch.
Four	Kiln.
... à chaux	Lime-kiln.

Four à coke	Coke oven.
Ganterie	Glove Factory.
Gare	Station.
Garenne	Warren.
Garnison	Garrison.
Gazomètre	Gasometer.
Glacerie	Mirror Factory.
Fabⁿ de glaces	Ice factory.
Glacière	
Gros	Chase.
Gué	Ford.
Guérite	Sentry-box, Turret.
... à signaux	Signal-box (Rly.)
Halte	Halt.
Hangar	Shed, Hangar.
Hôpital	Hospital.
Hôtel-de-Ville	Town hall.
Houillère	Colliery.
Huilerie	Oil factory.
Imprimerie, Impⁿ	Printing works.
Jetée	Pier.
Laminerie	Rolling mills.
Ligne de haute marée	High water mark.
Laisse de basse marée	Low
Maison Forestière Mⁿⁿ forⁿⁿ	Forester's house.
Malterie	Malt-house.
Marbrerie	Marble works.
Marais	Marsh.
Marais salant	Saltern.
	Salt marsh.
Marché	Market.
Maze	Pool.
Meule	Rick.
Minière	Mine.
Monastère	Monastery.
Moulin, Mⁿ	Mill.
... à vapeur	Steam mill.
Mur	Wall.
... crénelé	Loop-holed wall.

Nacelle	Ferry.
Orme	Elm.
Orphelinat	Orphanage.
Ormaie	Orme-bed.
Ouvrage	Fort.
Ouvrages hydrauliques	Water works.
Papeterie	Paper-mill.
Parc	Park, yard.
... aérostatique	Aviation ground.
... à charbon	Coal yard.
... à pétrole	Petrol store.
Passage à niveau P.N.	Level-crossing.
Passerelle, Pasⁿⁿ	Foot-bridge.
Pépinière	Nursery-garden.
Peuplier	Poplar tree.
Phare	Light-house.
Pilier, Pilⁿ	Post.
Plaine d'exercice	Drill ground.
Pompe	Pump.
Ponceau	Bridge.
Pont	Bridge.
... levis	Drawbridge.
Poste de garde	Guard.
Station	
Poteau Pⁿⁿ	Post.
Poterie	Pottery.
Poudrière, Poudⁿⁿ	Powder magazine.
Magasin à poudre	
Prise d'eau	Water supply.
Puits	Pitshaft, Eisait, Well.
... artésien	Artesian well.
... d'aérage	Ventilating shaft.
... ventilateur	
... de sondage	Boring.
Quai	Quay, Platform.
... aux bestiaux	Cattle platform.
... aux marchandises	Goods platform.
Raccordement	Junction.
Raffinerie	Refinery.
... de sucre	Sugar refinery.
Râperie	Beet-root factory.

Four à coke	Coke oven.
Ganterie	Glove Factory.
Gare	Station.
Garenne	Warren.
Garnison	Garrison.
Gazomètre	Gasometer.
Glacerie	Mirror Factory.
Fab^ue du glaces	
Glacière	Ice factory.
Grue	Crane.
Gué	Ford.
Guérite	Sentry-box, Turret.
,, à signaux	Signal-box (Ry.)
Halte	Halt.
Hangar	Shed, Hangar.
Hôpital	Hospital.
Hôtel-de-Ville	Town hall.
Houillère	Colliery.
Huilerie	Oil factory.
Imprimerie, Imp^ie	Printing works.
Jetée	Pier.
Laminerie	Rolling mills.
Ligne de haute	High water mark.
Laisse marée	
,, de basse marée	Low ,,
Maison Forestière	Forester's house.
Mon. fre.	
Malterie	Malt-house.
Marbrerie	Marble works.
Marais	Marsh.
Marais salant	Saltern, Salt marsh.
Marché	Market.
Mare	Pool.
Meule	Rick.
Minière	Mine.
Monastère	Monastery.
Moulin, M^in	Mill.
,, à vapeur	Steam mill.
Mur	Wall.
,, crénelé	Loop-holed wall.

Nacelle	Ferry.
Orme	Elm.
Orphelinat	Orphanage.
Oseraie	Osier-beds.
Ouvrages	Fort.
Ouvrages hydrauliques	Water works.
Papeterie	Paper-mill.
Parc	Park, yard.
,, aérostatique	Aviation ground.
,, à charbon	Coal yard.
,, à pétrole	Petrol store.
Passage à niveau P.N.	Level-crossing.
Passerelle, Pas^le	Foot-bridge.
Pépinière	Nursery-garden.
Peuplier	Poplar tree.
Phare	Light-house.
Pilier, P^r	Post.
Plaine d'exercice	Drill ground.
Pompe	Pump.
Poteaux	Posts.
Pont	Bridge.
,, levis	Drawbridge.
Poste de garde	Coast-guard station.
Station côte	
Poteau F^ie	Post.
Poterie	Pottery.
Poudrière, Poud^re	
Magasin à poudre	Powder magazine.
Prise d'eau	Water supply, Pit-head, Shaft, Well.
Puits	
,, artésien	Artesian well.
,, d'aérage	
,, métallurgique	Ventilating shaft.
,, de sondage	Boring.
Quai	Quay, Platform.
,, aux bestiaux	Cattle platform.
,, aux marchandises	Goods platform.
Raccordement	Junction.
Raffinerie	Refinery.
,, de sucre	Sugar refinery.
Râperie	Beet-root factory.

Remblai	Embankment.
Remise des aux Machines	Engine-shed.
Réservoir, Rés^r	Reservoir.
Route cavalière	Bridle road.
Rubanerie	Ribbon Factory.
Ruine	Ruin.
Ruines	
En ruine	
Ruiné	
Sablière	Sand-pit.
Sablonnière, Sablon^re	
Sapin	Fir tree.
Saule	Willow tree.
Saunerie	Salt-works.
Scierie, Sc^ie	Saw-mill.
Sondage	Boring.
Source	Spring.
Sucrerie, Suc^re	Sugar factory.
Tannerie	Tannery.
Tir à la cible	Rifle range.
Tissage	Weaving mill.
Tôlerie	Rolling mill.
Tombeau	Tomb.
Tour	Tower.
Tourbière	Peat-bog, Peat-bed.
Tourelle	Small tower.
Tuilerie	Tile works.
Usine à gaz	Gas works.
,, électrique	
,, d'électricité	Electricity works.
,, métallurgique	Metal works.
,, à agglomérés	Briquette factory.
Verrerie, Verr^ie	Glass works.
Viaduc	Viaduct.
Vivier	Fish Pond.
Voie de chargement	
,, de déchargement	
,, d'évitement	Siding.
,, de formation	
,, de manœuvre	
Zinguerie	Zinc works.

INSTRUCTIONS AS TO THE USE OF THE SQUARES.

1. The large rectangles on the map, lettered A, B, C etc., are divided into squares of 1,000 yards side, which are numbered 1, 2, 3, etc. Each of these squares is sub-divided into four minor squares of 500 yards side. These minor squares are considered as lettered a, b, c, d. (See Square No. 6 in each rectangle.) A point may thus be described as $lyi_{\cdot}$ within Square B.4 M.5.b. etc.

2. To locate a point within a small square, consider the sides divided into tenths, and define the point by taking so many tenths from W. to E. along Southern side, and so many from S. to N. along Western side; the S.W. corner always being taken as origin, and the distance along the Southern side being always given by the first figure. Thus the point E would be e5, i.e., 5 divisions East and 3 divisions North from origin.

3. When more accurate definition is wanted for the 1:20,000 or 1:10,000 scaled use exactly the same method, but divide sides into 100 parts and use four figures instead of two. Thus 8847 denotes 88 parts East and 47 parts North of origin. (see point X). Point X is 6825.

4. Use 0 but not 10; use either two or four figures; do not use fractions (¼, ½, etc.).

On squared maps all bearings should be given with reference to the vertical grid lines, which are parallel to the East and West edges of the sheet. Bearings should always be reckoned clockwise from 0° to 360°.

Grid bearings are less than compass bearings, the difference being called the deviation of the compass. To find out what this deviation is, take a compass bearing to a distant point, and measure on the map the grid bearing to that point. The difference between the two bearings is the deviation of the compass from Grid North. To obtain the grid bearing of any point this deviation must be subtracted from the compass bearing (adding 360° to the latter if necessary).

On this sheet the mean deviation of a normal compass is 11° 41'; but to obtain accurate results the exact deviation of each compass should be tested as described above, and this test should be repeated in each locality.

TABLE FOR CONVERTING METRES TO FEET.

Mtrs.	0	1	2	3	4	5	6	7	8	9
0		3·3	6·5	9·8	13·1	16·4	19·7	22·9	26·2	29·5
10	32·8	36·1	39·4	42·6	45·9	49·2	52·5	55·8	59·0	62·3
20	65·6	68·9	72·2	75·4	78·7	82·0	85·3	88·6	91·8	95·1
30	98·4	101·7	105·0	108·2	111·5	114·8	118·1	121·4	124·6	127·9
40	131·2	134·5	137·8	141·0	144·3	147·6	150·9	154·1	157·4	160·7
50	164·0	167·3	170·6	173·8	177·1	180·4	183·7	187·0	190·2	193·5
60	196·8	200·1	203·4	206·6	209·9	213·2	216·5	219·8	223·0	226·3
70	229·6	232·9	236·2	239·4	242·7	246·0	249·3	252·5	255·8	259·1
80	262·4	265·7	269·0	272·2	275·5	278·8	282·1	285·4	288·6	291·9
90	295·2	298·5	301·8	305·0	308·3	311·6	314·9	318·1	321·4	324·7
100	328·0	331·3	334·6	337·8	341·1	344·4	347·7	351·0	354·2	357·5

TRENCH MA[P]

BELGIUM & FRA[NCE]
SHEET 36 N.W.
EDITION 9. A

INDEX TO ADJOINING SHEETS

SCALE 20,000

WAR DIARY
Sept. 1918.

TRENCH MAP.
BELGIUM & FRANCE.
SHEET 36 N.W.
EDITION 9. A

SECRET.   Copy No. 32

40th DIVISION ORDER NO. 201.   10/9/18.

1. The 120th Infantry Brigade will relieve the 119th Infantry Brigade in the Outpost line on the 13/14th September.

2. The 119th Infantry Brigade on relief will move back to STEENWERCK area and will find the working parties for work on roads under 556 A.T.Coy. R.E.

3. Details of relief will be arranged between Brigadiers concerned.

4. 120th Infantry Brigade will forward a map showing their dispositions by companies by the morning of the 15th September.

5. Completion of relief will be notified to Divl. Headquarters.

6. ACKNOWLEDGE.

                                                                           Major,

                                          General Staff, 40th Division.

Issued at 4:30 pm

Copy No. 1 to G.O.C.
        2   119th I.Bde.
        3   120th I.Bde.
        4   121st I.Bde.
        5   C.R.E.
        6   17th Worc. R. (Pioneers).
        7   66th Divl. Arty.
        8   39th Bn: M.G.C.
        9   104th Bn: M.G.C.
       10   Signals.
       11   S.A.A.Section D.A.C.
       12   40th Div."Q".
       13   A.D.M.S.
       14   D.A.D.V.S.
       15   D.A.D.O.S.
       16   D.A.P.M.
       17   Div.Train.
       18   S.S.O.
       19   40th Div. M.T.Coy.
       20   Div. Gas Officer.
       21   Div. Claims Officer.
       22   Div. Reception Camp.
       23   64th Bde R.G.A.
       24   Major BELLAMY.
       25   31st Division.
       26   61st   "
       27   XV Corps G.
       28   XV Corps Q.
       29   XV Corps R.A.
       30   XV Corps H.A.
       31   War Diary
       32   "
       33   File

App 6

SECRET.   Copy No. 31

40th DIVISION ORDER NO. 202.   11/9/18.

1. Ref. 40th Division Order No. 200 dated 10/9/18, the relief need not now be completed until morning of 16th September.

2. Moves mentioned in paras. 3, 4, 5 and 8 will take place one day later than as therein laid down.

3. On completion of withdrawal to MORBECQUE, the 104th Bn: M.G.Corps will be in G.H.Q. reserve. On the 16th Sept. the 104th Bn: M.G.Corps will move from the MORBECQUE area to MILLAIN by route WALLON CAPPEL - BAVINCHOVE - NOORDPEENE - LEDERZEELE, starting at 9.30 a.m., with rations for consumption on the 17th.
    On arrival in MILLAIN area the 104th Bn: M.G.Corps will come under orders of the II Corps, remaining in G.H.Q. Reserve.

4. Any extra transport required for the move will be demanded from 40th Division "Q".

5. ACKNOWLEDGE.

J. H. Stafford

Major,
General Staff, 40th Division.

*****

Issued at 7.20 p.m.

To all recipients of 40th Division Order No.200.

SECRET.   Copy No. 22

          40th DIVISION ORDER NO. 203.   11/9/18.

1. The 66th Divl. Artillery will place the 330th Brigade
   R.F.A. tactically under the control of 31st Division from
   6 p.m. 11th September.

2. On the night 12th/13th September, the 330th Brigade
   R.F.A. will go into action in positions from which they
   can cover the right of the 31st Division and also the left
   of the 40th Division.

3. Arrangements for the move will be made by 66th Divl.
   Artillery with 31st Divl. Artillery direct.

4. 330th Brigade R.F.A. will remain under C.R.A. 66th D.A.
   for Administration other than the supply of ammunition.

5. ACKNOWLEDGE.

                                    J.H. Stafford.
                                              Major,
                              General Staff, 40th Division.

Issued at ..9.15 p.m..

Copy No. 1 to G.O.C.
         2   119th Inf. Bde.
         3   120th   ,,
         4   121st   ,,
         5   C.R.E.
         6   66th Div. Arty.
         7   31st Division.
         8   39th Bn: M.G.C.
         9   Signals
        10   40th Div. Q.
        11   A.D.M.S.
        12   D.A.D.O.S.
        13   D.A.P.M.
        14   Train.
        15   S.S.O.
        16   64th Bde R.G.A.
        17   XV Corps G.
        18   ,,   Q.
        19   ,,   R.A.
        20   ,,   H.A.
        21   War Diary
        22   ,,
        23   File

WD   App. 8   17

                                                    Copy No. 24
SECRET   12/9/18.
            40th DIVISION ORDER NO. 204.
            ****

1.   The 121st Infantry Brigade will move to-morrow 13th
     instant into billots in HAZEBROUCK in accordance with
     40th Div. S/145/C Q.

2.   Brigade Headquarters will be established at V.27.c.3.2.

                                    J. H. Stafford
                                              Major,
                            General Staff, 40th Division.
                                         *****

Issued at.... 6.30 pm.

     Copy No. 1 to G.O.C.
          2   119th Inf. Bde.
          3   120th   ,,
          4   121st   ,,
          5   C.R.E.
          6   66th Div. Arty.
          7   39th Bn: M.G.C.
          8   17th Worc. R. (P).
          9   104th Bn: M.G.C.
         10   Signals
         11   40th Div. "Q".
         12   A.D.M.S.
         13   D.A.D.V.S.
         14   D.A.D.O.S.
         15   D.A.P.M.
         16   Div. Train.
         17   S.S.O.
         18   40th Div. M.T.Coy.
         19   Div. Gas Officer.
         20   Div. Claims Officer.
         21   Div. Reception Camp.
         22   XV Corps G.
         23   War Diary
         24   ,,
         25   File

40th Div. No. 184/3 G.　　　　　　　　　　　　　S E C R E T.

40th DIVISION INSTRUCTIONS No.2.

The defensive arrangements on the Divisional Front (STEENWERCK Sector) will be organized as follows :-

1. The Divisional Front will be held by -

   One Infantry Brigade in Front Line.
   One Infanty Brigade in Support.
   One Infantry Brigade in Reserve.

FRONT LINE BRIGADE.

2. (a) The Front Line Brigade will be disposed in depth with

   One Battalion holding the outpost Line.
   One Battalion in Support.
   One Battalion in Reserve.

   (b) The Main Line of Resistance of the Front Line Brigade will be the ESTAIRES - LYS Line as far North as B.28.b.95.30 thence the NIEPPE System to Div. Northern boundary.

   (c) All ground in front of this line will be fought for.

   (d) The G.O.C., Front Line Brigade will employ all troops at his disposal to maintain the M.L.R. against hostile attack.

SUPPORT BRIGADE.

3. The Support Brigade will be located West of STEENWERCK and will be prepared -

   (a) To assemble in squares A.16, 22 and 28.

   (b) To move forward to support the Front Line Brigade.

   (c) To counter attack to restore the NIEPPE Line.

   (d) To occupy the STEENWERCK Switch Line.

   Orders for these moves will be issued by Div. H.Q.

   On alarm, the Support Brigade will send a mounted Officer with 2 cyclists or mounted men to the Front Line Brigade Headquarters to keep in touch with the situation.
   This Brigade will be at 1 hour's notice to move.

RESERVE BRIGADE.

4. The Reserve Brigade will be located in South HAZEBROUCK and will be prepared -

   (a) To assemble in an area East of the HAZEBROUCK - MORBECQUE Railway in D.11 and 17.

   (b) To move forward to an assembly area between DOULIEU and LE VERRIER. Transport arrangements for this move to be notified later

(c)

(c) To take the place of the Support Brigade if the Support Brigade moves forward of the STEENWERCK Switch.

(d) To occupy the 'Z' Line from K.4.a.5.0. to the Railway at E.4.c.7.2.

Orders for these moves will be issued by D.H.Q.,
On alarm the Reserve Brigade will send a Mounted Officer with 2 cyclists or mounted men to D.H.Q., to keep in touch with the situation.
The Brigade will be at 2½ hours' notice to move.

ARTILLERY. 5. (a) The 66th Div. Arty. (less one Brigade lent to 31st Div.) will be disposed in depth to cover the Front Line Brigade.

(b) The Artillery will be directly under the orders of C.R.A., 66th Div.

(c) The C.R.A., will arrange for the Artillery Brigade Commander to keep in direct touch with the Front Line Infantry Brigade Commander.

(d) Artillery Liaison Officers will be detailed as follows :-

One Captain at Infantry Brigade H.Q.
One Subaltern at Front Line Battalion H.Q.

(e) The 64th Brigade R.G.A. cover the front of 40th Division. The O.C. 64th Brigade will keep in touch with the G.O.C., Front Line Brigade.

MACHINE GUNS. 6. (a) The Companies of the Machine Gun Battalion will be disposed as follows :-

One Company with the Front Line Brigade.
One Company in Support.
One Company in Reserve about LE VERRIER.
One Company in Rest.

(b) The Company with the Front Line Brigade will have its guns echeloned in depth and will be actively employed in support of the Infantry.
This Company must keep a mobile reserve of one section under the immediate orders of the Brigade Commander.
The Company Commander will be responsible to the Brigade Commander for the whole of this defence. He will ensure that by reconnaissance and preparation, the reserve section is really mobile, has thoroughly reconnoitred the area, and is able to carry out any task which may be required of it.
The method of distribution of the forward guns must be adapted to the nature of the country. It is desirable to dispose guns in sections or pairs but in enclosed country this is sometimes impracticable and single guns may have to be used.

(c) The Company in Support will be responsible for the machine gun defence of the Artillery.
Sufficient guns will be kept in position to provide a a continuous belt of fire across the front of the Battery positions.
The General Line for this belt will be JESUS FARM - NIEPPE System in B.16.d.

(d)

3.

(d) The Company in Reserve will be prepared -

    (i) To assemble West of STEENWERCK.

    (ii) To move forward to support the Front Line Brigade.

    (iii) To support the counter attack by the Support Brigade.

    (iv) To take up positions to cover the STEENWERCK Switch.

(e) The Company in Rest will be located in the HAZEBROUCK area and will be prepared -

    (i) To assemble in an area East of the HAZEBROUCK - MORBECQUE Railway in D.11 and 17.

    (ii) To move forward to an assembly area between DOULIEU and LE VERRIER.

    (iii) To take over the duties of the Reserve Company if this Company moves forward of the STEENWERCK Switch.

    (iv) To take up positions to cover the 'Z' Line between K.4.a.5.0. to the Railway at E.4.c.7.2.

ROYAL ENGINEERS & PIONEERS.

7. The Field Companies R.E., and Pioneer Battalion will be prepared -

(a) To assemble in their present areas.

(b) Any Companies forward of the STEENWERCK Switch to come directly under the orders of G.O.C., Front Line Brigade for Defensive purposes.

(c) Companies West of the STEENWERCK Switch will be prepared to provide nucleus garrisons of this line and will act as Battle Stops and Guides.

    Orders for the necessary reconnaissance and for the move to be issued by C.R.E.,

J. H. Stafford.

Major,
General Staff, 40th Division.

16-9-18.

Copies to :-
    119th Infantry Bde.
    120th Infantry Bde.
    121st Infantry Bde.
    17th (P) Bn. Worc. R.
    C.R.A.,
    C.R.E.,
    Div. Signal Coy.
    39th Bn. M.G.C.,
    Div. Train.
    "Q"
    A.D.M.S.,
    D.A.P.M.,
    XV Corps "G".
    31st Division.
    61st Division.
    64th Bde. R.G.A.

O.

40th Div. No. 194/4 G.   S E C R E T.

40th DIVISION INSTRUCTIONS NO. 3.

1. The Divisional Commander has noticed that supporting troops have no fixed ideas of their action in case of a hostile attack. Commanders of Formations and Units will take immediate steps to see that the orders are made clear to subordinate commanders.

2. Posts will be made in the NIEPPE System by the C.R.E. in consultation with the G.O.C. Front Line Brigade.
    Intervening portions of the old Front Line trench of this System will be utilised as drainage channels and the command trench in rear drained into it.
    When the Command Trench has been drained and boarded, fire positions at intervals between the Posts will be made.

3. Positions for Shelter Trenches for the Support Battalion behind hedges will be selected by the G.O.C. Front Line Brigade and will be made by C.R.E. with shelters for the troops.   Labour to be found by Front Line Brigade.

4. These trenches will come into use at the next inter-battalion relief on 19th/20th September, when the dispositions of the Front Line Brigade will be :-

    <u>Front Line Battalion.</u>

            2 coys   ...   in outpost line.
            2 coys   ...   in NIEPPE System.

    <u>Support Battalion.</u>

            2 coys   ...   in ESTAIRES - LYS Line.
            2 coys   ...   in shelter trenches.

    <u>Reserve Battalion.</u>

            as at present.

J. H. Stafford.
Major,
General Staff, 40th Division.

17/9/18.

To :-

     119th Infantry Brigade.
     120th   ,,
     121st   ,,
     17th Worc. R. (Pioneers).
     C.R.A.
     C.R.E.
     Div. Signal Coy.
     39th Bn: M.G.Corps.
     "Q" 40th Div.

SECRET.   Copy No.......

                    40th DIVISION ORDER NO. 205.   18/9/18.
                    ****

1. The 121st Inf. Bde. will relieve the 119th Inf. Bde. in
    the Support Brigade area on the 21st September and 119th
    Inf. Bde. will withdraw to HAZEBROUCK area.

2. The move of dismounted personnel will be by train from
    HAZEBROUCK to BAILLEUL. The trains that take up the 121st
    Inf. Bde. will take back the 119th Inf. Bde.

3. On the 22nd/23rd September the 121st Inf. Bde. will relieve
    the 120th Inf. Bde. in Front Line. On relief, the 120th Inf.
    Bde. will withdraw to Support Bde. area.

4. Details of reliefs will be arranged between Brigadiers
    concerned.

5. The 121st Inf. Bde. will forward a tracing showing their
    dispositions by 25th September.

6. Completion of all reliefs to be notified to Divisional H.Q.

7. Command of the Front Brigade Sector will pass to G. O. C.,
    121st Inf. Bde. at 10. a.m. on 23rd September.

8. ACKNOWLEDGE.

                                          J. H. Stafford.
                                                        Major.
                                  General Staff, 40th Division.

Issued at 7.45.p.m.

Copy No.1 to G.O.C.
      2   119th Inf. Bde.
      3   120th Inf. Bde.
      4   121st Inf. Bde.
      5   C. R. E.
      6   66th Div. Arty.
      7   31st Division.
      8   61st Division.
      9   39th Bn. M.G.Corps.
     10   17th Bn. Worc. R.(P).
     11   Signals.
     12   S.A.A.Sec. 40th D.A.C.
     13   40th Div. "Q".
     14   A.D.M.S.
     15   D.A.D.V.S.
     16   D.A.D.O.S.
     17   D.A.P.M.
     18   Div. Train.
     19   S. S. O.
     20   40th Div. T.Coy.
     21   Div. Gas Off.
     22   Div. Claims Off.
     23   Div. Recep. Camp.
     24   64th Bde. R.G.A.
     25   Major BELLAMY
     26   XVth Corps G.
     27   XVth Corps Q.
     28   XVth Corps R.A.
     29   XVth Corps H.A.
     30   War Diary.
     31   War Diary.
     32   File.

SECRET.   Copy No. 20

40th DIVISION WARNING ORDER NO 206.   21/9/18.

1. The 40th Division will extend to the North and take over a portion of the 31st Div. front.

2. This front will be taken over by the 119th Inf. Brigade.

3. The front to be taken over will extend as far North as C.1.b.1.0. (where the PLOEGSTEERT - ARMENTIERES Road crosses the WARNAVE).

4. The Northern Divisional boundary will probably run from C.1.b.1.0. through B.8.b.0.5. - A.12.a.4.3. thence to present boundary at A.17.b.2.5.

5. The date on which this relief will take place is not yet settled, but arrangements will be made for the relief to take place not later than the night 23rd/24th Sept.

6. One Company 39th Battalion M.G.Corps will be detailed to support the 119th Infantry Brigade.

7. The 119th Infantry Brigade and one company 39th Bn: M.G.C. will move by rail from HAZEBROUCK on the morning of relief to BAILLEUL.
   The Brigade will move to a concentration area about LA CRECHE and move forward at dusk to carry out the relief.

8. Further orders will be issued later.

9. ACKNOWLEDGE.

                                        J.H. Stafford.
                                             Major,
Issued at 11 A.M.   General Staff, 40th Division.

Copy No. 1. to G.O.C.
        2.   119th I.B.
        3.   120th I.B.
        4.   121st I.B.
        5.   C.R.E.
        6.   66th Div. Arty.
        7.   17th Worc. R. (P).
        8.   39th Bn: M.G.C.
        9.   Signals.
       10.   Div. Train.
       11.   S.S.O.
       12.   "Q" 40th Div.
       13.   A.D.M.S.
       14.   D.A.P.M.
       15.   31st Division.
       16.   61st
       17.   XV Corps G.
       18.   XV Corps Q.
       19.   War Diary.
       20.   "
       21.   File.

SECRET.   Copy No. 31.

40th DIVISION ORDER NO. 807.   22/9/'18

In continuation of 40th Division Warning Order No. 806. -

1. The 119th Infantry Bde. will take over from the Right Battn. 94th Infantry Bde., 31st Division, on the night 23/24th.

2. The Northern Divisional Boundary will run from C.1.central - B.5.c.3.5. - along road to B.10.a.85.90. - B.8.b.1.4. - A.10.a. C.4. - A.16.a.6.6. thence along present boundary.

3. The 39th Bn. M. G. Corps will relieve guns of the 31st Bn. M. G. Corps in this area with one Company. Details to be arranged between Battalion Commanders. The Company at rest in HAZEBROUCK will be moved up to Support area on 23rd September.

4. The 119th Inf. Bde. and one Company 39th Bn. M. G. Corps will move by train from HAZEBROUCK to BAILLEUL on the morning of 23rd September. Detailed train time-table is being issued by 40th Div. "Q".

5. The 119th Infantry Bde. will move to a concentration area about BAILLEUL on detraining and will move forward to carry out the relief at dusk.

6. There will be no movement forward of DE SEULE before 7.pm.

7. 119th Infantry Bde. H.Q. will be established at B.7.c.1.1. The 31st Div. are arranging for the 170th Bde. R.F.A. to move out of these H.Q. by 2.pm. on 23rd instant.

8. Command of the new Section of Front Line will pass to G.O.C. 119th Infantry Bde. on completion of relief.

9. 119th Infantry Bde. and 39th Bn. M. G. Corps will forward a tracing shewing their dispositions by evening of the 25th.

10. Completion of reliefs will be wired to D. H. Q.

11. Div. H. Q. will close at LA MOTTE at 3.p.m. on the 24th September and will reopen at the same hour at A.21.b.2.8.

12. ACKNOWLEDGE.

                                                J. H. Stafford.
                                                    Major,
Issued at 5.30 p.m.   General Staff, 40th Division.

1	to G.O.C.	17	D.A.D.O.S.
2	119th I.Bde.	18	D.A.P.M.
3	120th ,,	19	Div.Gas Officer.
4	121st ,,	20	Div.Claims Officer.
5	C.R.E.	21	Div.Reception Camp.
6	60th D.A.	22	64th Bde R.G.A.
7	17th Worc.R(P)	23	Area Commandant, Right Div.
8	Signals	24	31st Division.
9	S.A.A.Sect.D.A.C.	25	61st ,,
10	Div. Train.	26	XV Corps G.
11	S.S.O.	27	,, Q.
12	40th Div.M.T.Coy.	28	,, R.A.
13	39th M.G.Bn:	29	,, H.A.
14	"Q"	30	War Diary.
15	A.D.M.S.	31	,,
16	D.A.D.V.S.	32	File.

SECRET.   Copy No. 22

40th DIVISION ORDER NO. 208.   22/9/1918.

1. A minor operation will be undertaken on the morning of the 24th September to clear the West bank of the LYS as far North as B.18.central.

2. The first objective will be the line of the River LYS to B.18.d.1.8. thence along along the road through B.18.a.8.5. to the WARNAVE at B.12.c.2.0. and to our present line at OOSTHOVE Farm.
   After this objective has been taken patrols will be pushed out as far as the ditch from B.18.d.7.9. - B.12.d.8.0. - B.12.b.1.0 - B.12.a.6.5. and will hold this line.

3. The attack will be carried out by one battalion of the 121st Infantry Brigade. G.O.C. 121st Infantry Brigade will also hold two companies in the NIEPPE Switch in readiness in case of necessity.

4. The attacking troops will form up on the line B.17.c.6.5. - B.23.b.6.4. behind the old trench line. Special parties will be detailed to mop up the area.
   As the advance progresses posts will be established on the line of the LYS River.

5. The 119th Infantry Brigade will establish touch with the 121st Infantry Brigade, first on the line B.12.c.2.0. - OOSTHOVE Farm, and subsequently on the line B.12.b.1.0. - B.12.a.6.5.

6. The attack will be carried out under a creeping barrage of two Brigades of Artillery.
   (a) The creeping barrage will come down on the line B.24.a.3.4. - B.17.d.10.97 and will move forward at the rate of 100 yards in five minutes.
   There will be a halt of seven minutes after the capture of the first objective, on the line B.18.b.9.0. - B.12.c.8.4. The barrage will cease after this seven minutes.
   The creeping barrage will consist of H.E. less 2 enfilade 18-pdr batteries which fire shrapnel.
   (b) 4.5" Hows.
   The intention is for three 4.5" How. batteries to put down smoke screen from B.24.c.05.40. to B.18.d.80.80. from zero to zero plus 74 mins.
   Should Hows. smoke shell not be available, Howitzer batteries will take part in the barrage, but 200 yards in advance of 18-pdrs barrage line.
   (c) Heavy Artillery.
   Will fire on buildings in B.18.c., B.18.a. within safety limits.

   Buildings about B.18.c. 68.30. - B.18.c.90.50.
   ,,   B.18.a. 35.20.
   ,,   B.18.a. 65.40.
   ,,   B.18.d. 00.80.
   ,,   B.18.d. 30.85. - 40.90.
   ,,   B.18.a. 87.77.

   (d) The detailed artillery programme will be issued to all concerned by 66th Div. Artillery.

7. The 121st Light T.M.Battery will engage the houses about
                                                              B.24.a.00.

-ii-

B.24.a.0.0. at zero with two guns.

Six guns will be emplaced to fire a smoke screen East of the LYS in B.24.c. This screen will not be required if the 4.5" Hows. can obtain smoke shell.

The 119th Light T.M. Battery will engage targets in the vicinity of C.1.d.4.1. with three guns, from zero to the cessation of the artillery barrage at zero plus 62.

8. A contact aeroplane will call for flares over the objective at zero plus three hours.

9. Watches will be synchronised at 121st Inf. Bde Headquarters at 6 p.m. on the 23rd under arrangements to be made by the Artillery with 121st Infantry Brigade.

The Artillery will arrange to synchronise their own batteries six hours before zero.

The Infantry time will not be altered after 6 p.m. on 23rd. It should be impressed on the infantry that zero hour will be the opening of the artillery barrage.

10. Zero hour will be notified later.

11. This operation will be referred to as "SAWDUST".

12. The 119th Infantry Brigade will take over from 121st Infantry Brigade on the night 24th/25th all ground captured North of a line through B.17.central - B.18.d.1.7.

13. ACKNOWLEDGE.

J. H. Stafford
Major,
General Staff, 40th Division.

Issued at 10/pm

****

```
Copy No.1 to G.O.C.
        2     119th I.Bde.
        3     120th I.Bde.
        4     121st I.Bde.
        5     C.R.E.
        6     17th Worc. R.(Pioneers).
        7     66th Div. Arty.
        8     39th Bn: M.G.Corps.
        9     Div. Train.
       10     "Q"
       11     A.D.M.S.
       12     D.A.P.M.
       13     'L' Special Coy. R.E.
       14     4th Squadron R.A.F.
       15     31st Division.
       16     61st      ,,
       17     XV Corps "G".
       18         ,,    "Q".
       19         ,,     R.A.
       20         ,,     H.A.
       21     War Diary
       22        ,,
       23     File
       24     Signals
```

SECRET.   Copy No. 31
                                                            23/9/18.
                    40th DIVISION ORDER NO.209.
                    ****

1.   The moves referred to in Division Order No. 207 of 22/9/18
     are postponed indefinitely. Any units that may have moved
     will return to their former locations.

2.   Paragraph 11 is cancelled. Further Orders will be issued
     regarding move of Divisional Headquarters.

3.   ACKNOWLEDGE.

                                                    P.P. Curtis
                                              /for/   Major.
                    General Staff, 40th Division.

Issued at 11.45. a.m. to all recipients of 40th Division Order
              No. 207 of 22/9/18.

                        ****

W.D.   App. 16   X

SECRET.   Copy No. 19.

        40th DIVISION ORDER NO. 210.   24/9/18.

1.   1 Company of 39th Bn: M.G.Corps will relieve 1 company of 31st Bn: M.G.Corps in the area to be taken over by 40th Division from 31st Division on night of 25/26th September.

    All details of relief will be arranged between Battalion Commanders concerned.

2.   The present M.G.Coy Headquarters at B.8.a.4.2. is required as a Brigade H.Q. for Left Brigade. 39th Bn: M.G.C. will arrange to leave this H.Q. vacant. M.G.Coy. Headquarters can be established on the North side of the road at present occupied by personnel of M.G.Corps.

3. ACKNOWLEDGE.

                                J.H. Stafford

                                        Major,

Issued at. 7.30pm

                            General Staff, 40th Division.

Copy No.1 to G.O.C.
       2   119th Inf. Bde.
       3   120th   ,,
       4   121st   ,,
       5   39th Bn: M.G.Corps.
       6   17th Worc. R. (P).
       7   C.R.E.
       8   66th D.A.
       9   Signals.
     10   Div. Train.
     11.   "Q".
     12.   A.D.M.S.
     13   D.A.P.M.
     14   31st Division.
     15   61st   ,,
     16   XV Corps G.
     17   ,,   Q.
     18   War Diary
     19   ,,
     20   File.

SECRET.

Copy No. 32
25-9-18.

40th DIVISION ORDER No. 211.

In continuation of 40th Division Order 207. -

1. The 119th Infantry Brigade will take over from the Right Battalion, 92nd. Infantry Brigade as far North as C.1.d.2.9 on the 26th/27th September.

2. The 119th Infantry Brigade will move by train from HAZEBROUCK to BAILLEUL on the morning of 26th September. Train time table has been issued by 40th Division "Q".

3. The 119th Infantry Brigade H.Q. will be established at B.8.a.4.2 and not at B.7.c.1.1.

4. Completion of Reliefs to be wired to D. H. Q.

5. Command will pass to G.O.C., 119th Infantry Bde on completion of relief.

J. H. Stafford.
Major,
General Staff, 40th Division.

Issued at 11:45 am.

1 to	G.O.C.,	17	D.A.D.O.S.
2	119th I.Bde.	18	D.A.P.M.
3	120th I.Bde.	19	Div. Gas Officer.
4	121st I.Bde.	20	Div. Claims Officer.
5	C.R.E.	21	Camp Cdt.
6	66th D.A.	22	Div. Reception Camp.
7	17th Worc.R (P)	23	64th Bde. R.G.A.
8	Signals.	24	Area Commandant, Right Div.
9	S.A.A.Sect.D.A.C.	25	31st Division.
10	Div. Train.	26	61st Division.
11	S.S.O.	27	XV Corps "G".
12	40th Div.M.T.Coy.	28	XV Corps "Q".
13	39th M.G. Bn.	29	XV Corps R.A.
14	"Q"	30	XV Corps H.A.
15	A.D.M.S.	31	War Diary.
16	D.A.D.V.S.	32	War Diary.
		33	File.

SECRET.   Copy No. 22

40th DIVISION ORDER No. 212.   25/9/18.

In continuation of 40th Div. Order No. 208.

1. This operation will take place on the morning of 27th September.

2. The creeping barrage will move at the rate of 100 yards in three minutes. The first lift will be at Zero plus 6.

3. 3" Stokes Mortars will fire a smoke barrage from B.24.c.05.40 to B.24.a.6.2.
   Two 4.5" How. Batteries will continue the smoke barrage Northwards from B.24.a.6.2. to B.18.d.8.8.

4. 59th Bn: M.G.Corps will fire a machine gun barrage in enfilade from positions in B.10. and B.5. This barrage will be 200 yards in advance of the Artillery barrage lines.

5. The 119th Infantry Brigade will take over from 121st Infantry Brigade on the night 27/28th all ground captured North of the line B.17.central - B.18.d.1.7.

6. The remainder of the scheme will be in accordance with 40th Div. Order 208.

7. ACKNOWLEDGE by wire.

J. H. Stafford
Major,

General Staff, 40th Division.

Issued at.... 6.30 p.m.

Copy No. 1 to G.O.C.
   2   119th I.B.
   3   120th I.B.
   4   121st I.B.
   5   C.R.E.
   6   17th Worc. R. (P).
   7   66th D.A.
   8   59th Bn: M.G.Corps.
   9   Div. Train.
  10   "Q".
  11   A.D.M.S.
  12   D.A.P.M.
  13   'L' Special Coy. R.E.
  14   4th Squadron R.A.F.
  15   31st Division.
  16   61st   ,,
  17   XV Corps G.
  18   ,,   Q.
  19   ,,   R.A.
  20   ,,   H.A.
21 & 22   War Diary.
  23   File
  24   Signals.

Z.2
War Diary

S E C R E T.

The operation referred to in 40th Division Order No. 288. will take place at 5.45 a.m. on 27th September.

J.H. Stafford, Major B.
fr. Lieut. Col.
General Staff, 40th Division.

26.9.18

40th Div. No.184/5(G).　　　　　　　S E C R E T.

40th DIVISION INSTRUCTIONS NO.4.

1. When the 40th Division has completed taking over from the 31st Division as far North as C.1.central, the front to be held including the line of the LYS from GOSPEL Villa will be about 7,500 yards.

2. This front will be held by two Infantry Brigades, with one Brigade in support West of STEENWERCK.

3. The Left Brigade will have two Battalions in the front line and close support and one battalion in reserve.

4. The Right Brigade will have one Battalion in the front line, one battalion in close support and holding the line of the LYS from the South Divisional boundary to the STEENWERCK - ARMENTIERES Railway, and one battalion in Reserve.

5. The Main Line of Resistance of the two forward Brigades will be the ESTAIRES - LYS Line to B.28.b.95.30. and thence the NIEPPE System to the Divisional Northern boundary.

6. The role of the Support Brigade will be as laid down in 40th Div. Instruction No.2.

7. There will be no additional artillery to support the 40th Division.
   The number of guns available does not permit of an S.O.S. barrage on both Infantry Brigade fronts.
   As the Northern flank is the most open to attack, 66th Divisional Artillery Commander will arrange to cover the most probable lines of approach between the LYS and the northern boundary.
   The interval between those lines will be dealt with by machine guns. Batteries must be able to switch on to the Right Brigade area if necessary.

8. The 39th Battalion M.G.Corps will site the Machine Guns in the Divisional area to support the two forward Brigades and the battery positions. A proportion of the battalion will be kept in reserve.
   Certain M.G's will have definite S.O.S. lines given to them. These lines will be :-

   <u>On Left Brigade front</u> - Intervals between the Artillery barrage lines.

   <u>On Right Brigade front</u> - Crossings over the River LYS.

9. A map will be issued to all concerned as soon as definite Artillery and Machine Gun positions and S.O.S. lines have been selected.

　　　　　　　　　　　　　　　　　J.M. Stafford.
　　　　　　　　　　　　　　　　　　　　　　Major,
25/9/18.　　　　　　　　　　General Staff, 40th Division.

119th Inf. Bde.	Div. Train.
120th　　"	"Q"
121st　　"	A.D.M.S.
17th Worc. R.(P).	D.A.P.M.
C.R.A.	XV Corps G.
C.R.E.	31st Division.
Div. Signal Coy.	61st　　"
39th Bn. M.G.C.	64th Bde R.G.A.

SECRET.   Copy No. 14

    40th DIVISION ORDER NO. 213.   27/9/18.

1. The Northern Corps of Second Army are attacking on J day at H hour. At the same time the XI Corps Artillery are assisting by engaging ARMENTIERES and the enemy Artillery to the South East.

2. Should the operations on the North cause the enemy to weaken on the PLOEGSTEERT Front the XV Corps is to press the enemy's retirement.

3. (i) The XV Corps is to form the right Flank Guard of the Second Army, the left of the Corps advancing between the WARNAVE and the DOUVE Rivers towards WARNETON.

   (ii) The 40th Division with two Brigades in line will hold the front from the right of the Corps to the PLOEGSTEERT - LE BIZET Road exclusive.

   (iii) The 31st Division is to be prepared to advance any time after H hour within 4 hours of the receipt of orders.

    (a) First Objective. From the right of the division along the WARNAVE to U.28.c.2.9. Northwards to U.22.a.2.5. - Cross Roads in U.15.b.4.1. - Road Junction U.15.b.3.8. - U.9.d.0.0. - U.8.central.

    Second Objective. Along the WARNAVE to its junction with the LYS U.23.b.6.5. - U.12.c.central, thence West along the DOUVE.

    In each case a defensive flank to be formed facing S.E. along the WARNAVE.

    (b) The time at which 31st Division are to advance to the First objective will be wired to all concerned by code message " WAR H + (number of hours and minutes).

   (iv) The 120th Infantry Brigade will be in Divisional Reserve during the operations in a constant state of readiness.

   (v) The defence of the front will be maintained in accordance with Div. Instructions No. 4.

4. (a) Provided the wind is favourable, smoke will be employed with the following objects :-

    (1) To cover batteries of the XV Corps during the bombardment of MESSINES.

    (2) To cover the assembly of troops of the 31st Div.

    (3) To cover the artillery supporting the 31st Division's attack.

   (b) For this purpose, smoke cloud will be formed between NIEPPE and the River LYS in accordance with 40th Div.No. 180/9(G) between H - 5 minutes to H plus 2 hours and from H plus 4 hours to H plus 6 hours.

                                      This...

-ii-

This smoke cloud will be continued for the purpose mentioned in para. 4 (a) 2 & 3 above from the period of 1 hour before to 2 hours after the attack of 31st Division is launched. The time at which this is to take place will be notified to O.C. "L" Special Company R.E. at 40th Div. Report Centre.

O.C. "L" Special Company will be at 40th Div. Report Centre at A.21.b.3.8. from H hour onwards.

5. The Artillery of XV Corps, less the Artillery with 40th Division will bombard certain areas about MESSINES from H - 5 minutes to H plus 2 hours and from H plus 4 hours to H plus 6 hours.
   The artillery will support the advance of the 31st Division to their objectives commencing at the hour mentioned in para. 3(b).

6. There will be a Staff Officer from 40th Division at Advanced Report Centre from H hour onwards.

7. ACKNOWLEDGE.

Issued at.... 7.50 p.m.

Lieut. Colonel,
General Staff, 40th Division.

****

Copy No. 1 to G.O.C.
       2   119th I.B.
       3   120th I.B.
       4   121st I.B.
       5   C. R. A.
       6   C.R.E.
       7   A.D.M.S.
       8   "Q"
       9   Signals
      10   39th M.G.Bn:
      11   D.A.P.M.
      12   "L" Special Coy. R.E.
      13   War Diary
      14
      15   File

40th Div. No. 184/6(G).   SECRET.

40th DIVISION INSTRUCTIONS NO.5.

1.   The dispositions laid down in 40th Div. Instructions No. 4 will be modified as follows :-

   (a) The left Brigade sub-sector will be held with one Bn. in the Outpost Zone, one in garrison of the NIEPPE System and one in reserve about TROIS ARBRES.

   (b) The Right Brigade sub-sector will be held as at present with two battalions distributed in depth between the outpost line and the NIEPPE system and one battalion in support between LA HANEGAT and l'HALLOBEAU.

   (c) The M.G. Battalion will be redistributed on a basis of 1 company being allotted to each Infantry Brigade in the line and two companies held in Divisional Reserve.
   A certain number of guns from the two companies in reserve will be posted so as to afford protection to the line of field guns in case of necessity.

   (d) The 331st Brigade R.F.A. will be divided into two groups each working with an Infantry Brigade in the line, but all batteries will be so placed that they can cover the front of either Infantry Brigades should the necessity arise.

2.   The possibility of a strong counter-attack on the part of the enemy from the direction of ARMENTIERES with a view to turning the right flank of the Second Army must be contemplated and it is very important that our defensive arrangements should be pushed forward with all the speed possible.

   The main Line of Resistance of the two forward Brigades will be the ESTAIRES - LYS line to B.28.b.95.30, and thence the NIEPPE System to the Divisional Northern boundary.

   All energies will be concentrated on completing the defenses of this line and arrangements for the necessary work will be made as follows :-

   (a) The C.R.E. will be responsible for erecting screens 300 - 500 yards in front of the NIEPPE System, leaving a ground clearance of at least 4 ft, as well as for the screening of the main roads in use in the forward area wherever necessary.
   For this purpose the two Field Companies in the line will be entirely at his disposal and the work will be completed in three days.

   (b)   Brigades in the line will be responsible for the defences of the NIEPPE System, labour for which must be found from their own resources, and the necessary pressure exerted on units with a view to getting the work done expeditiously.
   R.E. supervision will be provided under arrangements to be made by Brigadiers with the C.R.E.

3.....

3. Work will be carried out on the following lines :-

(a) The construction of sufficient fire positions for two battalions and two M.G.Companies in each Brigade sub-sector (i.e. 32 Platoon positions and 32 M.G. emplacements in each). These positions should not be "dressed" in a straight line but arranged chequer-wise so as to cover with fire the ground in front and afford one another mutual support; the whole forming a defended zone rather than a trench line.

(b) When this is done, arrangements for the provision of covered communications will be undertaken, those in the more exposed positions being commenced first.

(c) A certain number of platoon positions in the line have already been constructed by the Field Engineers. Details of the work completed and proposed will be given by the C.R.E. to the Brigadiers concerned.

(d) A considerable amount of duck-boards, timber and other material is lying about the forward area and this should be collected and utilised as far as possible.

4. Brigadiers will submit their plans for the consolidation of the NIEPPE System for approval and co-ordination by Divisional Headquarters.

5. Reliefs of Brigades in the line will be arranged on a basis of 12 days in and 6 days out.
The 121st Infantry Brigade will be relieved by the 120th Infantry Brigade in the right sub-sector on day and night of 2nd October and will in turn relieve the 119th Infantry Brigade in the left sub-sector on the day and night of the 9th October.

H.E. Black. Lieut. Colonel,

28/9/18. General Staff, 40th Division.

*****

119th Inf. Bde.	Div. Train.
120th "	"C"
121st "	A.D.M.S.
17th Worc. R. (P).	D.A.P.M.
C.R.A.	XV Corps G.
C.R.E.	31st Division.
Div. Signal Coy.	61st "
39th Bn: M.G.C.	64th Bde R.G.A.

SECRET.   Copy No......

    40th DIVISION ORDER NO. 214. 30/9/18.

1. Divisional Headquarters, 1st Echelon, will move forward to present Advanced Report Centre at A.21.b.2.8. and will open at 5 p.m. to-day.

2. The following will constitute the 1st Echelon for the purpose of this move :-

    "G" Office
    "A & Q" Office
    C. R. A.
    C. R. E.
    Camp Commandant.

3. The remainder will remain in their present locations until further orders.

4. ACKNOWLEDGE.

                Lieut. Colonel,
Issued at. 9.45 am
         General Staff, 40th Division.

```
Copy No. 1   to   G.O.C.
        2         119th I.B.
        3         120th I.B.
        4         121st I.B.
        5         C.R.E.
        6         66th D.A.
        7         17th Worc. R. (P).
        8         Signals
        9         S.A.A.Section D.A.C.
       10         Div. Train
       11         S.S.O.
       12         40th Div.M.T.Coy.
       13         39th M.G.Bn:
       14         "Q" 40th Div.
       15         A.D.M.S.
       16         D.A.D.V.S.
       17         D.A.D.O.S.
       18         D.A.P.M.
       19         Camp Commandant.
       20         Div. Gas Officer
       21         Div. Claims Off.
       22         Div. Reception Camp
       23         64th Bde R.G.A.
       24         Area Commandant, Right Div.
       25         31st Div.
       26         61st Div.
       27         XV Corps G.
       28             "     Q.
       29             "     R.A.
       30             "     H.A.
  31 & 32  War Diary
       33         File
       34         "L" Special Coy. R.E.
       35         Div. Employment Coy.
```

SECRET.   Copy No...26

            40th DIVISION ORDER NO. 215.   30/9/18.
            ****

1. The 120th Infantry Brigade will relieve the 121st
    Infantry Brigade in the Right Brigade front on the night
    1/2nd October.   120th Inf. Bde H.Q. will be established
    at TOUQUET PARMENTIER.

2. On completion of relief, 121st Infantry Brigade will
    move to billets in STEENWERCK and the neighbourhood.
    121st Inf. Bde. H.Q. will remain at LEWER Farm unless
    better accommodation can be found in STEENWERCK.

3. Details of relief will be arranged between Brigades
    concerned.

4. Command will pass on completion of relief.

5. Completion of relief will be notified to D.H.Q. by
    wire.

6. ACKNOWLEDGE.

                                    [signature]
                                              Lieut. Colonel,
Issued at 10.a.m.   General Staff, 40th Division.
                                    *****

Copy No. 1 to G.O.C.
         2   119th I.B.
         3   120th I.B.
         4   121st I.B.
         5   C.R.E.
         6   66th D.A.
         7   17th Worc. R.(P).
         8   Signals
         9   39th Bn: M.G.C.
        10   Div. Train.
        11   "Q".
        12   A.D.M.S.
        13   D.A.P.M.
        14   Div. Gas Officer.
        15   Div. Claims Off.
        16   Div. Reception Camp.
        17   64th Bde R.G.A.
        18   "L" Special Coy. R.E.
        19   31st Div.
        20   61st Div.
        21   XV Corps G.
        22   ,,   Q.
        23   ,,   R.A.
        24   ,,   H.A.
    25 & 26   War Diary
        27   File

CONFIDENTIAL   (Not to be taken forward of Bn: H.Qrs).

40th DIVISION DAILY INTELLIGENCE SUMMARY, No.10.
period 6 a.m. 1st - 6 a.m. 2nd Sept.1918.

(a) OUR OPERATIONS.

1. **INFANTRY.** Our infantry continued to follow up the enemy's retreat yesterday and by the evening had established a line running from A.29.a.30.95 along STEENWERCK SWITCH to about G.10.b.3.2. Touch was maintained with the Division on our left but was temporarily lost with the Division on our right. This was, however, regained this morning. The advance is continuing to-day and an unconfirmed report has been received to the effect that our men are through LA BOUDRELLE.

2. **ARTILLERY** At 10 a.m. movement reported by aeroplane in G.6., H.1. and A.27.d. was engaged. At Infantry request, LA KIRLEM and G.1.d.1.5. were engaged.
Harassing fire was maintained on roads and tracks throughout the 24 hours.

3. **AIRCRAFT.** Several reconnaissances were carried out by our 'planes over STEENWERCK - ARMENTIERES during the day at low altitude.

(b) ENEMY'S OPERATIONS

1. **INFANTRY.** Except for selected M.G. posts placed so as to harass our advance, no enemy activity has been reported.

2. **ARTILLERY.** There was some scattered field gun fire throughout the day on forward tracks and roads.
During the afternoon DOULIEU - PONT WEMEAU and the vicinity of AILERON FARM were shelled with about 50 rounds 10.5 cm How.
Otherwise enemy's artillery was inactive.

3. **GAS SHELLING.** A few gas shells fell in A.25 during the night and the area round F.29.a. during the morning.

4. **AIRCRAFT.** Five E.A. crossed our lines between 9.30 a.m. and 10 a.m. They attacked an R.E. 8, but were driven off by our Scouts and A.A. fire. Bombing 'planes were over our lines between 9.30 pm to 11.30 pm. A few bombs were dropped in the vicinity of LA MOT

5. **BALLOONS.**
Two Kite balloons were observed during the day on grid bearings of 78° and 114° from K.5.d.5.6.

(c) INTELLIGENCE.

1. **FIRES & EXPLOSIONS.** Numerous fires and explosions were again observed throughout yesterday.
Ammunition dump at A.12.b.3.3. was blown up at 5 p.m.

Chapman
for Lieut. Colonel,
General Staff, 40th Division.

P.T.O.

(Not to be taken forward of Battn. H.Q.)

CONFIDENTIAL

40th DIVISION DAILY INTELLIGENCE SUMMARY No.11.
Period 6 am. 2nd - 6 am. 3rd September, 1918.

(a) OUR OPERATIONS.

1. INFANTRY. Our troops followed up the enemy who continued his retreat yesterday. Little opposition was met with, with the exception of a certain amount of harassing fire by Machine Guns on our advancing tr[oops]
 The line now runs as follows from G.11.c.84 - G.12.c 67 - G.12.b.20 G.6 central along road to A.2.d.c 93 - B 19.c.46 - B.13.c.16 E. of TROISARBRES and astride Railway. Patrols on left working towards NIPPONBEND.

2. ARTILLERY. Active throughout the day and night. Harassing fire throughout the night by our Heavy Artillery. Hostile Battery positions were engaged by our Field Artillery at H.4.b, H.9.b. 18 pdrs also fired on Bridge at H.7.d and cross roads at FORT ROMPU.

3. AIRCRAFT. Usual reconnaissances by our aeroplanes were carried out during the day.

(b) ENEMY OPERATIONS.

1. INFANTRY. See above.

2. ARTILLERY. Intermittent shelling during night on CROIX DU BAC PETIT MORTIER was also heavily shelled during the night.
 Enemy searching fire on ground and houses on East and S.E. outskirts of CROIX du BAC. Harassing fire in vicinity of A.22.a by H.E. during the night.

3. GAS SHELLING. Sneezing gas in large quantities and a few mustard shells are reported.

4. MACHINE GUNS. Slight harassing fire on our advancing troops.

5. TRENCH MORTARS. Nil.

6. AIRCRAFT. 4 or 5 E.A. over our front during night. 6 or 7 E.A. observed over our front line and immediate rear during morning.

7. BALLOONS. A hostile Kite Balloon was observed to be brought down in flames at 6-10 am yesterday morning in the direction of CROIX du BAC.

(c) INTELLIGENCE.

1. EXPLOSION. A large explosion well behind the enemy lines was observe[d] in the direction of .. B.20.

for Lieut-Colonel,
General Staff, 40th Division.

Annexe to 40th Div. Daily Intelligence Summary No.11.

EXAMINATION OF PRISONERS AND DOCUMENTS OF I.R.140, captured near CROIX DU BAC.

ORDER OF BATTLE, North to South.

        4th Division   Infantry Regt. 49
             "   "   140

DISPOSITIONS. I.R.140 occupies a line from about 200 yds South of CROIX DU BAC to the road junction in G.18.d. The 5th Coy and 8th Coy were holding an outpost line (N. to S. 8th Coy 5th Coy.), the latter with 6 M.G's and two infantry posts.

RELIEFS The second Battalion relieved the 3rd Battalion in the front line on the night of the 27/28th August. Prisoner has heard that the Division is to be relieved shortly and that the relieving Division has already arrived in the area.

STRENGTH & LOSSES.
5th Coy.   Trench strength about 75
8th Coy.   "   "   " 140

During the last 12 day tour in the line near MERRIS the 5th Coy had about 20 casualties.

INTENTIONS. The outpost line had orders to retire in face of an attack to a line of resistance on the E. side of the LYS. A Battalion Order states that on relief the 3rd Bn: was to march via FLEURBAIX to its position in the ARMENTIERES line. From this it would appear that the enemy intends to stand on his original line.

LIGHT SIGNALS.
                        Destructive fire - White
                        Lengthen range   - Green
                        Shorten range   - Yellow.

*** ***
*

CAPTURED ENEMY ORDER OF I.R. 140 at CROIX DU BAC
TIMED 12.10 31st.

PATROL ORDERS.

1. The situation of the Division on our right appears uncertain. Continual touch and communication on your right with I.R.49 to be kept. Should the 49th withdraw then our right flank must conform.
   In case of enemy attack viz:- by smoke screen or drum fire all four patrols will withdraw to a line, German co-ordinates then given. In this line are outposts of line protecting artillery position.
   All communications should be addressed to me at FROID NID HOF

2. Patrols of 2nd line should always maintain distance of 300 metres behind patrols of 1st line.

CONFIDENTIAL.

(Not to be taken forward of Battn. H.Q.)

40th DIVISION DAILY INTELLIGENCE SUMMARY No. 12.
Period 6 am. 3rd - 6 am. 4th Sept. 1918.

(a) OUR OPERATIONS.

1. **INFANTRY.** During the night our Infantry continued to advance their line and by 6 am this morning had established themselves as follows :-
   JESUS FARM (B.26 d) WATERLANDS, VASCO FARM (B 27 a) TOUQUET PARMENTIER (B21 b)
   A slight increase of opposition by M.G. fire and sniping was noticed, particularly on our left flank.

2. **ARTILLERY.** During the period 18 pdrs carried out harassing fire on hostile battery positions at G.18, G.18 d and H.7 d. ERQUINGHEM was also registered on. 4.5" hows. expended 20 rounds on ERQUINGHEM CHURCH.

3. **AIRCRAFT.** Usual reconnoitring patrols were observed.

(b) ENEMY OPERATIONS.

1. **INFANTRY.** Nil.

2. **ARTILLERY.** Harassing fire during the night on CROIX du BAC - LE PETIT MORTIER, G.5.a.b.c.d. and intermittently on forward areas.
   During the early morning hostile harassing fire was carried out along roads in G.6.c.d and G.12 with 8" and 5.9.

3. **GAS SHELLING.** A few blue cross gas shells fell at SCANLAN CROSS Roads at 9 pm.

4. **AIRCRAFT.** E.A. attempted to carry out reconnaissance of our front line and immediate rear about 7 pm. but were driven off. Fairly active. One E.A. crossed our lines at 1 pm.

5. **MACHINE GUNS.** Increased activity from BAC ST.MAUR and G.17.b.

6. **TRENCH MORTARS.** Nil.

7. **BALLOONS.** A H.K.B was brought down in flames due East of our lines at 9-20 am (3rd instant).

(c) INTELLIGENCE.

1. **EXPLOSIONS.** Explosion was observed by aeroplane in FLEURBAIX at 6-30 am (4th).

2. **FIRES.** Fires still burning in FLEURBAIX and ERQUINGHEM.
   A fire was also observed in SAILLY at 8 pm.

D. G. Ridings
for Lieut-Colonel,
General Staff, 40th Division.

(Not to be taken forward of Battn H.Q.)

CONFIDENTIAL.

40th DIVISION DAILY INTELLIGENCE SUMMARY, No. 13.
Period 6 am. 4th - 6 am. 5th Sept. 1918.

(a) OUR OPERATIONS.

1. INFANTRY. Yesterday evening patrols advancing towards TAFFY FARM and THUNDER COTTS encountered considerable hostile M.G. and rifle fire from enemy posts located at PETIT MOULIN - RAILWAY CROSSING (B.28 b.27), B.28 a.6.3 and THUNDER COTTS and were unable to make further progress.

At 6 am. this morning the following line had been established :-
LE GIBET - B.22 a.32 - VASCO FARM - WATERLANDS - GRINGO FARM - JESUS FARM.

Later reports shew that our troops advanced again this morning and at 10 am. had reached the line JESUS FARM - PETIT MOULIN - L'EPINETTE RAILWAY CROSSING (B.28) and TAFFY FARM, with patrols pushing out towards the river.

2. ARTILLERY. Harassing fire was carried out on roads in S & E ARMENTIERES at intervals during the period. NOTRE DAME CHURCH, ARMENTIERES was engaged by 4.5" hows., direct hits being observed. Cross roads at H.5 B and B.30.c were also harassed intermittently.

3. AIRCRAFT. Usual daily reconnaissances were carried out.

4. TRENCH MORTARS. 28 rounds were fired at and around THUNDERCOTTS (B.28.a.35.80) from B.21.d.55 between 9-45 and 10-15 pm.

(b) ENEMY OPERATIONS.

1. INFANTRY. See above.

2. ARTILLERY. The enemy carried out harassing fire on forward areas intermittently throughout the day with H.E. and shrapnel. At 3-30 pm. 20-30 shells of 5.9 calibre fell in A.21.b and A.22 a & B BAC ST MAUR was heavily shelled at 6-20 pm. CROIX du BAC and PETIT MORTIER also received a certain amount of attention during the day.

3. MACHINE GUNS. Harassing fire from vicinity of B.28 a, B.22 a-c during the afternoon and night.

4. AIRCRAFT. Very active from 8 am. to 11 am.
E.A. made reconnaissance of our lines at about 8 pm last night. 8 E.A. flying low over our front early this morning but were driven off by A.A. fire.

5. TRENCH MORTARS. Nil.

6. BALLOONS. Three balloons were observed up opposite our front during the day. At 12.45 pm. a H.K.B. was observed to fall in flames on a grid bearing of 140° from B.19.c.22. Another balloon was destroyed at 2 pm.

7. FIRES & EXPLOSIONS. Nil.

for Lieut-Colonel,
General Staff, 40th Division.

CONFIDENTIAL.   (Not to be taken forward of Battn H.Q.)

40th DIVISION DAILY INTELLIGENCE SUMMARY, No. 14.
Period 6 a.m. 5th – 6 a.m. 6th September, 1918.

(a) OUR OPERATIONS.

1. **INFANTRY.** During yesterday's operations the enemy's resistance stiffened considerably, hostile M.Gs and rifle fire being encountered by patrols advancing towards the LYS.
   By this morning our troops had established the following line :-
JESUS FARM - PONTMOULIN - H.3.d.9.9. - H.4.b.4.7. - B.29.a.o.4 - MANCHESTER KEEP.
   One Company with which touch could not be obtained was reported to be at B.17.d.6.4.   Strong patrols have been sent out with a view to clearing PONT DE NIEPPE and establishing touch with them.

2. **ARTILLERY.** Harassing fire was maintained throughout the night against enemy roads, and tracks by 18 pdrs. 4.5" hows. registered NOTRE DAME Church and carried out harassing fire in B.30.c & d.
   At 11-30 am. PONT DE NIEPPE was shelled by our heavies for 10 minutes with a view to destroying possible M.G. nests. 6" How. Battery harassed areas around and in rear of ARMENTIERES.

3. **MACHINE GUNS.** Active against enemy planes during early part of evening.

4. **AIRCRAFT.** Usual formations observed during the period.

(b) ENEMY OPERATIONS.

1. **INFANTRY.** See above.

2. **ARTILLERY.** 24 shells directed against PETIT MORTIER from 4 pm.- 5-15 pm. of 4.2 and 5.9 calibre.
   Enemy harassed West side of the River LYS throughout day and night with 5.9 and 4.2. Enemy plane flew over Battalion Headquarters at HOLLEBEQUE FARM and dropped 2 Red Lights, immediately after which H.Q., was heavily shelled.

3. **GAS SHELLING.** A few gas shells were mixed with H.E. on West side of LYS during the night.

4. **TRENCH MORTARS.** Nil.

5. **MACHINE GUNS.** Active from PONT de NIEPPE and along East side of LYS near B.29.c.   Fairly active.

6. **AIRCRAFT.** A formation of 8-10 enemy planes carried out reconnaissance at high altitude over whole Brigade front between 6 pm. and 8 pm.

(c) INTELLIGENCE.

1. **FIRES & EXPLOSIONS.** Fires were observed in ERQUINGHEM during the morning. At 8-45 am. bridge at H.4.c. blew up.

D. G. Rylings. Lt.
for Lieut-Colonel,
General Staff, 40th Division.

CONFIDENTIAL. (Not to be taken forward of Battn. H.Q.)

40th DIVISION DAILY INTELLIGENCE SUMMARY No. 15.
Period 6 am - 6th - 6 am. 7th Sept. 1918.

(a) OUR OPERATIONS.

1. INFANTRY. Yesterday the enemy put up a stiffer resistance especially in PONT DE NIEPPE and though parties of our men established themselves in various posts in and around that place they could not clear the village. All these posts were withdrawn into the NIEPPE SYSTEM this morning preparatory to an organised attack.

Every effort was made by patrols both by day and by night to get touch with our isolated Company at B.17.d.6.4. but without success.

At 10 am. this morning the East Lancashire Regt. in conjunction with the 92nd Infantry Brigade on their left attacked PONT DE NIEPPE under a barrage, with the River LYS as theirn objective. At time of writing it is believed that our objective has been gained, but the troops on our left are understood to be held up on the line of the WARNAVE River. The operation is still proceeding.

2. ARTILLERY. Usual activity throughout the period, but no particulars to hand.

3. AIRCRAFT. Active.

(b) ENEMY OPERATIONS.

1. INFANTRY. See above.

2. ARTILLERY. Intermittent during the day. During the night H.E. and H.V. guns shelled the area B.22.c.6.0 - B.28.b.2.8.
24 77 mm shells were fired on the line B.22.d.0.2 to B.16.d,9.8. during the inter Brigade relief.

3. GAS SHELLING. Blue Cross Gas Shells were fired on the following areas during the night :-
B.21.a. (in the vicinity of OWL FARM), A.30.c. - H.1.b.6.8, A.24.a.central and G.4.a.

4. MACHINE GUNS. Fired intermittently during the night on the road approaches to the River LYS.

5. SNIPERS. Active during the period.

6. BALLOONS. Hostile balloon was brought down in flames beyond ARMENTIERES.

(c) INTELLIGENCE.

1. LIGHTS. Very few Very Lights were sent up during the night and these well beyond the E. bank of the River LYS. Some double green flares were seen at intervals - no action followed.

2. ROADS. Trees have been felled by the enemy and lie across the road junction at B.22.a.35.70, making it impassable at present.

3. MISCELLANEOUS At 6 pm. a long column of smoke appeared in the vicinity of FLEURBAIX.

Chapman Capt. G.S.
for Lieut-Colonel,
General Staff, 40th Division.

(Not to be taken forward of Battn H.Q.)

CONFIDENTIAL.

40th DIVISION DAILY INTELLIGENCE SUMMARY, No.16.
Period 6 am. 7th - 6 am. 8th September, 1918.

(a) OUR OPERATIONS.

1. **INFANTRY.** At 10 am. the East Lancashire Regt. in conjunction with the 92nd Infantry Bde. on the left attacked PONT de NIEPPE with a view to making good the line of the LYS. By 11 am. one Company had worked its way through PONT de NIEPPE and was established on the line of the River between B.24.c.0.8 and B. 24.a.6.8. Another Company prolonged our Right from B.24.c.0.8 in front of MANCHESTER KEEP back to the NIEPPE SYSTEM in B.28.b. The Brigade on our left were held up by the enemy on the line of the WARNAVE River. During the afternoon our exposed flank was driven in by a hostile counter-attack and in consequence of this we withdrew to the NIEPPE SYSTEM.

ARTILLERY. Our artillery assisted the above attack with a pre-arranged barrage from 10 am to 11.15 am.
 Harassing fire was also carried out during the day and night.
 One N.F. Call on I.2.a.7.3 was answered 8-30 am.

(b) ENEMY OPERATIONS.

1. **INFANTRY.** See above.

2. **ARTILLERY.** In reply to our Barrage the enemy bombarded NIEPPE - PONT de NIEPPE and B.13.b. area with all calibres between 10.15 am and 12 noon. An intense bombardment with 4.2" and 5.9" was carried out on B.21.a & B between 10-40 am. and 12 noon.
 Between 5 am and 6 am this morning a heavy barrage was put down on B.26.c - H.1.b and OWL FARM with 77 mm, 10.5 cm and 15 cm.
 Other areas shelled were B.19.d. - B.23.a & b - H.3.a & b and L'HALLOBEAU.

3. **GAS SHELLING.** Slight gas shelling of B.21.d.3.8 at 4 pm. and NIEPPE at 5 pm.

4. **MACHINE GUNS.** Very active from bank of canal during our operations M.G. posts are located at B.23.d.7.0 and H.4.b.70.55.

5. **AIRCRAFT.** Inactive. E.A. over at 9-15 am and 9-30 am. Driven off by A.A. fire.

6. **IDENTIFICATION.** One prisoner captured this morning at B.22.b.9.9. belongs to 88th I.R., 56th Division. Further particulars later.

for Lieut-Colonel,
General Staff, 40th Division.

Examination of Prisoner of the BAU KOMPAGNIE
I.R. 88 - 56th Division, captured at B.22.b.9.9., 7-9-18.

METHOD OF CAPTURE. Prisoner who was with a forward post near PONT de NIEPPE deserted to our lines after dark and entered an English post at B.22.b.9.9.

ORDER OF BATTLE.   56th Division.

     N. to S.   ... I.R. 186.
                      I.R. 88

Prisoner states that directly South of the 88 I.R., were troops of another Division (4th Division).

DISPOSITIONS. The 2nd Battalion is holding the line of the LYS from B.24.a. to the Railway in B.28.d., with all four Companies (order of Companies not known) forward and the BAU KOMPAGNIE which is attached to the 2nd Battalion in close support. Yesterday evening the West bank of the LYS was re-occupied by two outpost groups (each 1 N.C.O. and 8 men) from the BAU KOMPAGNIE and 1 or 2 groups of the 6th Company. On the right, these forward posts were in touch with a "Jadstaffel" of the 186th I.R.
    The 1st Bn. I.R., 88 has been inserted on the right of I.R. 186.
    Prisoner is not sure of the whereabouts of the 3rd Battalion but presumes it to be in rest.

COMPANY STRENGTHS. All the Companies of the 2nd Bn. are very weak their average fighting strength being about 35/40.

ENEMY INTENTIONS. Prisoner is of the opinion that the withdrawal is to be continued to the original line before the attack of April 9th; his reasons being that no defence work - even of a temporary nature, is being undertaken between the LYS and ARMENTIERES. ARMENTIERES is entirely empty of troops with the exception of one or two forward batteries of field guns, and a dressing station near the TOWN HALL.

HEADQUARTERS. The Headquarters of the 2nd Bn. is in ARMENTIERES. Regimental Headquarters and transport lines are at HOUPLINES.

FIELD KITCHENS. Warm rations are brought up each night from HOUPLINES to the centre of ARMENTIERES in field kitchens where they are met by ration parties furnished by the BAU KOMPAGNIE.

JAGDSTAFFEL. Consists of an Officer, 2 M.G. Groups and one Infantry Group and is composed of Volunteers. Their function is to cover the withdrawal of their own troops and to confuse and mislead the enemy by making a greater show of strength than is actually the case, by firing from alternate positions, plentiful use of Very lights, etc.
    In case of a determined attack they retire slowly on   to the main line of resistance.

BAU KOMPAGNIE. Men are drawn from all Companies of the Regiment to form the BAU KOMPAGNIE. They remain on the strength of their Companies but are detached from them for special pioneer work such as wiring, construction of dugouts, M.G. emplacements etc.
    It has two platoons consisting of about 70 men and one Officer.

LIGHT SIGNALS.   GREEN ... Destructive of Barrage fire.
                         RED   ... Lengthen Range.

MORAL. Poor. Prisoner who has served continuously for six years is tired of the War and deserted at first opportunity. He states that there is considerable dissatisfaction among the men of his Bn. owing to the length of time they had been kept in the line without any prospects of relief.

40th D.H.Q., 8-9-18.

(Not to be taken forward of Battn. H.Q.)

CONFIDENTIAL.

40th DIVISION DAILY INTELLIGENCE SUMMARY, No. 17.
Period 6 am. 8th - 6 am. 9th September, 1918.

(a) OUR OPERATIONS.

1. **INFANTRY.**
Patrols were sent forward at frequent intervals towards the Western bank of the LYS. The enemy was nowhere encountered. It is definitely ascertained that the Western bank of the river is clear of all enemy posts South of a line through B.23.c & d central.
Our line runs : JESUS FARM, B.26.d.37.00 - H.3.a. cent - WIGAN - H.3.b.90.65 - B.28.d.4.3. - B.28 cent. - thence along NIEPPE SWITCH to B.17.a.2.2. POSTS at B.28.d.70.65 and MANCHESTER KEEP.

2. **ARTILLERY.** The usual harassing fire was maintained throughout the period on enemy roads and tracks by 18 pdrs. During the day suspected enemy M.G. posts were subjected to concentrated bursts of fire. In response to N.F. calls a hostile battery at C.26.d.93 was engaged and effectively silenced.

3. **AIRCRAFT.** Owing to weather conditions little flying was possible.

(b) ENEMY OPERATIONS.

1. **INFANTRY.** The enemy's attitude has been quiet. He is, however, on the alert, and movement by troops in the forward area is quickly observed and subjected to fire from M.Gs snipers and 77 mm shells.

2. **ARTILLERY.** Hostile artillery showed a slight increase in activity. The following areas received special attention : B.13.c. & d - GRINGO FARM - POSTON FARM (B.20.b) and B.19 d. Roads in B.25 c. e were subjected to harassing fire at 9-30 pm. During the day the Railway Line and vicinity in B.28.b. was shelled with 77 mm. Tracks in A.24 d. were also subjected to light scattered shelling between 2 am. and 3-30 am.

3. **GAS SHELLING.** At odd intervals a few gas shells fell in our back areas.

4. **AIRCRAFT.** Inactive.

5. **M.Gs & SNIPERS.** Enemey M.Gs have been located at B.29.b.22 - B.23.d.19. There is also a M.G. situated at B.24.c.18 (Prisoner's statement).
Throughout the night our posts were frequently swept by M.G. fire. During the day M.Gs opened on our Infantry whenever they exposed themselves. Enemy M.Gs were firing from the ruins of ERQUINGHEM. Snipers were active.

(c) INTELLIGENCE.

1. **MOVEMENT.** Individual movement was observed in ruins at H.5.a.37 at 1-10 pm.

2. **ENEMY DEFENCES.** Railway Bridge at B.29 c. 70.65 is completely demolished. The bridge at B.29.b.20.15 is only partially destroyed and could be used for the passage of Infantry. Trench at B.17.c.75 was visited by a patrol and is reported to be waterlogged and in a bad state.
At the eastern end it is very shallow.

Major,
General Staff, 40th Division.

9-9-18.

CONFIDENTIAL.   (Not to be taken forward of Battn H.Q.)

40th DIVISION DAILY INTELLIGENCE SUMMARY, No. 18.
Period 6 am 9th - 10th September, 1918.

(a) OUR OPERATIONS.

1. **INFANTRY.** MANCHESTER KEEP was occupied during the day by 1 Officer & 10 O.R. This post was withdrawn at night.
Patrols. Our patrols have been active in the PONT de NIEPPE area.
 (i) A patrol left our lines at B.22.d.5.9 at 7-30 pm to reconnoitre the approaches to PONT de NIEPPE and houses in B.23.a. No opposition was met with.
 (ii) Patrol left B.16.d.8.5 at 7-30 pm to locate enemy posts in B.23.a. This patrol was fired on by M.Gs located in house at B.23.a.5.8./ of the village towards the cross roads and was again fired on by M.Gs from upper storeys of houses. Patrol then withdrew. A hostile party consisting of 8 men was observed on the return journey. /The patrol then proceeded up the main street

2. **ARTILLERY.** The usual harassing fire was carried out against enemy roads and tracks during the 24 hours. NOTRE DAME Church and the factory in B.29.b. also received attention. House at B.39 B.9.9. (suspected M.G. post) received direct hit.
Other targets included :-

 House B.24.c.05.70
 BOLTON KEEP B.29. c & d.
 House at B.29.b.9.9 and hedge running from H.5.b.05.90 to B.29.c.8.1

3. **TRENCH MORTARS.** Stokes guns fired towards B.27.b & d during the night.

4. **AIRCRAFT.** Owing to weather our aircraft was inactive.

(b) ENEMY OPERATIONS.

1. **INFANTRY.** The enemy's attitude remains quiet. Troops moving in our outpost lines were not subjected to any kind of fire.

2. **ARTILLERY.** Hostile Artillery was quiet during the day but shewed an increase of activity at night. Intermittent harassing fire was carried out by 4.2 & 5.9 in the following areas : B.13.a & b and B.19 MANCHESTER KEEP received a few rounds of shrapnel between 4 am & 5-30

2. **MACHINE GUNS.** Enemy M.Gs fired spasmodically during the night.

3. **AIRCRAFT.** An E.A. flew over our forward area at 7-30 pm.

4. **GAS SHELLING.** From 10-30 pm to 11-30 pm 15 cm hows fired yellow cross into B.14.

(c) INTELLIGENCE.

1. **MOVEMENT.** A man was seen walking along track at B.29.b.80.95 towards Bridge over River LYS at 2 pm.
A man walked at 4-15 pm. from behind a wooden hut at B.29.d.05.35 along track running S.W. and disappeared at B.29.c.75.00. (Ten minutes later he re-appeared and ran back).

2. **ENEMY DEFENCES.** The bridge at B.22.b.78 is intact. Bridges at H.4.c.15 and H.4.c.65 are both totally destroyed (patrol report). A new trench protected by wire runs from B.29.c.88.12 - B.29.c.75.00

3. **MACHINE GUNS.** Hostile posts are suspected at B.17.d.18, B.17.d.75 H.4.c.05.35. Enemy M.G. reported in yesterday's summary as located at E.29.b.22 should read B.29.b.22.

CONFIDENTIAL

(Not to be taken forward of Battn H.Q.)

40th DIVISION DAILY INTELLIGENCE SUMMARY No. 19.
Period 6 am. 10th - 6 am. 11th Sept. 1918.

(a) OUR OPERATIONS.

1. INFANTRY. Operations on the Divisional front during the past 24 hours have been confined to active patrolling both by day and night.

Daylight patrols leaving our lines in the morning and again in the afternoon made a thorough reconnaissance of PONT de NIEPPE without finding any signs of enemy occupation. Both patrols returned without being fired on.

A patrol consisiting of 1 Officer and 18 O.R. left our lines at midnight and patrolled the West bank of the River. The buildings were in good condition and unoccupied by the enemy. The patrol returned by the same route undisturbed.

At dusk a post of 1 platoon was established at Bridgehead B.23.d.9.8. Posts were also established at Bridgehead - H.4.c.58.55 and H.4.c.1.5.

2. ARTILLERY. Registration shoots were carried out during the day and S.O.S. lines checked. At intervals throughout the night harassing fire was maintained on selected roads and tracks. We replied vigorously to the hostile barrage which was put down on Right Divisional front at 5 am.

3. AIRCRAFT. Owing to unfavourable weather conditions little flying was possible.

(b) ENEMY OPERATIONS.

1. INFANTRY. Nil.

2. ARTILLERY. Hostile artillery activity has been below normal during the period. At 11-45 am. a few 77 mm shells fell into PONT de NIEPPE. The following areas also received attention. - PUNGENT FARM - H.1.b - B.20 - and H.3.a.

3. GAS SHELLING. At 2-30 pm. about 20 gas shells fell in the vicinity of PUNGENT FARM, B.26.a.20.53.

4. MACHINE GUNS Hostile M.G. was active from H.24.c.2.7 during the night. A M.G. has been located at H.4.d.05.60.

Enemy M.G. fired on our post at B.23.d.9.8 from B.24.c.2.7 during the night.

5. AIRCRAFT. Below normal. E.A. were observed over our lines at 3 pm and 5 pm. At 7-15 pm one E.A. patrolled our line from N. to S. for ½ hour and was engaged by A.A. fire.

(c) INTELLIGENCE.

1. MOVEMENT. Individual movement was observed at H.5.b.8.8. at 1-45 pm.
Four men were seen walking along the road at H.5.b.7.5 at 6-30 pm.

2. ENEMY DEFENCES Bridge at B.23.d.90.70 is in good condition (patrol report).

A close examination of the square in PONT de NIEPPE of which spot B.23.b.23.15 is the centre, discloses that it is a strongly fortified position. The M.Gs mounted in this position were responsible for holding up the attack of our Right Company on 7th September.

for Major,
General Staff, 40th Division.

CONFIDENTIAL

(Not to be taken forward of Battn H.Q.)

40th DIVISION DAILY INTELLIGENCE SUMMARY, No. 20.
Period 6 am. 11th - 6 am. 12th Sept. 1918.

(a) OUR OPERATIONS.

1. INFANTRY. During the night our line was advanced without opposition from the enemy as follows :-

From Railway Crossing B.28.b.8.3 - MANCHESTER KEEP - B.23.b.8. - along trench to B.17.c.7.5 to B.17.a.4.0 at which point junction was effected with Brigade on our left. Standing patrol at Bridge B.23.d.9.8 still remains.

Patrols this morning encountered the enemy about B.17.d.2.6 where a few enemy were killed. Patrols were unable to gain the road in B.18.a owing to casualties.

2. ARTILLERY. In conjunction with the Infantry during above advance of line our Artillery fired for 10 minutes on JUTE FACTORIES (B.29.b) and selected points between ARMENTIERES - PONT de NIEPPE Road and Railway.

We also fired on Roads and tracks, railway, NOTRE DAME CHURCH etc., during the night and early morning.

3. AIRCRAFT. Quiet.

(b) Enemy Operations.

1. INFANTRY. As above.

2. ARTILLERY. Quiet in the morning, more active in the evening.
B.13.c. was shelled with 200 rounds 15 CM Hows. between 3-30 pm. and 5-15 pm.

3. GAS SHELLING. 20 Gas shells on Support line during the night.

4. AIRCRAFT. One E.A. crossed our lines at about 8,000 feet at 6-45 pm. Heavily engaged by A.A. fire.

5. M.Gs. Hostile M.G. fired from B.24.a.15.80.

(c) INTELLIGENCE.

1. MOVEMENT. 3 men seen to walk from H.5.a.95.80 to H.5.b.70.75

2. LIGHT SIGNALS. During our bombardment this morning enemy put up double green lights at 5-45 am and double red lights at 5-50 am.

3. IDENTIFICATION. Shoulder strap taken off body of German killed about B.17.d.2.6 this morning, bears the number 77.

Major,
General Staff, 40th Division.

(Not to be taken forward of Battn H.Q.)

CONFIDENTIAL

40th DIVISION DAILY INTELLIGENCE SUMMARY, No. 21.
(period 6 am 12th - 6 am 13-9-18).

(a) OUR OPERATIONS.

1. INFANTRY. During the night 12th/13th we occupied the farm B.17.d.05.80 and established a post at B.17.d.0.9 without encountering enemy resistance.

   Patrols. (i) A patrol consisting of 1 Officer and 13 O.R and a Lewis Gun Section attempted to cross the R. LYS during the night at H.4.c.1.5. Our approach to the Bridge was perceived by the enemy. Flares were immediately sent up in quick succession and a party of about 20 strong was seen to run towards the bridge. By the light of the flares it was seen that the river was much swollen and no crossing could be made over the demolished bridge. Our Lewis Guns, therefore, opened heavy fire on the enemy position and eventually withdrew.

   (ii) Patrols sent out with the intention of crossing the river at B.23.d.90.75 and B.29.c.60.95 found the former bridge destroyed and the latter submerged. They were consequently unable to carry out their intended operations on the eastern bank.

2. ARTILLERY. During the period our artillery engaged the following targets :- B.24.c.25.70, JUTE FACTORIES (B29 b & d) and enemy post in house at B.29.b.98.90. Harassing fire was maintained during the night on enemy roads and tracks in and about the eastern outskirts of ARMENTIERES.

3. MACHINE GUNS. Our M.Gs carried out a programme of harassing fire.

(b) ENEMY OPERATIONS.

1. INFANTRY. See above.

2. ARTILLERY. Enemy artillery activity was normal. Throughout the 24 hours our forward area was subjected to light scattered shelling. Between 11 am and noon the NIEPPE SYSTEM was shelled by 4.2's. At 10.15 and 10.30 am PONT de NIEPPE was shelled with 10.5 cm howitzers and 77 mm. Other targets included STEENWERCK, B.13.c & B.27.b & d.

3. M.Gs. Enemy M.Gs continually swept our new outpost line. M.Gs were active during the morning from buildings at B.24.a.15.90. M.Gs were also located from houses at B.24.c.2.7 and B.24.c.4.1

4. AIRCRAFT. One E.A. was observed over our lines at 5-45 pm and was engaged by A.A. and M.G. fire.

(c) INTELLIGENCE.

1. MOVEMENT. Individual movement was observed at the following points:-
   H.15.b.70.75, B.29.c.85.30 and H.5.b.3.9.
   At 5-40 pm. a small party of men was seen at H.5.b.3.9.

2. LIGHTS. At 5-45 pm the enemy put up double green flares along the front on which our artillery was firing. At 5-50 pm these were followed by double red.

D. G. Rylings
for Major,
General Staff, 40th Division.

13-9-18.

CONFIDENTIAL. (Not to be taken forward of Battn H.Q.)

40th DIVISION DAILY INTELLIGENCE SUMMARY, No.22.
Period 6 am 13th - 6 am. 14th Sept. 1918.

(a) Our Operations.

1. **INFANTRY.** During the night 13th/14th September the 120th Infantry Bde relieved the 119th Infantry Bde in the Divisional Advanced Guard.

2. **ARTILLERY.** All Batteries carried out harassing fire on buildings in and around ARMENTIERES. Three hostile Batteries were engaged with short bursts of fire in response to aeroplane calls.

3. **AIRCRAFT.** Considerable activity was observed increasing towards the evening.

4. **TRENCH MORTARS.** Our Trench Mortar Battery having established itself in PONT de NIEPPE fired 64 rounds on buildings occupied by the enemy. Direct hits were obtained.

(b) ENEMY OPERATIONS.

1. **INFANTRY.** The enemy maintains a strictly vigilant attitude and is quick to observe our patrol movements. The buildings lying on the N.E. outskirts of PONT de NIEPPE which have previously been reported free of the enemy now appear to be re-occupied.

2. **ARTILLERY.** Hostile artillery was unusually quiet until 4 pm. after which time, activity increased to normal. At 5-30 pm the area about B.20.c.2.8 was shelled with 77 cm.
   (There had been troop movement just previously) At 7-30 pm a concentration of 5.9's was put down about B.19.c.7.7.
   During the night A.24.d and the vicinity of LOWER FARM received attention with 5.9's.
   The section of 10.5 cm hows. that fired on B.22.a appears to be close up and to be used solely for sniping.

3. **GAS SHELLING.** A few gas shells were mixed with H.E. on B.20.c. at 5.30

4. **AIRCRAFT.** At 8-30 pm an E.A. flying at a great height over our lines was engaged by A.A. fire and driven off.

5. **MACHINE GUNS.** Enemy M.Gs fired throughout the day on our posts in the forefield. Snipers were active, firing from buildings on outskirts of PONT de NIEPPE, B.24.a.20.15. Our Lewis Guns maintained a vigorous retaliation.

(c) INTELLIGENCE.

1. **ENEMY DEFENCES.** All footbridges across the LYS in B.23 d & B.29 d have been destroyed. (This includes that at B.23 d 90.70 reported intact by patrol on 11-9-18).
   A new length of trench has been dug from the light railway at H.9.b.6.9 to the old British Post at H.9 b 60.68 - also a short length has been dug S. from this post at H.9 b 71.53. The wire between H.10.b 2.2 & H.10.c.65.50 is now clearly shown. There may also be a belt between H.10 c 46.55 & H.10 d 0.9. (Photo 4 B 226).

14-9-18.
for Major,
General Staff, 40th Division.

War Diary

(Not to be taken forward of Battn H.Q.)

CONFIDENTIAL
40th DIVISION DAILY INTELLIGENCE SUMMARY No. 23.
Period 6am 14th - 6 am. 15th Sept. 1918.

(a) OUR OPERATIONS.

1. **INFANTRY.** Active patrolling was carried out during the night but no hostile movement was observed. An Observation Post was established at the Laundry B.29.c.5.9 from where excellent observation of both banks of the LYS is obtainable. Patrols reconnoitred the bridge at B.29.c.7.7, which was found demolished and the river still in flood.
The bridge at H.4.c.1.5 was also reconnoitred. The approaches and first 20 yards of the bridge were found to be in good condition but further reconnaissance was rendered impossible by heavy hostile M.G. fire across the bridge.

2. **ARTILLERY.** Harassing fire was carried out by 18 pdrs during the night on roads and tracks near the RUE MARLE Church (H 6 à) and on the South eastern outskirts of ARMENTIERES. The Laundry and roads in its vicinity also received attention.

3. **AIRCRAFT.** Usual formations were observed. At 1 pm one of our aeroplanes attacked and destroyed a hostile kite balloon E. of ARMENTIERES. A contact plane called for flares at 6-30 am and again at 6-45 pm.

4. **TRENCH MORTARS.** 20 rounds were fired round a suspected M.G. emplacement at B.23.b.95.55.

(b) ENEMY OPERATIONS.

1. **INFANTRY.** Nil. The enemy's attitude remains unchanged.

2. **ARTILLERY.** Hostile artillery activity was normal. Light field guns were active on NIEPPE and PONT de NIEPPE while 10.5 cm hows. paid some attention to square B.13. 50 rounds 77 cm were also fired on NIEPPE SWITCH about B.22 d 5.9

3. **GAS SHELLING.** About 300 gas shells fell into B.19.

4. **MACHINE GUNS.** Enemy machine guns were active during the night sweeping our posts from B.29 c 8.6 and the Laundries in H.5 a.

5. **TRENCH MORTARS.** A few rounds from a light trench mortar fell in the vicinity of LA HAYE.

6. **AIRCRAFT.** Enemy aeroplanes were active during the morning. At 6-15 am 1 E.A. and at 7 am. a formation of 9 E.A. were observed over our lines. All were engaged by A.A. fire.
At 7 am E.A. dropped flares just W. of our lines in B.23 b.

7. **BALLOONS.** Two H.K.B's were observed to ascend on bearings of 91° and 166° from LA HAYE FARM at 9-20 am.

(c) INTELLIGENCE.

1. **MOVEMENT.** Individual movement was observed about suspected M.G. position in A.23.b.95.55.

2. **MISCELLANEOUS.** Pigeons were seen to be released from tree at B.29.c. 90.25.

for Major,
General Staff, 40th Division.

Not to be taken forward of Battn H.Q.)
CONFIDENTIAL

40th DIVISION DAILY INTELLIGENCE SUMMARY, No.24.
Period 6 am 15th - 6 am. 16th Sept. 1918.

(a) Our Operations.

1. INFANTRY. Active patrolling was carried out during the night but there was nothing of interest to report. A liaison post has been established at Bridge H.3.c.3.7 and we are now in constant touch with the Division on our right.

2. ARTILLERY. The usual harassing fire was carried out by our field guns, particular attention being paid to ARMENTIERES and its southern outskirts and area north of the town along the bend of the LYS. About 20 rounds were fired on O.P. NOTRE DAME CHURCH (B.30 d).

3. AIRCRAFT. Usual formations were observed. About 5-30 pm our aeroplanes shot down an E.A. in the direction of JUTE FACTORY (B 29.b.) An enemy balloon was also destroyed S.E. of ERQUINGHEM on the evening of the 15th.

4. TRENCH MORTARS. 25 rounds were fired on selected targets including suspected M.G. emplacements and enemy posts.

(B) ENEMY OPERATIONS.

1. INFANTRY. Nil.
2. ARTILLERY. Hostile artillery displayed a slight increase in activity, the principal areas shelled being B.19.b NIEPPE & A.23.b. TAFFY FARM and the NIEPPE SWITCH received a few rounds of 7.7. cm
POSTON FARM (B.20.b.3.0) was heavily shelled between 2 pm & 7-30 pm with about 100 rounds of 5.9". During the night forward post were subjected to light scattered shelling with 7.7. cm.
3. GAS SHELLING About 8-30 pm about 20 gas shells fell into B.19 b & d.
4. TRENCH MORTARS. 20 rounds from a light trench mortar were fired into PONT de NIEPPE about 11 am from about B.24.c.2.2.
At 1-30 pm, 3 rounds fell at B.23.b.1.5.
5. MACHINE GUNS. Hostile M.Gs were fairly active during the night.
6. AIRCRAFT. Increased activity due to improved weather conditions. E.As crossed our lines at 8-45 am, 9-15 am, 2-30 pm, 3-20 pm and 5-15 pm and were engaged with A.A. and M.G. fire. At 6-30 pm a low flying plane flew over our lines but was driven off by A.A. fire
An enemy plane was brought down in our lines (B20) on the morning of the 16th.
7. BALLOONS. One H.K.B. was observed on a grid bearing of $81°$ from B.22 a. 4.0. A H.K.B. ascended at $131°$ grid from B.27.d.77.99.

(C) INTELLIGENCE.

1. MOVEMENT. Transport was heard during the night from post in GOSPEL VILLA.

2. ENEMY DEFENCES. Camouflage has been erected at B.18.c.2.4.

DG Rydings
Major,
General Staff, 40th Division.

(Not to be taken forward of Battn H.Q.)

CONFIDENTIAL.
40th DIVISION DAILY INTELLIGENCE SUMMARY, No. 25.
(period 6 am 16th - 6 am 17th Sept. 1918).

(a) Our operations.

1. INFANTRY. Our patrols were active during the night and the following hostile posts were located :- B.18.c.1.9. This post appears to be occupied by about 40 of the enemy. B.17.d.5.4. Three machine guns active from house. Cross firing with another at B.24.a.1.1.

2. ARTILLERY. Our artillery was active during the period under review. Harassing fire was continued during the night on enemy roads, tracks and buildings in ARMENTIERES and N.E. & S.E. outskirts,- special attention being paid to buildings at C.19.d.20.50 and road at C.25.a.60.99. 20 rounds were expended on a suspected battery position at H.6.b.central.

3. AIRCRAFT. Very active. Our scouts and reconnaissance machines flew over the enemy's lines continually throughout the day.

4. MACHINE GUNS. Suspected enemy posts and cross roads were engaged with intermittent bursts of fire.

(b) ENEMY OPERATIONS.

1. INFANTRY. Nil.

2. ARTILLERY. B.11.c was subjected to a concentration by 10.5 cm hows at 11 am. NIEPPE, PONT de NIEPPE & NIEPPE SWITCH received about 50 rounds of 7.7 cm at 12-30 pm.
Forward areas were intermittently shelled during the day by 7.7. cm. whilst at night harassing fire was normal. About 12 rounds of 10.5 cm. were directed at STEENWERCK at 10-30 pm.

5. GAS SHELLING. YELLOW CROSSING received a few gas shells at 10 pm. About 20 gas shells fell near STEENWERCK Station at 4 pm. Between 5 and 7 am. 40 rounds of Blue Cross fell into areas B.22 & B.19.

4. AIRCRAFT. Increased activity was displayed by hostile aircraft during the period, many attempts being made to cross our lines. At 11.45 am 1 E.A. escorted by 5 fighting machines crossed our lines at about 8,000 feet and patrolled for 20 minutes. 7-20 pm. one of our balloons was brought down in flames by E.A.

5. MACHINE GUNS. PONT de NIEPPE was swept at intervals during the night

6. TRENCH MORTARS. Trench Mortars were active at intervals. Light T.Ms were fired from B.18.c and B.16.d.5.0. Heavy T.Ms were fired from B.24.c.

(c) INTELLIGENCE.

1. ENEMY DEFENCES. Air photos of the 15th show -
An extension has been made to the existing trench in H.5. a & c from H.5.c.30.85 to the road at H.5.c.34.69. A short length of trench has also been dug on the S. side of the road at this point, and a track leads S. from it.

WIRE. Probably exists along the E. bank of the LYS in B.18.c &d and 24.a.

A short trench has been dug S. of the railway from H.5.c.75.08 to H.11.a.79.74. This is protected by one belt of wire and possibly a second along the ditch W. of above trench.

D.E.Rydings Lt
for Major,
General Staff, 40th Division.

17-9-18.

CONFIDENTIAL.   (Not to be taken forward of Battn H.Q.)

40th DIVISION DAILY INTELLIGENCE SUMMARY, No. 26.
Period 6 am 17th - 6 am 18th September, 1918.

(a) OUR OPERATIONS.

1. **INFANTRY.** Nil.

2. **ARTILLERY.** Harassing fire was continued throughout the 24 hours on roads and buildings in ARMENTIERES including NOTRE DAME CHURCH.
 At 5-30 am. two 18 pdrs batteries and one 4.5 howitzer battery fired on a standing barrage, along the line of WARNAVE River from B.12.b.40 to B.18.a.1.9 in support of a minor operation by the Division on our left.

3. **AIRCRAFT.** Very active during the day. Strong formations patrolling and crossing enemy's lines encountered heavy A.A. fire.

4. **MACHINE GUNS.** Our M.Gs fired on enemy posts roads and light railways during the period.

5. **TRENCH MORTARS.** Trench mortars expended 34 rounds on suspected M.G. and T.M. positions.

(b) ENEMY OPERATIONS.

1. **INFANTRY.** Nil.

2. **ARTILLERY.** Hostile artillery activity was below normal during the day, but active after 6 pm, particular attention being paid to battery areas and roads. Forward areas received the usual light scattered shelling, NIEPPE, B.19.a and B.21.b. & d received much attention throughout the day.
 A gun believed to be an 18 pdr fired 8 rounds on B.13.b.
 At 5-30 am. the enemy artillery replied vigorously on usual targets to our barrage on the left.

3. **GAS SHELLING.** B.19.b. received a few rounds of gas at 10-25 am. A few gas shells were mixed with H.E. in B.27 between midnight and 2 am.

4. **MACHINE GUNS.** Hostile machine guns wer active particularly on the right Company front.
 M.Gs were located firing from B.24.c.1.8 and from the ruins in ERQUINGHEM.

5. **TRENCH MORTARS.** The area B.28.b. was shelled by heavy T.M.s from 10-30 am to 11 am. and again from 8 pm. to 9 pm. Location of T.M. approximately B.18.d.1.8. Light T.Ms fired on our post at B.23.b.8.1 from B.24.c.2.2 PONT de NIEPPE was also shelled by L.T.Ms.

6. **AIRCRAFT.** E.A. repeatedly tried to cross our lines during the day, but were driven off each time by A.A. fire.

7. **BALLOONS.** Hostile Kite Balloons were observed as follows :-
 3 pm - 4-15 pm T.B. of 90° from B.28.b.49.58.
 5-25 pm.   G.B. of 97° from B.22.a. 70.65.

(c) INTELLIGENCE.

1. **MOVEMENT.** Individual movement was observed at enemy posts B.18.c.2.4 and B.24.c.1.8.

2. **LIGHTS.** Red Lights were fired along the Brigade front during our barrage at 5-30 am. No apparent enemy action followed.

for Major,
General Staff, 40th Division.

CONFIDENTIAL. (Not to be taken forward of Battn H.Q.)

40th DIVISION DAILY INTELLIGENCE SUMMARY, No.27.
Period 6 am. 18th - 6 am. 19th Sept. 1918.

(a) OUR OPERATIONS.

1. **INFANTRY.** Nil.

2. **ARTILLERY.** The usual number of rounds were expended on harassing fire. Targets included the buildings in the Square at ARMENTIERES and houses round the outskirts of the town, (C.19.d & I.1.c.)
In response to aeroplane calls 2 Batteries on the southern outskirts of ARMENTIERES were engaged by both 18 pdr & 4.5" howitzer Batteries.

3. **AIRCRAFT.** Normal. Usual reconnaissances were carried out. Flares were called for by a contact plane at 6-35 am.

4. **MACHINE GUNS.** Harassing fire was carried out at intervals, many targets being engaged.

5. **TRENCH MORTARS.** 17 rounds were fired on enemy positions at B.18.c.1.3 & B.17.d.7.5 during the day.

(b) ENEMY OPERATIONS.

1. **INFANTRY.** Nil.

2. **ARTILLERY.** Hostile artillery displayed normal activity during the day, increasing after dusk when cross roads and battery areas were harassed. NIPPON BEND was engaged by 10.5 cm and 15 cm howitzers during the afternoon and the south-eastern outskirts of STEENWERCK received attention at intervals after dark, a few gas shells being included.
Areas B.19.c, B.20.a & c and B.25.a received considerable attention especially during the night

3. **GAS SHELLING.** Area B.20.a & c received about 300 rounds of Yellow Cross between 1-15 am and 2-30 am, but the gas was carried away by the S.W. wind.

4. **MACHINE GUNS.** Hostile M.Gs were active searching the railway and roads in B.22.a. M.G. position was located at B.29.c.80.62.

5. **TRENCH MORTARS.** Quiet. A few rounds were fired on our post at B.28.b.9.5.

6. **AIRCRAFT.** Normal. 4 E.As flew over NIEPPE at a height of 6,000 feet at 6-25 pm. At 6-30 pm 1 E.A. flew over NIEPPE at about 2,000 feet and was driven off by A.A. fire.

7. **BALLOONS.** Hostile Kite Balloons were observed as follows :-
3 pm - 5-30 pm T.B. 92° from B.28.b.49.58.
12-30 pm - 3 pm T.B. 49° from B.27.b.70.10.
1-30 pm - 3 pm T.B. 90° from B.27.b.70.10

(c) INTELLIGENCE.

1. **MOVEMENT.** An enemy O.P. is suspected in tree across the river at B.29.c.90.65.

2. **FIRES.** Fire observed on bearing of 37° from B.27.b.70.10 from 4-15 pm to 5-5 pm.

3. **EXPLOSIONS.** Slight explosion at 11-30 am followed by clouds of grey smoke at bearing of 25° from B.27.b.70.10.

Major,
General Staff, 40th Division.

(Not to be taken forward of Battn H.Q.)
CONFIDENTIAL.

40th DIVISION DAILY INTELLIGENCE SUMMARY, No. 28.
Period 6 am 19th - 6 am 20th Sept. 1918.

(a) OUR OPERATIONS.

1. INFANTRY. Our patrols were active during the night. A patrol consisting of 1 Officer and 2 O.R. left our lines at H.3.a.5.1 to reconnoitre the bank of the LYS 400 yards to the right and left of H.3.c.5.7. The patrol returned without being fired on.

2. ARTILLERY. Roads and buildings in and around ARMENTIERES were subjected to the usual harassing fire during the night. In addition, 2 batteries co-operated with Heavy Artillery in firing 4 concentrations on 2 hostile batteries at I.1.c.36.41 and H.6.d.9.2. Seven short bursts of fire were put down on the road running from H.6.b.2.2. to H.6.d.7.3 (RUE MARLE) at ½ hour intervals in co-operation with the Heavy Artillery.

3. AIRCRAFT. Normal activity increasing during the afternoon when heavy A.A. fire was met with by our machines.

4. MACHINE GUNS. Our M.Gs carried out a programme of harassing fire during the night.

5. TRENCH MORTARS. Fairly quiet. 21 rounds were fired on enemy M.G. position in vicinity of B.17.d.7.4 at 5 am.

(b) ENEMY OPERATIONS.

1. INFANTRY. Nil.
2. ARTILLERY. Hostile artillery was very quiet during the day, increasing in activity during the evening. Particular attention paid to the following areas throughout the period :- B.15.b & d, B.16 a & c, B.21.d and B27.b.
   At 7-30 pm A.30.c. received 45 shells - 5.9" & 7.7 mm. Back areas were subjected to the usual night harassing fire with heavy calibre shells.
3. GAS SHELLING. 200 rounds of "Yellow Cross" are reported in the vicinity of HOLLEBECQUE FARM between midnight and 4 am.

4. MACHINE GUNS. Below normal.

5. TRENCH MORTARS. T.Ms were inactive with the exception of a few rounds in the vicinity of PONT de NIEPPE during the night.

6. AIRCRAFT. Normal.
   One E.A. flew over our lines at 8.55 am and was immediately driven off by A.A. fire.
   E.As flew over our lines at 4.25 pm., 5 pm and 5.25 pm and 6.15 pm. All were engaged by A.A. fire.

(c) INTELLIGENCE.

1. MOVEMENT. 2.25 pm. A party of five men was seen at B.29.a.9.1.

Major,
General Staff, 40th Division.

CONFIDENTIAL.

(Not to be taken forward of Battn H.Q.)

40th DIVISION DAILY INTELLIGENCE SUMMARY. No.29.
Period 6 am 20th - 6 am 21st September 1918.
****

(a) OUR OPERATIONS.

1. INFANTRY. A patrol consisting of 1 N.C.O. and 3 O.R. left our lines at B.17.d.3.0 to reconnoitre along trench to road at B.23.b.8.3. The patrol reports the trench clear of the enemy. No hostile fire was encountered from N.E. side of the trench. A M.G. opened fire from approximately B.23.b.9.5.

A second patrol was sent out to inspect our wire; route taken was from B.23.d.7.7 to B.29.a.05.75. The patrol reports a good belt of wire with occasional gaps.

2. ARTILLERY. During the 24 hours harassing fire was carried out at intervals on roads and buildings ARMENTIERES area, particular attention being paid to H.6.a and d, B.30.d and C.19.d. A suspected hostile battery position at H.6.a.80.25 was fired on by 4.5" hows.

3. MACHINE GUNS. Intermittent harassing fire was maintained throughout the night, 3,000 rounds being expended on cross roads and tracks.

4. AIRCRAFT. Usual formations were observed over our lines during the day, with more pronounced activity about 5 pm. Bombs were dropped on enemy forward areas at 11-30 am and again after nightfall.

5. TRENCH MORTARS. 30 rounds were expended on M.G. position at B.29.b.9.8.

(b) ENEMY OPERATIONS.

1. INFANTRY. Nil.

2. ARTILLERY. Normal activity. TAFFY FARM and VESCO FARM were harassed throughout the period. About 5 pm the former was heavily shelled by 7.7 mm for 45 minutes. Forward areas were subjected to light shelling by field guns and harassing fire was carried out on cross roads and battery positions in back areas during the night. Areas B.15.b, B.16.a, B.17.b and B.22 received particular attention.

15 cm howitzers fired air bursts on NIEPPE STATION. A heavy concentration lasting 10 minutes was put down on CROIX DU BAC at 9.15 pm by 15 cm.

3. GAS SHELLING. A few gas shells were reported in B.22 and B.27 c at 3.20 am.

4. AIRCRAFT. Below normal. At 6.45 pm 7 E.A. patrolled the line from S. to N. and were engaged by A.A. fire. Activity was confined to occasional bursts of fire during the night.

5. MACHINE GUNS. M.Gs were located firing from house at H.3.d.75.45 and H.4.b.65.65.

6. TRENCH MORTARS. Inactive.

7. BALLOONS. H.K.Bs were observed as follows :-
9.30 am to 11.40 am T.B. 93° from B.22.a.4.0.
5.30 pm to 6.55 pm T.B.168° from B.22.a.4.0.

(c) INTELLIGENCE.

1. MOVEMENT. Movement was seen in factory chimney in B.29.b.65.50. Noise of transport was heard at 10.30 pm at H.4.c.3.1.

2. FIRES. A fire was observed at T.B.133° from B.16.d.8.1. 8.30 pm. Fire in ARMENTIERES which burned throughout the night.

3. ENEMY DEFENCES. There are two short lengths of trench visible at B.24.c.13.22 and B.24.c.14.35 (photo 4 B.378). These are probably occupied. A light T.M. has been reported active in the vicinity of the first and a M.G. near the second.

D. G. Kyling
for Major,

General Staff, 40th Division.

(Not to be taken forward of Battn H.Q.)

CONFIDENTIAL.

40th DIVISION DAILY INTELLIGENCE SUMMARY, No. 30.
Period 6 am 21st - 6 am. 22nd September, 1918.

(a) OUR OPERATIONS.

1. INFANTRY. Nil.

2. ARTILLERY. Usual activity throughout the period at intervals between 8 pm. and 5 am., harassing fire was maintained on selected targets, particular attention being paid to the area between the LYS in B.18.c and 17 d.   One N.F. call from the air was answered.

3. AIRCRAFT. Considerable activity was displayed during the day. Strong formations were seen to cross the enemy's lines on several occasions.

4. MACHINE GUNS. 500 rounds were fired at suspected hostile M.G. positions in H.3.d.5.3, H.3.d.6.4 and H.3.d.7.4. In addition cross roads and tracks were searched at intervals during the night.

5. TRENCH MORTARS. Normal activity.   Our T.Ms fired on suspected M.G. and T.M. positions.

(b) ENEMY OPERATIONS.

1. INFANTRY. Nil.

2. ARTILLERY. Normal during the day. During the night, however, hostile harassing fire on battery areas increased; areas H.24.b & d and B.19.b being chiefly affected. Between 3-15 pm and 4-45 pm about 100 rounds of 5.9" fell in the vicinity of HOLLEBEQUE FARM. The same area was shelled with 5.9" again at 7.15 pm.
   At 8-15 pm our support lines were shelled with H.E. mixed with gas shells from 8 pm to 8.15 pm.

3. GAS SHELLS. A few gas shells are reported near the Railway Crossing in B.21.a.

4. MACHINE GUNS. Enemy M.Gs were rather more active than usual, sweeping our forward area throughout the night.   Roads in B.29.a were also subjected to searching fire.

5. TRENCH MORTARS. 15 rounds fell into PONT de NIEPPE at 6.30 pm., B.28.b.1.8 received 35 rounds about midnight.

6. AIRCRAFT. Normal.   Two E.A. attempted to cross our lines at 11-30 am but were driven off by A.A. fire. At 6.30 pm a formation of 6, flying from S. to N. over their own lines   were engaged by A.A. fire.   3 small bombs were dropped on NIEPPE at 10.22 pm.

7. BALLOONS. None observed.

(c) INTELLIGENCE.

1. GENERAL. An escaped Portuguese prisoner was found in our lines on the Railway in B.28.b. He is a Corporal of the 4th Inf. Regt. and was captured on 9th April at NEUVE CHAPELLE. He worked in ARMENTIERES prior to the enemy withdrawal (Aug.29/30), since when he has lived in a camp near St ANDRE, working on the ammunition dump there.
   No signs of evacuation soon, but has heard rumours of it from enemy soldiers. Civilians are stated to be working on ammunition dumps as well as roads near ST. ANDRE.
   No wiring or digging seen.   Some wire was being sent back from BONTEMS (?).

D. G. Rydings
for Major,
General Staff, 40th Division.

CONFIDENTIAL.   (Not to be taken forward of Battn H.Q.)

40th DIVISION DAILY INTELLIGENCE SUMMARY, No. 31.
Period 6 am. 22nd - 6 am 23rd September, 1918.

(a) OUR OPERATIONS.

1. INFANTRY. The 121st Infantry Bde. relieved the 120th Infantry Bde during the night of 22/23rd September in the Divisional Sector.
Patrols were pushed forward to cover the relief.

2. ARTILLERY. Normal harassing fire was carried out during the 24 hours on the whole front. 18 pdrs and 4.5" hows. paid particular attention to the area West of the LYS in B.18.c and B.17 d. 4.5" hows. fired on and silenced a hostile 77 mm gun at H.C.a.90.50.

3. MACHINE GUNS. 3,000 rounds were fired/on selected targets including enemy cross roads, road junctions and tracks.

4. AIRCRAFT. Below normal owing to weather conditions. Strong formations were observed at 6.30 am and 8 am.

5. TRENCH MORTARS. Nil.

(b) ENEMY OPERATIONS.

1. INFANTRY. Nil.

2. ARTILLERY. Fairly quiet in forward areas during the morning and early afternoon. Between 10.30 am and 11.30 am. areas B.14 & B.15 d received 15 rounds from a 10 cm gun.
KELLOW CROSSING was registered during the afternoon by shrapnel and air bursts. This resulted later in an area shoot by 4.2" and 5.9" calibres embracing B.13.a & b and B.14.
Normal night harassing fire was carried out on back areas and forward areas were subjected to light scattered shelling

3. GAS SHELLING. Gas was mixed with H.E. in A.24.c and B.19.a & c from midnight to 4 am.

4. MACHINE GUNS. Fairly quiet. Occasional bursts of harassing fire were directed against our forward posts. The crossing in B.28.b. and areas B.22. a & c were also swept by M.G. fire.

5. TRENCH MORTARS. Inactive.

6. AIRCRAFT. Normal. At 8 am. a reconnaissance machine protected by 7 scouts attempted to cross our lines, but was driven off by 3 of our scouts. 2 E.A. were observed at 10.30 am. and 1 E.A. at 11.45 am

7. BALLOONS. Nil.

D.G. Tyings Lt
for Major,
General Staff, 40th Division.

23-9-18.

(Not to be taken forward of Battn H.Q.,)
CONFIDENTIAL. 40th DIVISION DAILY INTELLIGENCE SUMMARY, No.32.
Period 6am 23rd - 6 am. 24th September, 1918.

(a) OUR OPERATIONS.

1. INFANTRY. Three patrols sent out during the night, established the fact that posts at B.24.a.1.1, B.24.a.0.5 and B.17.d.6.4 are still occupied.

2. ARTILLERY. For the third night in succession our Artillery harassed the area West of the Canal in B.18.c and B.17.d. 3 separate shoots lasting 2 hours each were fired.
   Otherwise normal activity.

3. MACHINE GUNS. Harassing fire was carried out throughout the night on roads, tracks, posts etc., around ARMENTIERES and E. of ERQUINGHEM.

4. AIRCRAFT. Usual activity.

(b) HOSTILE OPERATIONS.

1. INFANTRY. Nil.

2. ARTILLERY. Normal. Principal shelling on PONT de NIEPPE, NIEPPE and NIEPPE Station.
   One shoot of about 30 rounds 15 cm How. (of which, about 50% were duds) appeared to be directed against one of our Batteries in B.25.a.

3. GAS SHELLING. 6 pm. 2 rounds 10.5 cm gas on B.27.d.
   8.30 - 9.30 pm 5 rounds on B.19.b and 2 mustard gas shells on B.19.d.0.7.
   5.55 am 15 rounds 10.5 cm gas on B.27.b.

4. MACHINE GUNS. Occasional sniping round PONT de NIEPPE.

5. AIRCRAFT. Normal, increasing during late afternoon.
   Between 5 and 5.30 pm an aeroplane (believed to be German) brought down by A.A. fire S. of River LYS.

6. LIGHTS etc., Double red lights were sent up on our front at 7 pm and 11 pm. 3 Blue lights seen at about B.24.c. No apparent action followed.

for Major,
General Staff, 40th Division.

GERMAN LIGHT PISTOLS. No further German Light Pistols are now required.

ORDER OF BATTLE. A captured document shows that a relief was to take place last night in the 56th Division's area, and suggests that troops new to the area may be coming in.

P.T.O.

NEWS.

ST. QUENTIN FRONT.

The French have penetrated into the Woods North of LY FONTAINE, captured the Fort and Village of VENDEUIL and reached the OISE in that locality.

PALESTINE FRONT.

Prisoners captured by Allies now amount to 25,000 and 260 guns, and great quantities of transport and stores have also been taken but not yet counted. The whole of the 7th and 8th Turkish Armies have been accounted for.

MACEDONIAN FRONT.

British and Greek forces are reported to be advancing on both sides of LAKE DOIRAN, and between LAKE DOIRAN and the VARDAR; have captured the whole of the Bulgarian positions. Serbian troops are on the Western Bank of the VARDAR to a point N.E. of PRILEP.

MACEDONIA. (LATER).

The Bulgarians are in full retreat on a front of 150 kilos between LAKE DOIRAN and MONASTIR. French Troops are on a line between GYEVGYELI - GURINCHET and KOYNSKO.
2nd Serbian Army from DEMIRKAPU to GRAGSKO.
1st Serbian Army - RADOBILY - DREN - KALYANI (E. & S.E. of PRILEP).
French, Italian and Greek troops - KANATLARTSI - MOGILA (5 miles North of MONASTIR).
The Bulgarians are throwing away their arms, and the roads are full of columns in disorder which our aeroplanes are attacking. All the dumps are in flames or captured.
The 70th Bulgarian Regiment which was sent up in Support, fled and were fired on by German machine guns.

****

CONFIDENTIAL.   (Not to be taken forward of Battn H.Q.)

40th DIVISION DAILY INTELLIGENCE SUMMARY, No. 33.
Period 6 am. 24th - 6 am. 25th Sept. 1918.

(a) OUR OPERATIONS.

1. INFANTRY. During the night our patrols were active and posts were established at the following points :- B.17.d.1.9 - B.17.d.6.4 - B.23.b.7.3. - B.23.b.8.2 - B.24.a.1.1.
    Posts in B.23.b and B.24.a were established without opposition, but considerable resistance was met with before posts in B.17.d could be consolidated.

2. ARTILLERY. Special harassing fire was again continued on Square B.18 both E. and W. of the Canal. Houses in this area were shelled by 4.5 hows. One N.F. call from the air was replied to.

3. AIRCRAFT. Normal activity.

4. MACHINE GUNS. Harassing fire was maintained throughout the night, targets including roads and tracks W. of ARMENTIERES and the area E. of ERQUINGHEM.

(b) ENEMY OPERATIONS.

1. INFANTRY. See above. The enemy appears to be holding the road B.17.d.3.7 - B.17.d.6.6.

2. ARTILLERY. During the day hostile artillery was rather more active than usual. At 2.5 pm. B.14.c was subjected to an area shoot lasting for 15 minutes, howitzers and H.V. guns being used. Between 2 pm. & 5 pm. several heavy concentrations of 15 cm were put down in the vicinity of the railway in B.20.b & B.21.a.
    Night harassing fire was normal.

3. MACHINE GUNS. Fairly active. A Machine Gun firing from approximately H.5.a.50.75 was active on our forward posts during the night. The NIEPPE - PONT de NIEPPE road was harassed at intervals.

4. AIRCRAFT. Normal activity. Reconnoitring patrols were observed over our lines at intervals during the day. Two large formations of 8 and 6 E.A. respectively were heavily engaged and driven off by A.A. fire.

5. BALLOONS. One H.K.B. was observed in position on a bearing of 95° from B.18.b.5.5.

(c) INTELLIGENCE.

1. DEFENCES. Observers report newly dug trench running from H.5.b.3.8 - H.5.a.7.2. which was clearly seen yesterday, has now been carefully camouflaged. Fresh trench observed running from H.5.d.3.5 to road at H.5.c.3.6.

2. LIGHTS. Red and Yellow lights were put up by the enemy at 11-15 pm. No apparent action followed.

3. GENERAL. A German M.G. was found in a post at B.17.d.6.4.

Major,
General Staff, 40th Division.

CONFIDENTIAL.

(Not to be taken forward of Battn H.Q.)

40th DIVISION DAILY INTELLIGENCE SUMMARY, No. 34.
Period 6 am. 25th - 6 am. 26th Sept. 1918.
****

(a) OUR OPERATIONS.

1. INFANTRY. During the night posts were established along the road from B.17.d.1.9 - B.17.d.55.40 and at B.24.a.0.5.

2. ARTILLERY. The usual number of rounds were expended on harassing fire, special area shoots being carried out West of the LYS in B.18.c and 17.d. Field Artillery supported the Infantry in their establishment of posts in B.17.d. and B.24.a.

3. AIRCRAFT. Normal activity during the day increasing towards the evening. Bombs were released in ARMENTIERES at 9 pm.

4. MACHINE GUNS. The normal programme of harassing fire was carried out. 4,000 rounds were expended on the following targets:-
Roads in B.30.c.65.45.
Roads railway and tracks in H.10.b.30.30.
House and tracks in H.11.c.60.53.
Roads in H.5.b.10.85.
Open ground H.4.d.1.3.

(b) ENEMY OPERATIONS.

1. INFANTRY. Nil.

2. ARTILLERY. Normal activity displayed. The enemy fired a series of short concentrations W. of NIEPPE in B.15.b. During the afternoon a 7.7 mm fired at intervals on the Railway in B.21.d and 22.c. PONT de NIEPPE was harassed at intervals with 10.5 and roads in B.8.b, B.8.d and B.9.c received about 150 rounds of 10.5 cm and 15 cm how. during the morning.

3. GAS SHELLING. 50 Blue Cross shells fell in B.8.c. at 11.50 pm. PISTOL FARM was shelled with mustard gas during the night.

4. MACHINE GUNS. Active sniping in the vicinity of NIEPPE and PONT d NIEPPE Road during the day. Our forward areas were harassed during the night from B.29.b - H.5.a - and H.5.d. M.Gs were also reported active from ERQUINGHEM firing on roads in B.27.a and B.26.b.

5. AIRCRAFT. Normal. During the day E.A. carried out several high reconnaissances of our line, but failed to penetrate our back areas owing to A.A. fire.

6. BALLOONS. H.K.Bs were observed as follows :-
3.15 pm. 3 Balloons on bearings of 132°, 142° and 179° from B.27.d.77.99.
3-30 pm. 1 H.K.B. on/of 153° from B.25.a.50.05.
-6.15 pm.   G.B.

(c) INTELLIGENCE.

1. MOVEMENT. Between 9.15 am and 10.45 am individual movement was observed on road at B.18.c.6.2.
At 9.40 am red cross cart was seen on road at B.18.c.65.30 going N.E. At 9.52 am 1 man observed to be working on camouflage on road from B.18.c.5.1 - B.18.c.65.30.

2. LIGHTS. At 9-45 pm. green lights were observed to be fired as our planes crossed the enemy lines. At 5 am double red lights were put up by the enemy in front of ARMENTIERES. No apparent enemy action followed.

Major,
General Staff, 40th Division.

(Not to be taken forward of Battalion H.Qrs).

CONFIDENTIAL.

40th DIVISION INTELLIGENCE SUMMARY NO.35.
Period 6 a.m. 26th - 6 a.m. 27th Sept.1918.
****

(a) OUR OPERATIONS.

1. INFANTRY. Patrols. Patrol of 1 officer and 6 O.R's reconnoitred the ground from B.28.d.2.5. Eastwards towards the LYS. Ground in the vicinity of the LYS is extremely marshy. Patrol skirted marshy ground and reached the road running towards the LYS at B.29.c.3.7. No enemy were encountered.

Patrol of 2 officers and 4 O.R. left our lines at B.11.d.6.5. at 2.30 a.m. proceeding in the direction of the WARNAVE. On reaching B.11.d.95.05. hostile machine guns opened at point blank range from B.12.c.05.10. The hostile party(about 20 strong)advanced towards our patrol throwing bombs and firing rifles. Patrol engaged this party with rifle fire and forced them to withdraw. Hostile machine gun fire then re-opened, and patrol returned to our lines. One of the patrol was wounded but was brought back with patrol.

Patrol of 1 officer and 4 O.R's proceeding between posts of Left Battalion, Left Brigade at 2.30 a.m. was attacked by hostile party (approx. strength 10) at B.12.b.30.75. Hostile party threw bombs wounding the officer of the patrol and one N.C.O. Hostile party then hurriedly withdrew across the WARNAVE. The N.C.O. who was wounded was last seen crawling into a shell hole but has not yet been discovered.

At 5.45 a.m. this morning, Right Brigade attacked under a creeping barrage from positions N. of PONT DE NIEPPE. Definite news has not yet been received of the results of this attack but 24 prisoners are known to have been captured. See preliminary examination.

2. ARTILLERY. Special programme of harassing fire was maintained throughout the day on ground W. of the LYS in B.17.d., B.18.a.c & d. and B.24.a. At 5.45 a.m. a creeping barrage and a smoke barrage was put down by our artillery in support of the attack by Right Brigade.

3. AIRCRAFT. Normal.

4. MACHINE GUNS. On left brigade front fired in conjunction with the Artillery barrage put down in support of our attack.

(b) ENEMY OPERATIONS

1. INFANTRY. See under our patrols.

2. ARTILLERY. Enemy's artillery maintained normal activity. Back areas harassed during the night with H.E. and a proportion of gas.

3. MACHINE GUNS. Hostile M.G's fire was above normal about GOSPEL VILLA and in B.28.b. during the night. The NIEPPE - PONT DE NIEPPE Road was swept at intervals during the night.

4.AIRCRAFT....

4. AIRCRAFT. Four hostile 'planes were over our lines at 10 a.m. on the Right Brigade front. One hostile 'plane crossed our lines at 5.30 a.m., was engaged by A.A. fire and driven off.

(c) INTELLIGENCE.

5. MOVEMENT. At 1.45 a.m. four men seen in the vicinity of B.24.c.3.1. At 5 p.m. one man seen on road at H.5.b.7.6. Individual movement seen throughout the day on the road and in the buildings about B.18.c.

6. ENEMY DEFENCES. Artillery report strong belt of wire running East of the LYS between ERQUINGHEM and ARMENTIERES. Belt is about 100 yards from the LYS and runs parallel to the river. Left Brigade report bridge at B.17.b.1.0. destroyed. There is a bridge at B.17.b.3.2. This bridge is of wood and wide enough to allow troops to cross two a-breast .

7. LIGHTS. Red flares were put up at intervals during the night with no apparent result.

8. PRISONERS. Five prisoners of 186 I.R. surrendered to Right Battalion of Left Brigade at 6.10 a.m. this morning. Point of capture B.17.d.central.
Prisoners to date in our attack this morning,15 unwounded, and 2 wounded of 88 I.R., 2 wounded of 186 I.R. Preliminary examination gives Order of Battle North to South -

       118 I.R. 1st Battalion.
       186 I.R. 1st Battalion.
       88 I.R. 1st Battalion

 88th I.R. holds the line West of the LYS with all three companies forward, 3rd Battalion in support on the line through LE BIZET, 2nd Battalion in rest near FRELINGHIEN. All Battalions of 186th and 88 I.R. now reduced to three companies. 56th Division received a draft of 500 men on the 21st from the Recruit Depot at ALTER. Average trench strength per company is 80. Prisoners know of no intention of further withdrawal.
  Light signals in force are -
    RED - longthen range.
    GREEN - barrage fire.

                 Lieut. Colonel,
            General Staff, 40th Division.

               *****

(Not to be taken forward of Battn H.Q.)

CONFIDENTIAL.

40th DIVISION DAILY INTELLIGENCE SUMMARY, No. 36.
Period 6 am 27th - 6 am 28th September, 1918.

(a) OUR OPERATIONS.

INFANTRY. At 5-45 am a minor operation was carried out by the Lancs Fusiliers with a view to making good the line of the LYS as far as B.18.d. Attack progressed at first on the flanks but met with considerable resistance in the centre and our troops were eventually forced to withdraw to their original line. There was considerable machine gun resistance from the Laundry in B.18.c, Brickworks in B.24.a. & Custom House B.18.a. Total prisoners captured were 25 of whom 5 were wounded and 5 gave themselves up to our left Brigade when the barrage opened.

2. ARTILLERY. At 5-45 am all Batteries fired a creeping barrage and put down a smoke screen in support of the minor operation by our right brigade. Further barrages were fired subsequently at request of the Infantry.
Harassing fire was carried out at night on roads in B.18.a and c and B.17.d.

3. AIRCRAFT. Normal activity. One aeroplane seen to fall over ARMENTIERES at 9 am, thought to be British.

4. MACHINE GUNS. In addition, to normal harassing fire machine guns carried out a special programme in support of the above operation.

(b) ENEMY OPERATIONS.

1. INFANTRY. See above.
2. ARTILLERY. Enemy artillery fire in response to our barrage fell on the road through B.17 a and d. According to one prisoner's statement their barrage also fell on their own troops, causing considerable casualties. On the left brigade front scattered harassing fire was maintained during day and night. The area West of a line running B.1. cent.- B.8.b.20.40 - B.15.b.20.48 received particular attention towards nightfall. A little counter battery work was carried out against batteries in A.23.d.
3. AIRCRAFT. Enemy planes were less active than usual during the day. A low flying E.A. crossed our line at 8-30 pm and dropped flares. Shortly afterwards the road B.10.b.cent - B.11.c.4.2 was heavily shelled. At 1 am. E.A. dropped bombs in the vicinity of B.16.d.
4. MACHINE GUNS. Hostile M.Gs were quieter than usual during the night except on PONT de NIEPPE and GOSPEL VILLA. M.Gs were active from C.1.c 05.10, B.12.b.40.35 and ERQUINGHEM.
5. GAS SHELLING. A few gas shells fell in B.6.c. B.10.b and B.21.a during the night.

(c) INTELLIGENCE.

1. MOVEMENT. A small party of enemy was seen to enter farm at C.1.c.05.10 at 7-30 pm.
2. DEFENCES. There is a thick belt of wire running from B.24.c.30.00 to B.29.b.central about 3'6" high and 12-15 feet wide.
3. LIGHTS. At 7-30 pm. double red flares were put up. No apparent enemy action resulted.

Lieut-Colonel,
General Staff, 40th Division.

(Not to be taken forward of Battn H.Q.)

CONFIDENTIAL.

40th DIVISION DAILY INTELLIGENCE SUMMARY, No. 37.
Period 6 am 28th - 6 am 29th September, 1918.

(a) OUR OPERATIONS.

1. INFANTRY. Patrols from our right Brigade reconnoitred the following areas without encountering enemy opposition :-

    (i) B.17.d.1.9.
    (ii) Road running N.E. in B.23.b to B.17.c.8.8.
    (iii) Area B.18.c.15.05 and B.24.a.4.9.

Bridges were established across the WARNAVE at B.17.b.8.6 - B.12.c.4.3 and B.12.c.8.8 during the night by the left Brigade. A patrol crossed the bridge at B.17.b.8.6 but encountered a superior hostile party at B.18.a.3.7 and was obliged to withdraw. An enemy patrol was also active at B.18.a.1.9.

2. ARTILLERY. Owing to active patrolling normal harassing fire was curtailed, batteries only firing at the request of the infantry. One call from the air was replied to.

3. AIRCRAFT. Our planes were active, frequent reconnaissances being made over enemy lines and back areas.

4. MACHINE GUNS. The usual harassing programme carried out during the night on the following targets :-
    Bridge   C.25.a.60.95
    Jute Factory   B.29.b & d.
    Roads, tracks and Railways   H.10.b.95.70.
    Houses and roads   H.5.d.30.40.

(b) ENEMY OPERATIONS.

1. INFANTRY. The enemy maintains a strictly alert attitude and patrols were active at B.18.a.3.7 and B.18.a.1.9.

2. ARTILLERY. Hostile artillery displayed normal activity during the period. STEENWERCK received about 50 rounds from 10 cm H.V. gun between 7 - 8 am. Other areas shelled include B.11 d, B.19.c, B.16.d and B.22.c. NIEPPE and PONT de NIEPPE were harassed at intervals during the afternoon by 7.7 cm and 15 cm. A long period of inactivity was noticed in the PONT de NIEPPE sector during the night. The front line in B.28.d was shelled for 10 minutes at 3-55 pm.

3. GAS SHELLING. Fifteen gas shells fell in B.23.b.3.6 at 3-40 pm. About 50 blue cross are reported in B.5.a. and B.4.a between 5-30 & 6-30 am.

4. AIRCRAFT. Below normal. 3 E.A. crossed our lines between 1 am and 4 am.

5. MACHINE GUNS. Normal activity on right sector, slightly above normal on left 2 M.Gs fired intermittent bursts from ERQUINGHEM during the night. Two M.Gs were also located at B.12.b.4.5.

6. BALLOONS. Two Balloons were observed during the morning N & W of ARMENTIERES.

(c) INTELLIGENCE.

1. MOVEMENT. At 12-15 pm 2 men were seen to leave a supposed M.G. emplacement at B.24.c.4.3.

2. ENEMY DEFENCES. New earth has been thrown up at B.24.c.4.3.

3. EXPLOSIONS. 2 explosions were seen about 9 pm in the vicinity of ARMENTIER

4. LIGHTS. A large number of green lights were sent up on the left during the night.

5. GENERAL. Foot bridge at B.24.c.1.1 has been destroyed. A smoke barrage was put up by us on Divisional front during morning and afternoon.

Lieut-Colonel,
General Staff, 40th Division.

(Not to be taken forward of Battn H.Q.)

CONFIDENTIAL.

40th DIVISION DAILY INTELLIGENCE SUMMARY, No. 38.
Period 6 am 29th - 6 am 30th September, 1918.

(a) OUR OPERATIONS.

1. INFANTRY. At dusk on the evening 29th/30th September patrols were pushed forward by our Left Brigade in order to maintain touch with the enemy. The hostile covering screen was driven in and the following line established :-

    C.1.c.15.60 - C.1.c.10.23 - C.1.c.05.10 - C.7.a.2.9 - C.7.a 40.55 - B.12.b.90.15 - B.12.d.2.5 - B.18.a.95.60 - B.18.b. 05.20.

Considerable hostile M.G. fire was encountered from the line B.18.b.25.85 - B.18.d.4.9.

Patrols from our right Brigade advanced in conjunction with the left and the line LAUNDRY - CUSTOM HOUSE was found unoccupied. Patrol operating in B.29.c encountered no opposition.

2. ARTILLERY. Harassing fire was carried out during the period on roads and cross roads in ARMENTIERES and northern outskirts. Hostile Batteries were subjected to neutralising fire during the day and destructive fire directed against enemy M.G. emplacements.

Several N.F. calls were received and answered.

3. AIRCRAFT. Very active all day especially between 6 - 8 am. At 11 am a H.K.B was observed to be brought down by one of our aeroplanes.

4. MACHINE GUNS. Intermittent harassing fire was maintained on the ERQUINGHEM area and in the vicinity of the JUTE FACTORY.

5. TRENCH MORTARS. 74 rounds were directed against suspected M.G. emplacements in B.18.

(b) ENEMY OPERATIONS.

1. INFANTRY. See above.
2. ARTILLERY. Hostile artillery activity was below normal during the day. NIEPPE and vicinity received attention with 7.7 cm and 10.5 cm at intervals during the day. From 4.20 pm to 5.20 pm road junctions in B.10.d and B.11.c were shelled with 15. cm hows. Other targets included Battery areas in B.7 & 8 and areas B.5 and B.28.d and B.27.
3. AIRCRAFT. Normal activity.
4. MACHINE GUNS. Enemy M.Gs were active during the night sweeping forward areas and harassing roads. Guns were located at B.18.b.7.5 and B.18.d. central.
5. SNIPERS. Enemy snipers became very active in the left sector at daybreak.
6. GAS SHELLING. A few blue cross shells fell into B.16.d at 5 am.
7. GENERAL. A pigeon was observed flying towards enemy's lines from the direction of NIEPPE. It is believed to have been released from enemy plane which was over our lines at 10-30 am

                                        for Lieut-Colonel,
General Staff, 40th Division.

NEWS

PALESTINE.

Australian Mounted Divisions took EL KUNEITRA at 2 p.m. yesterday, and are making for DAMASCUS. Our troops have joined up with Arabs at DARAA.

MACEDONIA.

Unofficial report from G.H.Q. says "BULGARIA has asked for peace and hostilities cease 12 noon to-morrow (1st)".

ARGONNE FRONT.

All enemy counter attacks yesterday were repulsed and the French have continued their advance, particularly East of GRATEUIL.

The Americans have also advanced.

FRENCH FRONT.

First French Army (South of ST.QUENTIN) have captured URVILLERS and CERIZY.

Between the AILETTE and the AISNE French line runs East of PONT ARCY - West of MOUSSY - West of BRAYE - West of PARGNY - North of CHAVIGNON - thence along AILETTE to West of ANEZY.

CAMBRAI - ST.QUENTIN. As a result of attacks by the 1st, 3rd and 4th Armies our line now runs :- AUBENSCHEUL - AU BAC - BLECOURT - TILLOY - Western edge of CAMBRAI - Fbg. de PARIS - RUMILLY - MASNIERES - LES RUES DES VIGNES - along Canal to BANTEUX - GONNELIEU - VILLERS GUISLAIN - VENDHUILE - BONY (excl.) - BELLICOURT - JONCOURT (excl.) - LEVERGIES - LE TRONQUOY - GRICOURT - all places inclusive unless otherwise marked.

Enemy counter attack in neighbourhood of BAECOURT but no details yet received.

PRISONERS. 3rd Army morning 27th - 6 a.m. 29th.
8,400 prisoners and 125 guns.
4th Army for 29th - 6,500 (estimated).
46th Division yesterday - 4,000 prisoners and 40 guns.

FLANDERS. Since this morning's report our men have been reported in the following places :-
MOORSLEDE (incl.) East of GHELUWE - on the COMINES - WARNETON Railway.

31st Division line runs as follows :-
Left Brigade approaching WARNETON.
Right Bde on line of LYS in 28/U.17.d. and U.23.b. thence along WARNAVE River to 36/C.1.central.

40th Division line runs :-
36/ C.1.central - C.1.c.2.5. - C.1.c.1.1. - along hedge to C.7.a.central - along road to B.12.b.9.1. - B.12.d.2.5. - B.12.d.1.0. - B.18.a.9.7. - B.18.a.9.1. - B.18.c.9.6. - B.18.c.8.2. - B.24.a.4.9. - B.24.a.1.5. to B.23.b.8.4., thence as before.

Captain,
General Staff, 40th Div.

30/9/18.

(Not to be taken forward of Battn H.Q.)
CONFIDENTIAL

40th DIVISION DAILY INTELLIGENCE SUMMARY, No. 39.
Period 6 am 30th Sept. - 6 am 1st October, 18.

(a) OUR OPERATIONS.

1. **INFANTRY.** Our troops continued to follow up the enemy and at nightfall the following line had been established by our Left Brigade :-
B.12.d.8.6 - B.12.b.95.05 - C.7.a.6.8 - C.1.d.4.1.
Patrols were pushed forward later and in spite of considerable hostile M.G. fire by 3 am our troops had established themselves on a line running C. 13.c.4.7 - C.13.a.3.4 - C.13.a.2.9 - C.7.c.3.4 - C.7.c.8.6 - C.7.d.1.9 - C.7.B.6.2. - C.7.b.9.4 with a defensive flank lying from B.18 cent to C.13.c.4.7.
Posts were established by the right Brigade at B.18.d.1.8 - HOSPITAL-LAUNDRY - B.24.a.3.9 and touch obtained with the right and left flanks.

2. **ARTILLERY.** The usual harassing fire was carried out in the vicinity of ARMENTIERES, and enemy centres of resistance were engaged at the request of the Infantry.
Batteries also co-operated with the H.A. in concentrations on two hostile batteries.

3. **AIRCRAFT.** Owing to unfavourable weather conditions our planes were inactive.

4. **MACHINE GUNS.** Harassing fire was carried out during the night. This was chiefly confined to the right sector.

(b) ENEMY OPERATIONS.

1. **INFANTRY.** During the afternoon patrols operating in B.12.b & d encountered the enemy, bombs being thrown. A hostile patrol also made an attempt to approach one of our posts in B.13 a. One of the enemy was killed the remainder then withdrew.

2. **ARTILLERY.** Enemy artillery activity was below normal. Forward posts in B.12.b were subjected to a little scattered shelling by 7.7 cm at intervals during the period. NIEPPE received attention from 6 - 7 am - 10 - 11 pm. and again from 4-30 - 6 am. Roads in B.7.d, B.5.a & d and B.11 received a few odd rounds of 10.5 cm during the night.

3. **AIRCRAFT.** Inactive. One E.A. made a reconnaissance of our lines at 6-25 am. A. H.K.B. was brought down by one of our planes east of LE BIZET at 10 am.

4. **MACHINE GUNS.** Hostile M.Gs continually swept our lines in the left sector. By day movement was quickly noticed and close range fire directed on it. Slight activity is reported in the NIEPPE sector and guns in ERQUINGHEM were less active than usual.

5. **SNIPERS.** Hostile snipers were active.

6. **TRENCH MORTARS.** A few rounds fell about B.28.b.7.0 between 10 and 11 pm.

(c) INTELLIGENCE.

1. **FIRES.** Two fires were observed at 10-50 pm in a north easterly direction. from B.17.d.5.2. A fire was also observed in ARMENTIERES at 11-45 pm and an explosion at 9-45 am (1st Oct) about C.19.c.20.30.

2. **LIGHTS.** Fewer very lights than usual were observed.

3. **MOVEMENT**

2.

3. **MOVEMENT.** One man was observed near ruined farm at C.13.c.95.50.

4. **DEFENCES.** House at C.13.c.50.75 appears to be occupied by enemy troops. Sentry observed standing by the gate.

5. **IDENTIFICATIONS.**

Two prisoners belonging to the 3rd Company, I.R. 186, 56th Division were captured this morning in C.13.a.
Prisoners who recently arived from the Recruit Depot with a draft were unable to give any information with regard to the order of battle or dispositions.
They were left behind as a Company reserve with about 12 others at ST. ANDRÉ when the 1st Battalion went into the line, about 8 days ago, and on the night of 29/30th September were ordered up to strengthen the Company. Prisoners had heard that a withdrawal was to take place but knew nothing definite. Beyond confirming statements of prisoners captured on 27th no fresh information was obtained.

Chapman
Capt-GS
for Lieut-Colonel,
General Staff, 40th Division.

CONFIDENTIAL.   ORIGINAL.

WAR DIARY

40th Division

GENERAL STAFF BRANCH

VOL. XXIX

FROM:- 1st October, 1918.
To :- 31st October, 1918.

_____ Major General,
Commanding 40th Division.

According to the Daily Summary of operations attached to this diary, the line shown here was occupied during the night 1/2nd October and not night 30th/1st.
Also see G.S Diary 30/9/18 [inid] which gives line at 3 am (1st Oct) B 17/24.

SECRET.   Copy No. 19

40th DIVISION ORDER NO. 213.   13/10/18.

1. As a result of operations to be carried out farther North on the morning of October 14th, the Corps on our left may be enabled to occupy PAUL BUCQ and BOUS BECQUE by the evening of that day or the morning of October 15th.

2. The 121st Infantry Brigade will be prepared, by the evening of the 14th, on receipt of orders from Div. H.Qrs. to push forward three fighting patrols of not less than 25 men each along the best avenues of advance.

   (a) These patrols must be prepared to fight their way through any light outpost line of resistance they may meet.

   (b) They will be closely supported by Artillery and M.G's.

   (c) Their objective is to maintain close touch with the enemy in his retirement.

   (d) Rifle grenadiers should form part of each of these patrols and should be freely used when opposition is met with from M.G. fire within their range.

3. In the event of an advance the 331st Brigade R.F.A. will move forward with the advanced Guard Brigade under orders of the Brigade commander.
   The 330th Brigade R.F.A. will stand fast in their present positions.

4. The Company of the M.G.Battalion at present under the orders of the Advanced Guard Brigade will similarly be prepared to advance.
   The remaining three companies will be held in readiness to move at 1 hour's notice.

5. The 119th and 120th Infantry Brigades will be held in readiness to move at 1 hour's notice on receipt of orders from Div. H.Q.

6. ACKNOWLEDGE.

                                                    Chapman
                                                    Captain,

Issued at 19.45   General Staff, 40th Division.

Copy No. 1 to G.O.C.   13 D.A.P.M.
        2   119th Inf. Bde.   14 64 Bde R.G.A.
        3   120th   ,,   15 31st Division.
        4   121st   ,,   16 59th   ,,
        5   C.R.E.   17 XV Corps G.
        6   66th D.A.   18   ,,   H.A.
        7   17th Worc. R. (B).   19 War Diary
        8   Signals.   20   ,,
        9   39th Bn: M.G.Corps.   21 File
       10   Div. Train.
       11   "Q" 40th Div.
       12   A.D.M.S.

SECRET.

Copy No. 25.

40th DIVISION ORDER NO. 220.

15/10/18.

App. 8

1. All indications point to the enemy carrying out an early withdrawal in front of 40th Division.

2. The 40th Division will be ready to advance in an Easterly direction in conjunction with the advance of 59th and 31st Divisions on both flanks, and will vigorously press the retreating enemy.

3. The objectives allotted to the Division are as follows :-
FORT DE LOMPRET (J.8.b.) - Buildings J.3.c.4.8. - LA TULLERIE FARM (D.27.d.0.7.) - LE CŒUR JOYEUX (D.22.b.0.7.) - QUESNOY (exclusive).

4. The Advanced Guard of the Division will be formed of the following troops :-

    Advanced Guard Commander - Brig.Gen. G.C.STUBBS, D.S.O.

    121st Infantry Brigade.
    331st Brigade Royal Field Artillery.
    "B" Company 39th Battalion Machine Gun Corps.

5. (a) Intermediate objectives will be given to each battalion and company of the Advanced Guard, to which they will advance on the first signs of enemy withdrawal without waiting for further orders.

    (b) G.O.C. 120th Infantry Brigade will be prepared to support the 121st Infantry Brigade or to move through the 121st Infantry Brigade if the situation admits of and requires it. He will keep in close touch with the situation and be prepared to move at short notice on orders being received from Divisional Headquarters.

    (c) G.O.C. 119th Infantry Brigade will be prepared to move forward to the area at present occupied by 120th Infantry Brigade.
    He will keep in close touch with G.O.C. 120th Infantry Brigade and be prepared to move on receipt of orders from Divisional Headquarters.

6. After the advance has commenced the 330th Brigade Royal Field Artillery will come into Divisional Reserve and be moved forward as the situation demands under orders from Divisional Headquarters.

7. The O.C. 39th Battalion Machine Gun Corps will arrange for companies to accompany the Brigades to which they are already attached and for the fourth company to remain in Divisional Reserve in its present location.

8. Units will endeavour to establish communication as early as possible by wireless, pigeon, visual and runner.
Attention is directed to Chapter III S.S.191.

9. Two main forward roads and one lateral road will be maintained by the C.R.E. in the area over which the advance will be carried out.

10. Location of Divisional Headquarters and the date of move will be notified later.

11. A C K N O W L E D G E.

Issued at... 20.00.

Major,
General Staff, 40th Division.

P.T.O.

```
Copy No. 1 to G.O.C.
     2      119th Infantry Brigade.
     3      120th         ,,
     4      121st         ,,
     5      C.R.E.
     6      66th D.A.
     7      40th D.A.
     8      Signals
     9      39th Bn: M.G.C.
    10      17th Worc. R. (P).
    11       Div. Train.
    12      "Q" 40th Div.
    13      A.D.M.S.
    16      D.A.P.M.
    17      64th Bde. R.G.A.
    18      31st Division.
    19      59th Division.
    20      XV Corps G.
    21         ,,    Q.
    22         ,,    R.A.
    23         ,,    H.A.
    24      War Diary
    25         ,,
    26      File
```

40th Div. No. 184/11 (G). SECRET.

App. 9

40th DIVISION INSTRUCTIONS NO. 10.

1. When unable to push on, units will state in their reports the position of the troops who have been checked, the position and estimated strength of the enemy opposing them, and how they are dealing with the situation.

2. One Stokes Mortar and 40 rounds of ammunition will accompany each Battalion Headquarters; a proportion of one round of smoke will be carried to every 5 rounds.

3. The above instructions will be made known to all commanders down to Company Commanders.

JHWailes Major,

16/10/18. General Staff, 40th Division.

119th Inf. Bde.   C.R.A.
120th   ,,   39th Bn: M.G.C.
121st   ,,   "Q"

"A" Form.
MESSAGES AND SIGNALS.

Army Form C. 2121. (In pads of 100.)

TO: All recipients Div. Order 220

Sender's Number	Day of Month	In reply to Number	AAA
GC 588	16		
Reference	40th	Div.	Order
220	aaa	40th	Div.
will	advance	at	once
and	gain	objectives	laid
down	in	para	B
aaa	If	strong	enemy
resistance	is	met	Advance
Guard	supported	if	necessary
by	120th	Brigade	will
make	organised	attack	with
Artillery	support	at	1700
to-day	aaa	120th	Brigade
will	move	at	once
and	occupy	area	vacated
by	121st	Brigade	aaa
C.R.A.	will	arrange	for
move	of	230th	Artillery

"A" Form

Army Form C. 2121
(in pads of 100.)

MESSAGES AND SIGNALS.

No. of Message ....

Prefix .... Code ....m.	Words.	Charge.	This message is on a/c of:	Recd. at ....m.
Office of Origin and Service Instructions.	Sent		...............................Service.	Date ....
File	At...................m.			From .... Copp 21
	To			
	By		(Signature of "Franking Officer.")	By ....

TO				
	120	Bde	G	
	ACE 3 (Bon)		CRE	

Sender's Number.	Day of Month.	In reply to Number.	AAA
* GB 124	19		

In	continuation	[illegible]	GB [illegible]
[illegible]	18th	AAA Daily	from
[illegible]	1½ Bns	[illegible]	[illegible]
and	1½ Bns	[illegible]	[illegible]
to	[illegible]	[illegible]	[illegible]
[illegible]	[illegible]	[illegible]	[illegible]
[illegible]	[illegible]	[illegible]	[illegible]
[illegible]	[illegible]	[illegible]	[illegible]
[illegible]	AAA	[illegible]	120 Bde
[illegible]	ACE 3	G	CRE

From	40 Div		
Place			
Time			

The above may be forwarded as now corrected. (Z) [illegible] Maj

Censor. Signature of Addressor or person authorised to telegraph in his name

* This line should be erased if not required.

(2599). Wt. W3253/P511. 100,000 Pads. 1/18. H. C. & L., Ltd.

SECRET.   Copy No. 34

Ref. sheet
36. 1:40,000   40th DIVISIONAL ORDER No. 222.   19-10-18.

                                                     App. 22

1. Divisional Headquarters (1st Echelon) will move to-morrow to ROUBAIX F.21.c.7.7 and will open at midday.

2. For the purpose of the move 1st Echelon will consist of:-

      G.O.C.,
      G. Office
      A & Q Offices.
      C.R.E.,
      A.D.M.S.,

3. Remainder of Divisional Headquarters will follow on the 21st October.

4. 40th Divisional Artillery and 39 Bn M.G.C., will concentrate in an area about WAMBRECHIES for rest and training.

                            E.H.S.Black

                                    Lieut-Colonel,
Issued at 2000.   General Staff, 40th Division.

Copy No. 1 to G.O.C.,
     2   119th I.B.
     3   120th I.B.
     4   121st I.B.
     5   C.R.E.,
     6   40th D.A.
     7   17th Worc R.(P)
     8   Signals
     9   S.A.A. Section D.A.C.
    10   Div. Train.
    11   S.S.O.,
    12   40th Div.M.T.Coy.
    13   39th M.G.Bn.
    14   "Q" 40th Div.
    15   A.D.M.S.
    16   D.A.D.V.S.
    17   D.A.D.O.S.
    18   D.A.P.M.
    19 Camp Commandant.
    20   Div. Gas Officer.
    21   Div. Claims Officer.
    22   Div. Reception Camp.
    23   45th Bde R.G.A.
    24   Area Commandant, Right Div.
    25   "L" Special Coy. R.E.
    26   Div. Employment Coy.
    27   31st Div.
    28   59th Div.
    29   XV Corps G
    30   XV Corps Q.
    31   XV Corps R.A.
    32   XV Corps H.A.
  33 & 34   War Diary.
    35   File.

SECRET.   Copy No. 15

    40th DIVISION ORDER NO. 223.   23/10/18.

1.   119th Infantry Brigade will move to an area about BONDUES to-morrow.

2.   No restrictions as to time of march or roads to be used.

3.   Administrative orders follow.

4.   ACKNOWLEDGE.

                                        for Lieut. Colonel,
                          General Staff, 40th Division.

Issued at 11.15

    Copy No. 1 to G.O.C.
          2   119th I.Bde.
          3   120th I.Bde.
          4   121st I.Bde.
          5   C.R.E.
          6   Div. Train.
          7   A.D.M.S.
          8   Signals
          9   40th D.A.
          10   39th M.G.Bn.
          11   D.A.D.V.S.
          12   D.A.P.M.
          13   "Q"
          14   XV Corps G.
          15   War Diary
          16   "
          17   File

SECRET.   Copy No. 30

     40th DIVISION ORDER NO. 224.   24/10/18.   App.24

Ref. Map 1/40,000,
Sheets 36 and 37.

1. The 40th Division will relieve the 31st Division in the line on 26th and night 26th/27th October.

2. Movements and reliefs by Infantry, Artillery, 39th M.G.Battalion and Pioneer Battalion will be carried out in accordance with attached movement table.

3. Only one Brigade of Divisional Artillery will move up : the other remaining in present location until further orders.

4. C.R.E. will take over work from the C.R.E. 31st Division and arrange for the movement of his Field Companies accordingly.

5. Relief of Field Ambulances will be arranged by the A.D.M.S.s concerned.

6. The 120th Infantry Brigade will continue work on Railway up to and including 27th instant.

7. Command will pass at 10.00 27th October.

8. ACKNOWLEDGE.

                              [signature] . Lieut. Colonel,
Issued at 21.15   General Staff, 40th Division.

                                    ******

Copy No. 1 to G.O.C.   17 to D.A.D.O.S.
        2   119th I.B.   18   D.A.P.M.
        3   120th I.B.   19   Div. Gas Officer.
        4   121st I.B.   20   Div. Claims Off.
        5   C.R.E.   21   Div. Reception Camp.
        6   40th D.A.   22   Div. Employment Coy.
        7   17th Worc. R. (P).   23   14th Division.
        8   Signals   24   31st Division.
        9   39th Bn: M.G.C.   25   XV Corps "G".
       10   S.A.A.Section.   26   ,,   "Q"
       11   Div. Train.   27   ,,   R.A.
       12   S.S.O.   28   ,,   H.A.
       13   40th Div.M.T.Coy.   29   War Diary
       14   "Q" 40th Div.   30   ,,
       15   A.D.M.S.   31   File.
       16   D.A.D.V.S.

MOVEMENT TABLE to accompany 40th Div. Order No. 224.

Date	31st Division.			40th Division		
	Formation	From	To.	Formation	From.	To.	Remarks
25th Oct.	92nd I.Bde.	WATTRELOS	CUERNE	121st Inf. Bde.	CROIX	Staging area about LEERS.	Not to enter L'ANNOY before 13.00
	94th I.Bde. 31st Bn:M.G.C. (less 1 coy)	L'ANNOY. LEERS	MOUSCRON CUERNE	39th Bn:M.G.C.	WAMBRECHIES	LEERS via CROIX.	- do -
26th Oct.	94th I.Bde.	MOUSCRON	CUERNE	119th I.Bde.	BONDUES	WATTRELOS	Route via MOUVAIX ROUBAIX.
	170 Bde.RFA.	A.29 & 30.	-do-	"A" Bde RFA 40th Divn.	WAMBRECHIES.	A.29 & 30.	To via CROIX. To take over from 170th Bde RFA.
Night 26/27th October.	93rd I.Bde. 1 coy 31st Bn: M.G.C.	Line	MOUSCRON	121st I.Bde. 1 coy 39th Bn: M.G.C.	LEERS area	Line.	In relief of 93rd I.Bdo. Details to be arranged between Brigadiers concerned. Maps of the area will be taken over.
27th Oct.				17th Worc.R(P).	F.27.a.6.9.	L'ANNOY.	
28th Oct.				120th I.Bde.	ST.ANDRE	L'ANNOY.	via LA MADELEINE and CROIX

CONFIDENTIAL (Not to be taken forward of Battn H.Q.)

40th DIVISION DAILY INTELLIGENCE SUMMARY, No. 51.
Period 0600 12th - 0600 13th October, 1918.

(a) OUR OPERATIONS.

1. INFANTRY. The line gained yesterday was consolidated and posts established to connect/up with the main line on the left. The general line now runs as follows :- C.22.c.7.1 - C.28.b.2.4 - C.28.d.8.7. C.28.d.7.2 I.5.a.3.7 - I.5.c.2.9, I.5.c.5.5, I.5.d.00.30.

INCANDESCENT TRENCH to the railway at I.11.a.6.3 where we are in close liaison with troops on our right. Th area to a depth of 500 yards in front of our line from I.5.a.3.7 to I.5.c.9.3 is a complete bog.

Patrolling was carried out during the night but no hostile movement seen.

2. ARTILLERY. Roads tracks and occupied areas in C.15.d., C.18.a & C C.23.b., C.24. a & b., C.30. a & d., I.6.a & b., I.7.c. I.13.b were harassed by 18 pdrs and 4.5" hows. during the night and early morning. The M.G. at C.29.c.80.70 reported by patrols on 11th inst was engaged with H.E. by three 18 pdr batteries.

Hostile battery at D.26.a.32.65 - 36.59 was harassed with bursts of fire at intervals.   No N.F. Calls were received.
3. AIRCRAFT. Unfavourable weather conditions prevented flying.
4. MACHINE GUNS. Normal. Usual harassing fire was carried out.

(b) ENEMY OPERATIONS.

1. INFANTRY. Nil.
2. ARTILLERY. Fairly quiet throughout the day; activity increasing after nightfall. HOUPLINES and LE BIZET were harassed by field guns with H.E. mixed with a little gas.

At 0530 this morning the enemy again put down a barrage similar to that reported for the last 4 days. It extended approximately from HOUPLINES Northwards dwelling at first on the Support Line area, then lifting eastwards to our front line on which it rests till it ceases. The duration of the shoot varies from 30 minutes to 1 hour according to the amount of shooting we have been doing during the night.

On the Right Group front Battn H.Q. in C.26.b. was shelled by 10.5 cm Hows. Otherwise the front was quiet.
3. AIRCRAFT. Inactive.
4. MACHINE GUNS. Machine Guns were located firing from I.5.b.4.2 and I.5.d.5.8 during the morning. Occasional bursts were fired from the direction of FRELINGHIEN and C.17.d.
5. GAS SHELLING. Gas was occasionally mixed with H.E.
6. BALLOONS. None observed.

(c) INTELLIGENCE.

1. LIGHTS. Green lights were fired by enemy throughout the night. No apparent enemy action followed.

2. GENERAL. INCANDESCENT TRENCH was found to be in a very bad state, being nothing more than a chain of shell holes.

for Captain,
General Staff, 40th Division.

To Cop.
13-10-18.

NEWS.

LENS FRONT.

North of the SENSEE River ARLEUX, ESTREES and CORBEHEM have been cleared of the enemy: we hold HARNES and ANNAY. We have also captured PLANQUE and COURCELLES, and are on the W. outskirts of DOURGES.

CAMBRAI-ST.QUENTIN FRONT.

Enemy counter attacked strongly North of the LE CATEAU. Our troops are east of SELLE River just north of MONTAY thence West of River through Southern half of NEUVILLY to Railway East of River - BRIASTRE inclusive - thence line continues South and West of ST PYTHON - HAUSSY - SAULZOIR - HASPRES (all exclusive) - HOUDAIN (incl). North of SCARPE line runs CORBEHAM - CUINCY - COURCELLES - HARNES - ANNAY (all incl). Elsewhere no material change. French have reached line of AISNE River between VOUZIERES and BERRY-AU-BAC.

FRENCH FRONT.

The enemy is retreating hurriedly North and North-east of RHEIMS. French troops have entered BOUZIERES. Westward the line runs North of the VOUZIERS - VAUVRES Road - TAGNON - VIEUX-lez-ASFELD.
North of the AILETTE the French hold TRUCY and MONANPTEUIL, and West of the BASSE FORET DE COUCY the enemy has been driven out of SEPTVAUX.

AMERICAN FRONT.

East of the AIRE American troops are on the outskirts of ST. JUVIN - ST. GEORGES - LANDRES. East of the Meuse they hold MOLLEVILLE Farm (4 km due East of SIVRY-sur-MEUSE).

GENERAL NEWS.

It is reported the German Government in conjunction with the Austro-Hungarian Government has agreed to President Wilson's demand for the evacuation of all occupied territories.

LATER.

Wire from Second Army timed 1540 begins aaa First Army report situation midday aaa Our troops are reported in SAULZOIR aaa We attacked East of the SCHELDT Canal towards LIEU ST AMAND progress was delayed through heavy M.G. fire aaa Hostile counter attack North of AUBIGNY-au-BAC was repulsed and prisoners taken HAUTE DEULE Canal was crossed North of COURCELLES in face of considerable opposition and line now runs AUBY (excl) -- COURCELLES (incl)- NOYELLE - GODAULT (incl) -- DOURGES (excl) - COURRIERES (excl) thence 500 yards South of HAUTE DEULE Canal to ANNAY ends aaa G.H.Q. Situation report 1500 aaa We have made some progress in the SELLE VALLEY and hold BELLEVUE and BRIDGEHEAD in N. portion of ST PYTHON and between ST PYTHON and HAUSSY. Otherwise no material change on British Front. French have occupied LAON this morning, and 12000 civilians found in the town. French have reached VERSIGNY about 6 km E. of LA FERE.

40th D.H.Q.
13-10-18.
Timed 20.00

for Captain, G.S.

CONFIDENTIAL.
(Not to be taken forward of Battalion H.Q.)

40th DIVISION INTELLIGENCE SUMMARY, No. 52.
period 06.00 13th - 06.00 14th Oct. 1918.

(a) OUR OPERATIONS.

1. INFANTRY. Patrols were out during the night but no information of importance was obtained. Enemy wire in front of our posts is reported to be very thick and intact.

2. ARTILLERY. During the day activity was maintained on areas likely to be occupied by the enemy. All calibres carried out harassing fire on enemy roads, tracks and buildings during the night.

3. AIRCRAFT. Below normal, owing to weather conditions.

4. MACHINE GUNS. Normal.

(b) ENEMY OPERATIONS.

1. INFANTRY. A hostile party about 20 strong attempted to work round our post at I.5.d.0.3. whilst another party with a machine gun tried to creep up a communication trench. Fire was opened on both parties who immediately made a hasty retreat. Casualties were inflicted on the enemy.
   The enemy continues to maintain an alert attitude. M.G. fire is opened as soon as our patrols approach his positions.

2. ARTILLERY. Normal activity during the day. From 04.45 to 06.00 hostile shelling was heavy on both forward and back areas, particularly on the left sector. Both LE BIZET and HOUPLINES were subjected to short concentrations of H.E. and blue cross. Other areas receiving considerable attention throughout the period were :- C.20.b., I.1.a & b., I.2.a., I.9.c., H.12.a., and C.26. and 27.

3. AIRCRAFT. Inactive.

4. MACHINE GUNS. Normal activity. Intermittent bursts of fire on our posts during the night.

5. GAS SHELLING. Gas was occasionally mixed with H.E. especially in vicinity of HOUPLINES.

(c) INTELLIGENCE.

1. GUN FLASHES. At 14.20 a field gun battery was active from wood in J.8.c. Gun flash was observed on a T.B. of 109½° from C.27.c.1.5.

D.G. Rydings
for Captain,
General Staff, 40th Division.

(Not to be taken forward of Battn H.Q).

CONFIDENTIAL.

40th DIVISION DAILY INTELLIGENCE SUMMARY, No. 53.
Period 0600 14th - 0600 15th October, 1918.

(a) OUR OPERATIONS.

1. **INFANTRY.** At 0530 this morning fighting patrols from each outpost company were sent out with a view to occupying the German front line and maintaining touch with the enemy.
The situation at 1230 is reported as follows :- A post has been established in INANE TRENCH, and INCANDESCENT SUPPORT occupied as far as I.5.d.45.50. Our centre patrol is reported to have reached C.29 central. On the left our patrol penetrated as far as C.23.a.17 where it was held up by M.G. fire from CELT TRENCH. Steps are being taken to deal with this by Artillery.

2. **ARTILLERY.** During the period both 18 pdrs and 4.5" hows carried out harassing fire on roads and tracks in enemy forward areas. Special area shoots were carried out on C.29.b - I.12 a & b - C.18.c and C.24.a at infantry request and howitzers of the left group engaged in wire cutting in front of FRELINGHIEN for the Division on our left
No N.F. calls were received.

3. **AIRCRAFT.** Our aeroplanes were very active throughout the day. Numerous large formations were observed; enemy lines being frequently reconnoitred in the direction of LILLE.

(b) ENEMY OPERATIONS.

1. **INFANTRY.** Nil.

2. **ARTILLERY.** There was an increase in hostile artillery over the previous day.
Occasional heavy bursts of fire were directed against HOUPLINES and CHAPELLE D'ARMENTIERES during the morning. ERQUINGHEM was fired on by a 15 cm gun and ARMENTIERES received some attention.

3. **AIRCRAFT.** During the morning 6 E.A. were active over forward areas

4. **GAS SHELLING.** A few scattered gas shells were mixed with H.E. during the above shelling

5. **MACHINE GUNS.** Between 14.30 and 15.30 M.Gs were active against our planes from I.5.d. Occasional bursts of fire during the night. From the sound of M.G. fire the enemy is apparently considerably more advanced by night than by day.

Major,
General Staff, 40th Division.

CONFIDENTIAL.   (Not to be taken forward of Battn H.Q.)

40th DIVISION DAILY INTELLIGENCE SUMMARY, No. 54.
Period 0600 15th - 0600 16th October, 1918.

(a) OUR OPERATIONS.

1. **INFANTRY.** During the day our troops succeeded in occupying the old German front line.
   At dawn to-day advanced guard troops continued to follow up the enemy's withdrawal and according to the latest reports reached the following points without encountering opposition :- The centre patrol has reached C.30.a.5.1 and flank platoons are moving forward in support.   According to a verbal report the right patrol has reached I.6.c.8.0 and the left patrol C.18.d. central.

2. **ARTILLERY.** Normal. Night harassing fire was maintained on roads, tracks, etc. All available artillery successfully engaged two enemy M.Gs which were holding up the advance on our left.

3. **AIRCRAFT.** Very active between 0700 and 1100. At the latter time bombs were heard dropping behind enemy lines.

(b) ENEMY OPERATIONS.

1. **INFANTRY.** A withdrawal by the enemy along the whole front is apparently in process.

2. **ARTILLERY.** Enemy artillery was inactive throughout the period, only a few scattered rounds on forward areas being reported.

3. **AIRCRAFT.** Inactive. No hostile planes seen.

4. **MACHINE GUNS.** M.G. fire was heard, but from the sound it appeared to be much further back than on the previous night

(c) INTELLIGENCE.

1. **IDENTIFICATION.** A shoulder strap bearing a K and a Crown was found by one of our patrols at I.5.c.5.3 and another with figures "88" (I.R.88) was taken from a dead German in I.5.d. This is a normal identification of the 56th Division.

2. **LIGHTS.** Very few lights were put up by the enemy during the night.

Major,
General Staff, 40th Division.

Confidential.   Original.

WAR DIARY.

GENERAL   STAFF   BRANCH.

40th DIVISION.

VOL: XXX

FROM :-   1st NOVEMBER, 1918.
TO   :- 30th NOVEMBER, 1918.

                                             Major-General,
                            Commanding 40th Division.

(6392) Wt. W6192/P875 1,500,000 4/18 McA & W Ltd (E 2815) Forms W3091/4. Army Form W.3091.

Cover for Documents.

Nature of Enclosures.

Notes, or Letters written.

WAR DIARY

GENERAL STAFF BRANCH.

40th Division.

VOL. XXX

FROM :- 1st November, 1918.
TO   :- 30th November, 1918.

INDEX

Pages 1 - 4 ...   War Diary.
      5 - 20...   Appendices.
                  Map.

Army Form C. 2118.

WAR DIARY
INTELLIGENCE SUMMARY
(Erase heading not required.)

40th DIVISION.   NOVEMBER, 1918.

Instructions regarding War Diaries and Intelligence Summaries are contained in F. S. Regs., Part II. and the Staff Manual respectively. Title pages will be prepared in manuscript.

Place	Date	Hour	Summary of Events and Information	Remarks and references to Appendices
LANNOY.	1/11/18.		The Disposition at the beginning of the month was as follows :- The 121st Infantry Brigade, (Advanced Guard Brigade) held a line of outposts along the West bank of the River L'ESCAULT from just South of PECQ to the ESPIERRES canal on the North.	
			After an Artillery preparation our patrols pushed forward and occupied the post at I.2.b.6.4, the enemy evacuating same as a result of the bombardment. One wounded prisoner was captured and one Machine Gun. Two dead Germans were also found in the post. The enemy counter-attacked and endeavoured to recapture the post but was repulsed. Patrols crossing the River East of WARCOING met with strong resistance from hostile M.G's.	
			Telegram G.C.736 (Orders for establishment of posts East of the River North of WARCOING) issued. Appendix I.	Appx. 1
			The 119th Infantry Bde. moved to the LEERS NORD area.	
"	2.		Our patrols established posts on the East side of the River opposite WARCOING. A party of the enemy was encountered and dispersed by our Lewis Gun fire. Casualties were inflicted and a subsequent search of the ground resulted in a Machine Gun being brought in. With Artillery co-operation the post at C.21.c.15 was successfully occupied, the enemy evacuating same on approach of our infantry. Heavy T.M. and Artillery fire subsequently necessitated the withdrawal of our troops from this post, as also from the post on the road East of the River opposite PECQ.	
			Order No. 227 (relief of 121st Infantry Bde. by the 119th Brigade in the line) issued. Appendix. 2.	Appx. 2.
"	3.		Two more posts were established on the East bank of the River opposite WARCOING. A slight increase was noticeable in hostile artillery activity.	
			Order No. 228 (moves of 121st and 120th Infantry Brigades, interchanging areas) issued. Appendix. 3.	Appx. 3.

Army Form C. 2118.

WAR DIARY
INTELLIGENCE SUMMARY
(Erase heading not required.)

40th DIVISION. NOVEMBER, 1918.

Instructions regarding War Diaries and Intelligence Summaries are contained in F. S. Regs., Part II. and the Staff Manual respectively. Title pages will be prepared in manuscript.

Place	Date	Hour	Summary of Events and Information	Remarks and references to Appendices
LANNOY.	4.		Usual patrolling carried out East of PECQ and WARCOING. The 119th Infantry Bde. relieved the 121st Infantry Bde. in the line, night 4th/5th.	
"	5.		Instructions No. 13 (Action to be taken in the event of enemy's resistance weakening) issued. Appendix 4.	Appex. 4.
"	6.		In consequence of a reported enemy withdrawal from the division on our right, attempts were made by our troops to penetrate towards HERRINES, also East of PECQ towards the railway, both along the RIVAGE and from the South, but met with very considerable opposition from Machine Guns, T. M's. and Artillery fire; in one instance they penetrated within 100 yards or so of HERRINES. Patrols East of PECQ encountered considerable M.G. opposition. 120th Infantry Bde. moved into Support (LEERS) area and 121st Infantry Bde. into Reserve at LANNOY.	
"	7.		Order No. 229. Readjustment of Divisional Front (1000 yards of left front being handed over on night of 6th/7th to the 14th Division) issued. Appendix 5. Platoon training and firing practice at the range carried out daily by Support and Reserve Brigades.	Appex. 5.
"	8.		The situation was unchanged. Preparations were made for the forcing of a passage over the River L'ESCAULT in face of strong enemy opposition (if encountered) by frontal attack. 40th Division Order No. 4/170. G. (attachment of 113th A.F.A.Bde. to the Division) issued. Appendix 6.	Appex. 6.
"	9.		A patrol occupied the crater at U.21.c.o.5. during the morning. Further activities on the part of our patrols invariably met with resistance from enemy M.G's, but there were indications that the enemy resistance was weakening and late in the day some of our troops penetrated through HERRINES, some M.G. opposition still being encountered. Anticipating a withdrawal, our troops pushed forward beyond HERRINES and East of PECQ now	

— WAR DIARY —

WAR DIARY

40th Division

GENERAL STAFF BRANCH

VOL. XXIX

FROM:- 1st October, 1918.
TO:-   31st October, 1918.

INDEX

Pages 1 - 6 ... ... War Diary.
"   7 - 37 ... ... Appendices.
"   38 - 58 ... ... Intelligence Summaries.
Map.

Army Form C. 2118.

WAR DIARY
or
INTELLIGENCE SUMMARY

(Erase heading not required.)

40th DIVISION   **OCTOBER, 1918.**

Instructions regarding War Diaries and Intelligence Summaries are contained in F. S. Regs., Part II. and the Staff Manual respectively. Title pages will be prepared in manuscript.

Place	Date	Hour	Summary of Events and Information	Remarks and references to Appendices
36/A.21.b.3.8. nr STEENWERCK.	1st.		During the night 30th/1st the envelopment of LE BIZET was continued and our line runs :- Sheet 36/C.13.c.4.7. - C.13.a.5.4. - C.13.a.2.9. - C.7.c.6.6. - C.7.d.1.9. - C.7.d.4.9. - C.7.d.8.6. - C.8.c.1.4. - C.8.c.4.1. - C.8.d.9.2. - Posts were also established at LE BIZET Convent, WALLABY Post and junction of STATION AVENUE and Railway Switch at C.15.a.50.87. Two prisoners belonging to 3rd Company, 186th I.R., 56th Division, were captured in C.13.a.	
,,	2nd.		Left Brigade occupied LE BIZET and reached the Northern outskirts of ARMENTIERES without opposition, and the line now runs :- River LYS at C.19.d.5.3. along E. edge of houses in C.19.d.and b. - LA FLENQUE Post - LYS Farm. Right Brigade moved across River LYS at ERQUINGHEM on news being received that the Div. on the right had gained the ERQUINGHEM Switch. They took over the part of this switch held by 61st Division from River LYS to H.10.b.5.0. and then pushed forward South of ARMENTIERES to a line I.1.a.1.2. - I.1.c.0.0. - I.7.a.0.0. at which point they were in touch with the 61st Division. Order No. 216 issued (method of taking ARMENTIERES and the principle upon which the line would then be held).	App.1.
,,	3rd.		During the night a foot-bridge was thrown across the River LYS at C.15.d.50.75. and portions of the original British Front Line were occupied. During the day our line was established in the old British Front Line from the River LYS to C.29.a.2.0. thence along QUEENSLAND Road and trenches in I.4.a., I.3.d. and I.9.b. Touch was gained with the Division on right at I.9.b.6.0. A hostile M.G. nest gave trouble during the day in I.3.d. but on approach by our men were seen to retire on to I.10.b.	
,,	4th.		No further advance in the line was made, but a post was established at I.4.d.9.4., and touch was maintained with hostile forward positions all the time.	
,,	5th.		Instructions No. 6 (120th Infantry Brigade to take over duties of Advanced Guard Brigade) were issued. We occupied Gd.PORTE EGAL Farm (I.10.b.) and at 18.00 our Right Brigade moved forward along......	App.2

Army Form C. 2118.

WAR DIARY
or
INTELLIGENCE SUMMARY
(Erase heading not required.)

40th DIVISION   OCTOBER, 1918.

Instructions regarding War Diaries and Intelligence Summaries are contained in F. S. Regs., Part II. and the Staff Manual respectively. Title pages will be prepared in manuscript.

Place	Date	Hour	Summary of Events and Information	Remarks and references to Appendices
56/A.21.b.3.8. Nr SEENWERCK	5th. (continued) 6th.		along CENTRAL AVENUE and occupied HEADQUARTERS WALK from I.10.b.3.5. to LOTHIAN AVENUE.	
"	6th.		At 05.00 the enemy after putting down a heavy barrage along our front, raided a post at C.23.a.1.6. One N.C.O. and seven men were afterwards found missing and the body of a dead German belonging to the 118th I.R. (56th Div.) was found in the post. The 120th Infantry Brigade relieved the 119th Infantry Brigade, relief being complete by 0100 (7th).	
"	7th.		During the night 6th/7th our line was slightly withdrawn in accordance with 40th Divisional Instructions No.7 (issued 6.10.18). G.O.C. 120th Infantry Brigade assumed command of Advanced Guard at 10.00. The following posts were established during the night 7th/8th :- L.G. - C.16.c.75.05, C.22.c.95.80, C.28.a.95.95, C.28.c.90.90. Inf. - C.22.b.10.45, C.28.b.10.35, I.5.c.20.20 , I.11.a.00.60, I.11.a.4.4. The last post is in touch with 59th Division on right.	App. 3.
"	8th.		40th Division Instruction No.8 (Defence of Divisional area) issued. Quiet day. Usual patrolling carried out without encountering any opposition. Posts were established at C.22.b.40.45. (L.G.) and C.22.a.95.80. (Infantry).	App. 4.
"	9th.		As a result of an aerial combat between two British scouts and a hostile two-seater, one of our scouts crashed at A.23.d.7.5. and the E.A. made a forced landing at A.24.a.5.2. The two occupants (Officer observer and Serjeant Pilot) belonging to Feld-Flieger Abt.13 were taken prisoner. Quiet day, only patrol activity to record.	
"	10th.		Only patrol activity recorded. Results show that the enemy hold the old German front and support trenches in some strength. 40th Division Order No. 217 (relief of 120th Infantry Brigade by 121st Infantry Bde) issued. 40th Div. Instructions No. 9 (alteration in main line of resistance) issued.	App. 5. App. 6.
"	11th.		During the afternoon patrols established our line as follows :- along old British Support......	

Army Form C. 2118.

WAR DIARY
or
INTELLIGENCE SUMMARY

40th DIVISION.   (Erase heading not required.)   OCTOBER, 1918.

Place	Date	Hour	Summary of Events and Information	Remarks and references to Appendices
36/A.21.b.3.8. nr STEENWERCK (Continued).	11th		Support Line to C.22.c.8.2. - C.28.b.1.8. - C.28.b.1.4.- C.28.d.8.8. - C.28.d.8.2. - I.5.a.3.7. - I.5.c.8.8.; thence along Old British Front Line to Railway at I.11.a.0.3. Liaison post with 59th Division, still at I.11.a.4.2. Patrol attempting to work along INCANDESCENT TRENCH from the Railway met with considerable M.G.resistance and had to withdraw. Otherwise a quiet day.	
,,	12th		A minor operation was carried out by the 120th Infantry Bde. at 05.15, resulting in the capture of INCANDESCENT TRENCH. The general line now runs as follows :- C.22.c.7.1. - C.28.b.2.4. - C.28.d.8.7. - C.28.d.8.7.2. - I.5.a.3.7. - I.5.c.2.9. - I.5.c.5.5.- I.5.d.0.3., thence along INCANDESCENT TRENCH to the Railway at I.11.a.6.3. and our troops are in touch with the Brigade on their right.	App.7.
,,	13th		Patrols were out during the night but no enemy were encountered. 40th Div. Order No. 218 (121st Inf. Bde. to be prepared to send forward fighting patrols, to push through the enemy outpost line if necessary - in the event of success by the Corps on our left.) issued.	
,,	14th		A hostile raiding party about 20 strong attempted to work round our post at I.5.d.0.3. and another party with a machine gun tried to creep up a communication trench. The enemy were repulsed by rifle fire and casualties inflicted. Considerable enemy artillery fire directed on HOUPLINES area. G.O.C. 121st Infantry Bde. assumed command of Advanced Guard on completion of relief of 120th Infantry Bde.	App.8.
,,	15th		Patrols were sent forward to occupy the old German front line. The left patrol was temporarily checked by M.G.fire but this was dealt with by artillery fire and the line was established as follows :- INCANDESCENT TRENCH to I.5.d.45.40 - IRENE TRENCH to I.5.b.2.5. - Posts at C.29.a.0.0. and C.23.b.5.8. Order No. 220 (allotting further objectives for the pursuit and harassing of the enemy in the event of his withdrawal) issued.	
,,	16th		Our line was again advanced to I.12.central - C.30.central - C.18.d.central and patrols entered CROIX-AU-BOIS. 40th Div. Instructions No. 10 (methods to be adopted when patrols checked by the enemy) issued.	App.9.

Army Form C. 2118.

WAR DIARY
or
INTELLIGENCE SUMMARY

(Erase heading not required.)

40th DIVISION. OCTOBER, 1918.

Instructions regarding War Diaries and Intelligence Summaries are contained in F. S. Regs., Part II. and the Staff Manual respectively. Title pages will be prepared in manuscript.

Place	Date	Hour	Summary of Events and Information	Remarks and references to Appendices
36/A.21.b,5,8 nr.STEENWERCK. (Continued).	16th		Telegram G.C.586 reference Order 220 (organized attack to be made if necessary to gain objectives laid down in above order) issued.	App.10.
			Telegram G.B.527 (objectives to be gained by 121st Infantry Bde. on 17th inst.) issued.	App.11.
"	17th		The line was advanced to the Railway running S.E. from QUESNOY - Patrols entered WAMBRECHIES and a post was established at the Bridge (E.26.d.5.3.) which was destroyed. Addendum (wire G.B.530) to Order No. 220, reference move of D.H.Q. to ARMENTIERES, issued.	App.12.
			Order No. 221 (reference relief of 66th Divisional Artillery by 40th Divisional Artillery) issued.	App.13.
			Instructions No. 11, regarding further advance to be made on 18th inst. issued.	App.14.
			Telegrams (G.B.536 and G.C.610, instructions for the advance on 18th inst) issued.	App.15.
ARMENTIERES.	18th		Divisional Headquarters moved to ARMENTIERES.	
			Our line was again advanced to road K.10.b.2.0. - K.5.a. - FORT de BONDUES, E.29.a., and later, patrols penetrated through CROIX, L.10.c. and eventually to a line, L.23.b.central - L.18.a.9.8. No hostile opposition encountered. ROUBAIX was evacuated by the enemy and entered by our troops.	
			The 66th Divisional Artillery was relieved by the 40th Divisional Artillery.	
			Warning Order, telegram G.B.112 (for 119th and 120th Infantry Bdes. to furnish working parties for work on roads and railways) issued.	App.15 A
			Telegram G.B.104 (attachment of party of XV Corps Cyclists to 121st Infantry Bde. for operations) issued.	App.16.
			Instructions No. 12 (reference discipline of troops in towns recaptured from the enemy) issued.	App.17.
			Telegram G.B.103 (giving 40th Divid on objective for 18th, and boundaries) issued.	App.18.
			Telegram G.B.114 (detailing working parties from 119th Infantry Bde.) issued.	App.19.
			Telegram G.B.119 (orders for relief of 40th Division in the line) issued.	App.20.
"	19th		Patrols advanced early, reached L'ANNOY/(G.28.d) TOUFFLERS (G.23) LEERS (G.6.c) LEERS NORD (H.2.a), but during the day, relief of 121st Infantry Bde. (by the taking over of their front by the 93rd Infantry Bde., 31st Division on the left and 176th Infantry Bde. (59th Division) on the right) was completed, and the Division was withdrawn from the line.	
			Six prisoners were taken in ROUBAIX (two of them wounded in Hospital - 4 of them deserters) Telegram...	

Army Form C. 2118.

WAR DIARY

or INTELLIGENCE SUMMARY

(Erase heading not required.)

40th DIVISION.   OCTOBER, 1918.

Instructions regarding War Diaries and Intelligence Summaries are contained in F. S. Regs., Part II. and the Staff Manual respectively. Title pages will be prepared in manuscript.

Place	Date	Hour	Summary of Events and Information	Remarks and references to Appendices
ARMENTIERES (continued)	19th.		Telegram Gb124 (orders regarding parties to be detailed by 120th Infantry Brigade for work on Railways) issued.	App.21
			Order No. 222 (move of D.H.Q. to MOUVEAUX F.21.c.7.7.) issued.	App.22
MOUVEAUX F.21.c.7.7.	20th.		Divisional Headquarters moved to F.21.c.7.7. (MOUVEAUX). One prisoner (deserter) taken. 119th and 120th Infantry Brigades employed on roads and railway repair.	
	21st.		Division resting, training, and employed on roads and railway repair.	
	22nd.		- ditto -	
	23rd.		Order No.223 (move of 119th Infantry Brigade to BONDUES Area) issued.	App.23.
	24th.		119th Infantry Brigade moved to BONDUES area, E.17.c. Order No.224 (Relief of 31st Division by 40th Division in the line) issued.	App.24.
	25th.		121st Infantry Brigade and 39th Bn: Machine Gun Corps moved to staging area at LEERS and LEERS NORD.	
	26th.		119th Infantry Brigade (less 1 Battalion which moved to CROIX (L.9.a.) for work on railways) moved to WATTRELOS Area. 121st Infantry Brigade relieved 93rd Infantry Brigade (31st Division) in the line. The front extended from WARCOING to PECQ (2,500 yards along the Western bank of the River L'ESCAUT).	
LANNOY	27th.		D.H.Q. moved to LANNOY and command of the Divisional Sector passed to G.O.C. 40th Division. There was intermittent hostile shelling and some heavy gas shelling for 15 minutes on the right of the Divisional front. Order 225 (extension of Divisional front up to the ESPIERRES CANAL) issued.	App.25.
	28th........			

Army Form C. 2118.

WAR DIARY
or
INTELLIGENCE SUMMARY
(Erase heading not required.)

Instructions regarding War Diaries and Intelligence Summaries are contained in F. S. Regs., Part II. and the Staff Manual respectively. Title pages will be prepared in manuscript.

Place	Date	Hour	Summary of Events and Information	Remarks and references to Appendices
LANNOY	28th.		At 09.00 hours a daylight patrol crossed the River L'ESCAUT, East of PECQ, and proceeded to I.2.a.8.4. Here they met with opposition from machine guns and Trench Mortars, and also rifle fire. The patrol subsequently withdrew and the Machine Guns and Trench Mortar which they located were dealt with by the Artillery.	
	29th.		120th Infantry Brigade moved to LANNOY. 1 Battalion of 119th Infantry Brigade previously working on Railways at CROIX rejoined its Brigade at WATTRELOS. At dawn the R.E. attempted to throw a footbridge across the River in C.20.d. but were prevented from doing so by the heavy Machine Gun and Artillery fire directed against them. Our artillery shelled suspected M.G. positions and a T.M. emplacement. Two of our aeroplanes came down on the East side of the River in C.20.c. Both pilots reached our lines; one of them who was wounded, was rescued by an officer of the 23rd Lancashire Fusiliers swimming across the River L'ESCAUT under M.G. fire and swimming back with him. The other swam the River unaided. A daylight patrol proceeded along the LE RIVAGE Causeway to bring in a serjeant previously shot and located a strong enemy post at I.2.b.4.3.	
	30th.		A daylight patrol crossed by a footbridge constructed by the R.E. at C.20.c.7.5. WARCOING, proceeded along the road in C.20.d. and surprised an enemy post, shot the sentry and brought back 4 prisoners (including the wounded sentry). An enemy party was dispersed by another of our patrols who had crossed the river further North. Patrols who crossed the river opposite PECQ met with considerable opposition, crept forward and bombed the post and withdrew. Prisoners (above referred to) belonged to the 12th Bavarian Division, indicating a relief opposite the Divisional front.	
	31st.		Patrols made attempts to push along the roads East of PECQ and WARCOING and to rush the enemy post (Artillery co-operating) at I.2.b.4.3. but again met with considerable opposition and withdrew. Order No. 226 (instructions for further advance in the event of enemy withdrawal and for resting artillery to come into action) issued.	App.26

Lieut. Colonel,
General Staff, 40th Division.

SECRET.   Copy No. 20   App. 1

             40th DIVISION ORDER NO. 216.   2/10/18.
             ****

1. The enemy is withdrawing rapidly and it is believed that he
   is going back to the line of the Hte.DEULE Canal, which runs
   N.E. and S.W. along the Western face of LILLE.

2. All Divisions are to follow up the enemy, harassing and impeding
   his retirement.

3. For the forward move Inter-Divl. boundaries will be as follows :-

   NORTHERN BOUNDARY.   Grid line from C.16.central to C.18.central and
                         Eastwards.

   SOUTHERN BOUNDARY.   Grid line from H.10.central - H.12.central -
                         I.8.central and Eastwards.

4. Troops of the 40th Division will act as follows :-

   119th Infantry Brigade. Will work round North of ARMENTIERES and
         clear up the situation East of that town as far South as the
         ARMENTIERES - LILLE Railway, keeping in contact with the
         retreating enemy.

   120th Infantry Brigade will take over such portion of the line as is
         now held by troops of the 61st Division North of the Divl.
         boundary and will work round South of ARMENTIERES, gaining
         touch with the 119th Infantry Brigade, but keeping South
         of the LILLE - ARMENTIERES Railway.

         This Brigade will conform with the movements of the Brigade
         on its right (which from to-night will be the 178th Brigade
         of the 59th Division).

         When the advance reaches the point where the LILLE -
         ARMENTIERES Railway cuts the Divl. boundary, the 120th Inf.
         Brigade will become automatically sqeezed out and will
         remain in support echeloned on the right rear of the Divl.
         sector.

   121st Infantry Brigade will remain in Divl. reserve in its
         present locations.

   The Divl. Artillery Commander will arrange for his Brigades
         to cover the forward movement of 119th and 120th Infantry
         Brigades, but no batteries will cross the LYS without
         reference to Divl. H.Qrs.

5. The Machine Gun Companies now attached to forward Brigades will
   accompany those Brigades in their advance.

6. As ARMENTIERES has been placed out of bounds and is not to be
   entered, Brigades during their forward movement will arrange for
   the protection of their inner flanks.

                                          Lieut. Colonel,
                                  General Staff, 40th Division.

Issued at 20.00

                                                          P.T.O.

Copy No.1 to G.O.C.
       2   119th I.B.
       3   120th I.B.
       4   121st I.B.
       5   C.R.E.
       6   66th D.A.
       7   17th Worc. R.(P).
       8   Signals
       9   39th Bn: M.G.C.
      10   Div.Train.
      11   "Q"
      12   A.D.M.S.
      13   D.A.P.M.
      14   64 Bde R.G.A.
      15   "L" Special Coy. R.E.
      16   31st Division.
      17   61st   ,,
      18   59th Division.
      19   XV Corps G.
      20   ,,   Q.
      21   ,,   R.A.
      22   ,,   H.A.
      23   War Diary
      24   ,,
      25   File

40th Div. No. 184/7(G).   S E C R E T.

40th DIVISION INSTRUCTIONS NO.6.

1. The 120th Infantry Brigade will relieve the 119th Infantry Brigade in the position East of ARMENTIERES on the day and night of the 6th instant and will operate as the Advanced Guard to the Division.

2. For this purpose the following troops will be placed under the orders of the G.O.C. 120th Infantry Brigade :-

    331st Brigade R.F.A.
    A company of 39th Bn: M.G.Corps.
    ½ Coy. XV Corps Cyclist Bn:

3. The 119th Infantry Brigade will be withdrawn into the supporting position in the NIEPPE System and will be responsible for the upkeep and, in case of necessity, the defence of this system, from the Divisional Northern boundary to the River LYS.

    Responsibility for the defence of the NIEPPE System South of the River LYS will for the present remain with the Advanced Guard Brigade.

4. 330th Brigade R.F.A. will be prepared in case of necessity to take up positions covering the NIEPPE System and the River Line.

5. O.C. 39th Bn: M.G.Corps will place 1 company at the disposal of the G.O.C. 119th Infantry Brigade for the defence of the NIEPPE System. The M.G's of this company will be in position at all times.
    The remaining two companies of the M.G.Battalion will be held in Divl. reserve, but reinforcing positions for the defence of the NIEPPE System will be selected and made known to all ranks concerned.

6. The following communications are being opened up and maintained under the direction of the C.R.E:-

    (a) A Main Route running forward through ORVILLE JUNCTION - ERQUINGHEM - Southern edge of ARMENTIERES - CHAPELLE D'ARMENTIERES.

    (b) Supplementary Route through LE BIZET - C.14.a. c. and d. to C.20.b. & d. to Bridge at C.20.d.9.0. A connection with the Main Route will be made East of the LYS as soon as possible.

    (c) Pontoon bridges exist at :-

        H.2.c.1.9.
        H.3.c.4.7.
        H.4.c.1.4.
        C.20.d.9.0.

    (d) Foot bridges exist at :-

        H.3.d.5.5.
        C.15.d.6.8.

                                                    Another....

-ii-

Another is under construction at C.21.d.3.5.

7.   In two or three days time R.E. assistance will be available for the improvement of forward and second line defences.

8.   Working parties totalling 300 men per day will be required from the Supporting Brigade for work on communications under the direction of the C.R.E.

                                            (signed)   Lieut. Colonel,

5/10/18.   General Staff, 40th Division.

                                         ***

To :-
    G.O.C.
    119th Inf. Brigade.
    120th   ,,
    121st   ,,
    17th Worc. R. (Pioneers).
    C. R. A.
    C. R. E.
    Div. Signal Company.
    39th Bn: M.G.Corps.
    Div. Train.
    "Q"
    A.D.M.S.
    D.A.P.M.
    XV Corps G.
       ,,   H.A.
    31st Division.
    59th   ,,
    64th Bde R.G.A.

40th Div. No. 184/8(G).   S E C R E T

40th DIVISION INSTRUCTIONS NO.7.

40th Division Instructions No.6 will be modified as follows :-

1. During the relief to-night the G.O.C. 119th Infantry Brigade will arrange to throw back the left of his Outpost Line to the Support Line of the old British System running South from the River LYS to the Redoubt in C.28.c.6.2. Thence the Outpost Line will run along AVENUE ROAD to GRANDE PORTE EGAL Farm where touch will be gained with the post of the 17th Infantry Brigade in PETIT PORTE EGAL Farm.

2. The relieved Outpost Battalion will be withdrawn into Support West of the River LYS, special parties being detailed to protect the bridges over the LYS North of ARMENTIERES in case of necessity.

3. When this supporting battalion is relieved to-morrow the G.O.C. 120th Infantry Brigade will arrange for two companies to be posted behind the LYS N.E. of ARMENTIERES in support of the left of the Outpost Line, and two companies S.E. of ARMENTIERES in support of the right of the Outpost Line.
    The Reserve Battalion of the Advanced Guard Brigade will be posted in or about the ERQUINGHEM Switch.

4. The 330th Brigade R.F.A. will remain in action about LE BIZET, forming a sub-group under the direction of the commander of the Advanced Guard Artillery.

                         Lieut. Colonel,

6/10/18.   General Staff, 40th Division.

To:-
    G.O.C.
    119th I.Bde.
    120th I.Bde.
    121st I.Bde.
    17th Worc. R. (P).
    C.R.A.
    C.R.E.
    Signals
    39th Bn:M.G.C.
    Div. Train.
    "Q".
    A.D.M.S.
    D.A.P.M.
    XV Corps G.
       ,,   H.A.
    31st Division.
    59th   ,,
    64th Bde. R.G.A.

40th Div. No. 184/9(G).   S E C R E T.

40th DIVISION INSTRUCTIONS NO. 8.

1. The Outpost Line of Resistance will follow the Reserve trench of the old British system from the River LYS in C.21.c., East of Nouvel Houplines, through C.2.central and along the South-eastern outskirts of ARMENTIERES to the Corps Southern boundary at I.7.a.0.0.

2. The Advanced Guard Commander will maintain this line with all the resources at his disposal unless and until orders for withdrawal are received from Divl. Headquarters.

3. If and when such orders are received the withdrawal will be carried out in a South-Westerly direction towards ERQUINGHEM. Two companies only will be maintained in a position about C.20.central and C.21.a., whose rôle it will be to prevent the enemy crossing over the LYS N.E. of ARMENTIERES, and to keep touch with the troops of the Division on our left.
    Before any withdrawal commenced the Advanced Guard Commander would give orders for the destruction of the pontoon and foot bridges over the LYS N.E. of ARMENTIERES.

4. The Main Line of Resistance will be the line of the WARNAVE to the NIEPPE System and thence Southwards to the ERQUINGHEM Switch.
    Schemes for the defence of this line will be prepared by the Supporting Brigade and the defences improved.

5. The Reserve Brigade will continue its training near STEENWERCK, but G.O.C. and Brigade Staff will acquaint themselves with the nature of the defences in the Main Line of Resistance and with the routes leading thereto.

                                                  Lieut. Col.

8/10/18.   General Staff, 40th Division.

G.O.C.   D.A.P.M.
119th I.Bde.   XV Corps G.
120th I.Bde.   ,,   H.A.
121st I.Bde.   31st Division.
17th Worc. R.(P).   59th ,,
C.R.A.   64th Bde. R.G.A.
C.R.E.
Signals
39th Bn: M.G.C.
Div. Train.
"Q"
A.D.M.S.

SECRET. Copy No. 25

40th DIVISION ORDER NO. 217.   10/10/18.

1. The 120th Infantry Brigade will be relieved in the Advanced Guard by the 121st Infantry Brigade on the night 13/14th October and G.O.C. 121st Infantry Brigade will take over command of the Advanced Guard at 10 00. on 14th October.

2. Details of relief will be arranged between Brigadiers concerned.

3. Preliminary to the relief 119th Infantry Brigade and 121st Infantry Brigade will change places in Support and Reserve respectively during the day of the 12th October.

4. ACKNOWLEDGE.

                                                                               Lieut. Colonel,
                                     General Staff, 40th Division.

Issued at 20.00

Copy No. 1 to G.O.C.
      2   119th I.Bde.
      3   120th I.Bde.
      4   121st I.Bde.
      5   C.R.E.
      6   66th D.A.
      7   17th Worc. R. (P).
      8   Signals
      9   39th Bn: M.G.Corps
     10   Div. Train.
     11   "Q"
     12   A.D.M.S.
     13   D.A.P.M.
     14   64th Bde. R.G.A.
     15   "L" Special Coy. R.E.
     16   Div. Gas Officer.
     17   Div. Claims Officer.
     18   Div. Reception Camp.
     19   31st Division.
     20   59th   ,,
     21   XV Corps G.
     22   ,,   Q.
     23   ,,   R.A.
     24   ,,   H.A.
     25   War Diary
     26   ,,
     27   File

40th Div. No. 184/10(G).   S E C R E T.

40th DIVISION INSTRUCTIONS NO.9.

1. With reference to 40th Div. Instructions No. 8, the Main Line of Resistance of the Division will, North of the LYS be brought forward to the old River Line Defences running through B.28.d., B.28.b., B.23.c. to PONT DE NIEPPE. Thence the line will run to LA CLEF DE LA BELGIQUE (B.18.a.8.4), posts being sited so as to cover the river, and from LA CLEF DE LA BELGIQUE it will turn back to the WARNAVE in B.12.c.

2. Special arrangements will be made for the protection of the high level bridge at PONT DE NIEPPE.

Lieut. Colonel,

10/10/18.   General Staff, 40th Division.

Issued to all recipients of 40th Div. Instructions No.8.

"A" Form.
MESSAGES AND SIGNALS.

Army Form C. 2121.
(In pads of 100.)

			AAA
Brigade	so	that	its
support	will	be	available
for	any	organised	attack
aaa	Acknowledge aaa		Addressed
all	receipients	of	Div.
Order	220		

From: **40th Division.**

"A" Form.
MESSAGES AND SIGNALS.

Army Form C. 2121.
(In pads of 100.)

PRIORITY to
120 & 121.I.B.

From **APO 11**

TO: and to all concerned.

AAA

Following objectives will be gained to-morrow advanced Guard line of LA BASSEE DEULE K.9.a.6.0. River to K.3.a.1.9. WAMBRECHIES BELLE FARM E.18.c. aaa 120th Brigade will move forward to I.6.a. C.20. central C.18.d. units to be concentrated about these co-ordinates so that subsequent advance can be quickly effected along roads aaa units of 120th Brigade to be clear of present locations by 1000 to-morrow aaa Acknowledge addressed 120th and 121st Brigades repeated all concerned

From
Place 40th Division.
Time 22.30

(Z)

Major.

"A" Form
MESSAGES AND SIGNALS.

Army Form C. 2121 (In pads of 100)

By ~~wire to Corps~~
~~and flank divs.~~
~~D.R. to remainder~~

App. 12

TO: All recipients of 40th Div. Order 220.

Sender's Number.	Day of Month.	In reply to Number.	
* GE 530	17		AAA

~~Reference~~ para 10 40th
~~Div.~~ Order 220 of
~~15th~~ October aaa Div.
Headquarters will move 18th
instant to ARMENTIERES B.30.b.6.6.
and open there at
1100 aaa Acknowledge aaa
Addressed all recipients of
D.O. 220 and Camp Commandant.

Place: 40th Division.

(sd) H.F. WALLIS

G.S.

SECRET.   Copy No........

Ref. sheet   40th DIVISIONAL ORDER NO. 231.   17/10/18.
36. 1:40,000   ##############################

The relief of the 66th Div. Artillery by the 40th Divisional Artillery will be carried out on 18th October as under :-

1. **40th Divisional Artillery.**

    (a). "A" Brigade R.F.A. to area about road C.30.central - J.1.d. - D.20.d. where they will remain in readiness as Advanced Guard Artillery under the orders of O.C. Advanced Guard. Move to be completed by 16.00 hrs.

    (b) "B" Brigade R.F.A. to area about RUE MARLE where on arrival they will come into Divisional reserve. Move to be completed by 15.00 hrs.

    (c) D.A.C. and T.M.Batteries will move to STEENWERCK. Move to be completed by 16.00 hrs.

    (d) Headquarters of 40th D.A. will open at B.30.b.6.6. at 12.00 hours.

2. **66th Divisional Artillery.**

    (a) 330th Brigade R.F.A. will move to PONT D'ACHELLES area. Not to start until the arrival of "B" Brigade R.F.A., 40th Divisional Artillery at RUE MARLE.

    (b) 331st Brigade R.F.A. (now Advanced Guard Artillery) will withdraw to wagon lines as soon as "A" Brigade 40th Divisional Artillery are in position of readiness (vide para. 1(a) above).

    (c) D.A.C. (less No. 2 section) will move to STEENWERCK area - movement to start at 14.00 hours. No.2 section D.A.C. remains at ERQUINGHEM.

3. Head of 40th Divisional Artillery (less D.A.C.) will be at ERQUINGHEM PONTOON BRIDGE at 12.00 hours.

4. Details regarding the relief will be arranged between C.R.A's concerned.

5. Command of the Artillery covering the Divisional front will pass from C.R.A. 66th Division to C.R.A. 40th Division at 16.00 hours, 18th October.

6. ACKNOWLEDGE.

                                         Lieut. Colonel,
Issued at 18.45   General Staff, 40th Division.

Copy No. 1 to C.C.C.   16 to 64th Bde. R.G.A.
      2   119th I.B.   17   Camp Comdt.
      3   120th I.B.   18   D.A.D.O.S.
      4   121st I.B.   19   Div. Claims Off.
      5   C.R.E.   20   Div. Gas Officer.
      6   66th D.A.   21   M.T.Company.
      7   40th D.A.   22   S.S.O.
      8   Signals   23   Div. Reception Camp.
      9   17th Worc.R.(P).   24   Div. Employment Coy.
    10   39th Bn. M.G.C.   25   Area Comdt. Right Div.
    11   Div.Train.   26   "L" Spec. Coy. R.E.
    12   "Q" 40th Div.   27   31st Division.
    13   A.D.M.S.   28   59th   ,,
    14   D.A.D.V.S.   29   XV Corps G.
    15   D.A.P.M.   30   ,,   Q
                                  31   ,,   R.A.
                                  32   ,,   H.A.
                     33 & 34   War Diary
                         35   File

40th Div. No. 184/12(G).   S E C R E T.

Ref.sheet   40th DIVISION INSTRUCTIONS NO. 11.
36:1/40,000.

App. 14

1. Enemy Rear Guards are reported to be on the Western edges of TURCOING.

2. The Outpost line of troops on our left runs from RONCQ South through CROIX BLANCHE (F.7.a.) to E.29.central.

3. (a) The Advanced Guard of the Division will continue the outpost line from FORT DE BONDUES (E.29.a.) inclusive along road through K.5.a. to Southern boundary at K.10.b.2.0. With this in view 1 battalion will be disposed on N, E, and S. edges of WAMBRECHIES and remainder in close support.

   (b) 120th Infantry Brigade will move forward to-morrow morning to area D.22. and D.28. Troops to be located in available accommodation near roads.

   (c) 119th Infantry Brigade will move forward to-morrow morning to I.6.c.3.0. and C.24. with units concentrated near roads where accommodation is available.

4. To-morrow evening Brigades of 40th Divisional Artillery will be disposed as follows :-

   "A" Brigade R.F.A. under the orders of the Advanced Guard Commander at C.30.central, J.1.d., and D.20.d.

   "B" Brigade R.F.A. in Divisional Reserve in area about RUE MARLE.

5. PICQUETS. In the event of ROUBAIX and TURCOING having been evacuated, all the Western entrances to those towns will be picquetted.
   The following will be the picquet line in this Division's area:-

   LILLE - TURCOING road from Divl. S. boundary at K.12.b.8.0. to F.21.c.7.9. thence along MOUVAUX - CROIX - BLANCHE road through cross roads at F.21.a.0.5. to F.14.central.

   Only Intelligence (B) and French Mission officials and formed bodies of troops under the command of an officer are allowed to pass the picquet line.

   The Advanced Guard will arrange for the necessary picquets to be posted.

6. Signal Communications in TURCOING and ROUBAIX. (a) Existing lines will be taken over by special detachments detailed by XVth Corps who, in due course, will allot lines to units as required.
   (b) All underground cables leading towards enemy's lines which are found will be cut and a report of such action forwarded to Divisional Headquarters.
   (c) Telephone and telegraph instruments will not be removed from any buildings.

7. ACKNOWLEDGE.

17/10/18.

Lieut. Colonel,
General Staff, 40th Division.

P.T.O.

DISTRIBUTION.

        G.O.C.
        119th Inf. Bde.
        120th Inf. Bde.
        121st Inf. Bde.
        17th Worc. R. (P).
        C.R.A. 68th Div.
        C.R.A. 40th Div.
        C.R.E.
        Signals.
        39th Bn: M.G.Corps.
        Div. Train.
        "Q".
        A.D.M.S.
        D.A.P.M.
        XV Corps G.
        31st, Division.
        59th   ,,
        64th Bde R.G.A.
        XVth Corps H.A.

"A" Form
MESSAGES AND SIGNALS.

Army Form C. 2121
(in pads of 100.)

Date: Apl 15

TO	178 Bde	OC	XV Corps	31 Div
	119 Bde	CRE	Signals	59 Div
	120 Bde			

Sender's Number: G 536

Corps outpost line runs from RONCQ S through CROIX BLANCHE F 7 a to F 29 Central AAA Advance Guard will establish Outpost line FORT DE BONDUES inclusive along road through K 5 a to boundary at K 10 b 20 AAA Forward Bn to be located on N E and S edges of VAMBRECHIES and remaining 2 Bns to be located in suitable area close behind AAA 120 Bde will move to-morrow morning to area

"A" Form
MESSAGES AND SIGNALS.

Army Form C. 2121
(in pads of 100)

Prefix	Code	Words	Charge	This message is on a/c of	Recd. at ... m.
Office of Origin and Service Instructions		Sent At ... m. To By		Service (Signature of "Franking Officer.")	Date From By

TO All recipients of GB 536

Sender's Number.	Day of Month.	In reply to Number.	AAA
* GB 10	17		

Reference	GB 536	of	to-day
AAA	119	AAA	will
move	to	F6	C 30
not	C 24	for present and	
not	120	By	as
stated	herein	AAA	acknowledge
AAA	Queen	119	and
120	repto	AAA	(Cancelled)

From: HQ SW
Place:
Time:

The above may be forwarded as now corrected. (Z)

Censor. Signature of Addressor or person authorised to telegraph in his name.
* This line should be erased if not required.

(1539). Wt. W3033/P511. 200,000 Pads. 2/18. H.C. & L., Ltd.

"A" Form
MESSAGES AND SIGNALS.

TO	119 Bde.	"Q"	3" M.G.Bn:
	1% Bde.	CRE	
	121 Bde.	CRA	50 Div.

| Sender's Number. | Day of Month. | In reply to Number. | AAA |
| GS 110 | 16 | | |

Warning order aaa 119th Brigade will be prepared to find working parties on Railway in ARMENTIERES and PEREMONIES and 120th Brigade similar parties in ST. ANDRE K.14. aaa 1 bn: 119 will be prepared to move ARMENTIERES and 2 Bns: 120 Brigade to ST.ANDRE to-morrow morning aaa Units will take as many shovels as possible aaa Brigades will reconnoitre accommodation in ARMENTIERES and ST.ANDRE aaa acknowledge aaa Addressed 119 Bde 127 Bde repeated C.R.E.   Q   50 Div. C.R.A.   50 M.G.Bn:

From
Place: 40th Division.
Time

(sd) H. ......LES Major
G.S.

"A" Form
MESSAGES AND SIGNALS.

Army Form C. 2121 (in pads of 100.)

App 16

TO	121 Bde	Q	31 Div
	120 Bde		XV Corps
	119 Bde		

| Sender's Number. | Day of Month. | In reply to Number. | AAA |
| G 104 | 18 | | |

1st Platoon Corps Cyclists has been ordered by VOZO to report at Cross roads E.28.c.3.8 at 13.00 to-day or earlier if possible. They will be attached to Advanced Guard and Send representative with their orders to above Place. Are likewise has Advised 172 Bde upto XV Corps 31 Div and all concerned

From: DAQA
Place:
Time: 10.45

40th Div. No. 184/13(G).   S E C R E T

40th DIVISION INSTRUCTIONS NO. 12

1. With reference to 40th Division Instructions No. 11, para. 5.
   The Corps Commander does not wish to place any restrictions on troops being billeted in the towns through which the Corps is likely to move. All commanders however will issue such instructions as will ensure that the inhabitants are not unduly interfered with. The troops must realise that the inhabitants have been under German rule for over four years and will reasonably expect that their own Allies will treat them with courtesy and respect.

2. Entering of houses without authority will be treated as an attempt to loot.

3. Brigade billeting areas will be as concentrated as possible, and communications by Cyclists between Brigade Headquarters and Battalions, as well as Battalions Headquarters to Companies must be so organised that the Brigade can be assembled in a short time. Communication by telephone will not be practicable in towns, nor is this necessary if the cyclist orderlies are properly organised. In no case should Battalion Headquarters be more than a quarter of a mile from Brigade Headquarters when in towns or villages.
   All units must have a place of assembly termed the "Alarm Post", at which the troops must fall in when ordered or when the bugle sounds the assembly.

4. Troops in towns must be properly dressed outside their own billets and must not leave their Brigade areas without Passes.

5. All troops must be warned that should it be found that these instructions are not being complied with, the indulgence of billeting in towns occupied by inhabitants will have to cease.

                                        Lieut. Colonel,
18/10/18.   General Staff, 40th Division.

G.O.C.
119th Infantry Brigade.
120th   ,,
121st   ,,
40th D.A.
C.R.E.
"Q" 40th Div.
40th Div. Signal Coy.
39th Bn: M.G.C.
17th Worc. R. (P).
A.D.M.S.
D.A.P.M.

"A" Form
MESSAGES AND SIGNALS.

Army Form C. 2121
(In pads of 100.)

Prefix......Code......m	Words	Charge	This message is on a/c of:	Recd. at......m
Office of Origin and Service Instructions	Sent		......Service.	Date............
	At ......m			App 18
	To			From......
	By		(Signature of "Franking Officer")	By......

TO	119 Bar	CRO	39th...	
	120	CRA	31 S.D.	
	121	by Bar RGA		

Sender's Number	Day of Month	In reply to Number	AAA
SB.133	18		

DADA'S			
			VUZE
TURCOING		cavalry	
MARIE	R.H		
	HEM		
			MOUVAUX
	CANAL JUNCTION		

From ......
Place ......
Time ......

The above may be forwarded as now corrected. (Z)

Censor. Signature of Addressor or person authorised to telegraph in his name
* This line should be erased if not required.

Order No. 1625 Wt. W3253/ P 511. 27/2 H & K., Ltd. (E. 2634).

"A" Form
MESSAGES AND SIGNALS.
Army Form C. 2121 (in pads of 100.)

Prefix ...... Code ......m.	Words. / Charge.	This message is on a/c of.	Recd. at ......m.
Office of Origin and Service Instructions.	Sent		Date App 19
	At ......m.		From
	To		
	By	(Signature of "Franking Officer.")	By

TO: 119 FB Q CRE

Sender's Number	Day of Month	In reply to Number	AAA
* G6-114	18		

Following duly working parties
will be found by
you from 19th and
aaa 1½ Coy to
report 277 Divway Coy
at PERENCHIES Stn at
0900 and 1½ Coys
at same place 1300
bringing as many shovels
as possible each party
work four hours less
B.... not required alterations
hour ... Rly pits Road
119 Coy CRE
Q

From 40 Div
Place
Time 18/...

Censor. Signature of Addressor or person authorised to telegraph in his name.

"A" Form
MESSAGES AND SIGNALS.

Army Form C. 2121

PRIORITY
to 121
Brigade

TO		
121 Bde.	59 Div.	Q
XV Corps	CRA	
31 Div.	CRE	

Sender's Number.	Day of Month.	In reply to Number.	AAA
* Gb1.19	18		

VOZO is to relieve your advanced troops
to-morrow on front TOUFFLERS LEERS and
G.O.C. MAKU has received instructions
to gain touch with you and arrange
relief aaa DADA will relieve those
troops South of LANNOY to-morrow aaa
Advanced troops as relieved will
assemble at CROIX pending further
instructions aaa Your Support and
Reserve Battalions will remain where
they are aaa Acknowledge aaa Addsd 121
Bde reptd XVth Corps flank divisions CRA
CRE and Q

From DAFA
Place
Time 2330

(sd) H.F.WAILES, Major.
GS

SECRET.   Copy No. 20 app 25

40th DIVISION ORDER NO. 225.   27th Oct. 1918.

Ref. Sheet 37. 1/40,000.
----

1. On the night 27th/28th October the 121st Infantry Brigade will extend its front Northwards and take over from 42nd Infantry Brigade (14th Division) up to the ESPIERRES CANAL (exclusive to 121st Inf. Bde.).
   Details of relief will be arranged direct between G.O's.C. Infantry Brigades concerned.

2. The Northern Divisional boundary from 0600 28th October will be as follows :- E. and W. grid line through B.13.c.0.0. to B.17.d.15.00. thence along S. bank of CANAL DE L'ESPIERRE to C.9.d.1.3. thence Eastwards through C.11.d.1.3.

3. Command of the new front will pass at 0600 28th October.

4. Redistribution of the artillery covering the front will be arranged direct between C.R.A. 40th Division and C.R.A. 14th Division.

5. Completion of relief to be reported to Divisional Headquarters.

6. ACKNOWLEDGE.

                                          Lieut. Colonel,
Issued at... 11.-.15   General Staff, 40th Division.

                              ****

Copy No. 1 to G.O.C.
     2   119th I.B.
     3   120th I.B.
     4   121st I.B.
     5   C.R.E.
     6   40th D.A.
     7   17th Worc. R. (P).
     8   Signals
     9   39th Bn: M.G.C.
    10   "Q" 40th Division.
    11   A.D.M.S.
    12   D.A.P.M.
    13   14th Division.
    14   59th   ,,
    15   XV Corps G.
    16   ,,   Q.
    17   ,,   R.A.
    18   ,,   H.A.
    19   War Diary
    20   ,,
    21   File

SECRET.   Copy No. 30

40th DIVISION ORDER NO. 232.   31/10/18.

app. 26.

1. The enemy is continuing his preparations for the destruction of roads and railways East of the SCHELDT. The attack which is being delivered by the troops to the North of us may hasten the withdrawal of the enemy opposite this front.

2. Should the enemy defence weaken, the Divisions in the line are to –

   (a) Establish Advanced Guards East of the Inundations.

   (b) Be prepared to carry out a further advance to capture the Spur which runs Northwards from I.17. through D.15. and D.3.

3. With this in view –

   (a) The Advanced Guard Brigade will continually test the enemy defences. Patrols if successful in crossing the Inundations will be supported and any success gained exploited.

   (b) The arrangements already made for a main crossing at PECQ and a subsidiary crossing E. of WARCOING will be maintained in a state of complete readiness.

4. Forward boundaries so far as can be laid down at present will be as follows :-

   With Division on Right.

       I.8.central due East.

   With Division on Left.

       C.10.c.0.0. to D.20.central.

5. The 119th Infantry Brigade will move forward to-morrow to the LEERS NORD area. There are no restrictions as to time or route of march.

6. All resting Artillery of the Division will move into action to-night.

7. ACKNOWLEDGE.

                                Lieut. Colonel,

Issued at.....10.30A.   General Staff, 40th Division.

Copy No.				
1	to G.O.C.	17	to D.A.D.O.S.
2	119th I.B.	18	D.A.P.M.
3	120th I.B.	19	Div. Gas Officer.
4	121st I.B.	20	Div. Claims Off.
5	C.R.E.	21	Div. Reception Camp
6	40th D.A.	22	Div. Employment Coy.
7	17th Worc. R.	23	14th Div.
8	Signals	24	59th Div.
9	39th M.G.Bn:	25	XV Corps G.
10	S.A.A.Sect.	26	,, Q.
11	Train	27	,, R.A.
12	S.S.O.	28	,, H.A.
13	M.T.Coy.	29	War Diary
14	"Q"	30	,,
15	A.D.M.S.	31	File
16	D.A.D.V.S.		

(Not to be taken forward of Battn H.Q.)

CONFIDENTIAL.

40th DIVISION DAILY INTELLIGENCE SUMMARY, No.40
Period 6 am 1st - 6 am 2nd October, 1918.

(a) OUR OPERATIONS.

1. INFANTRY. During the night the envelopment of LE BIZET was continued. Our line runs C.13.c.4.7 - C.13.a.5.4 - C.13.a.2.9 - C.7.o.3. C.6.6 - C.7.d.1.9 - C.7.d.3.9 - C.7.d.8.6 - C.8.c.1.4 - C.8.c.4.1 - LE BIZET CONVENT, WALLABY POST - C.15.a.50.87.

At time of writing it is believed that our patrols occupy LE BIZET, LA FLENQUE POST and LYS FARM and there are very few (if any) of the enemy N. of the River LYS.

2. ARTILLERY.
Both Brigades fired 100 rounds per hour special harassing fire on a line through C.7.d.25.25 - C.13.b.18 - C.13.b.30.45 in support of infantry operation, commencing at 20.00. Two hurricane bombardments of 4 minutes duration were fired during the afternoon by the Brigade covering our left sector on C.7.b - 13.b. & d and 14 a & d.

3. AIRCRAFT. Normal activity during the day increasing towards evening. Large formations passed over our lines at 6 pm.

4. MACHINE GUNS. The usual programme of harassing fire was carried out during the night.

(b) ENEMY OPERATIONS.

1. INFANTRY. See above.
2. ARTILLERY. Hostile artillery was generally quiet throughout the 24 hours. At 11.00 about 20 rounds 10.5 cm fell in the vicinity of ORVILLE JUNCTION fire probably being drawn by a working party on the road. PONT de NIEPPE received a few rounds of 7.7 cm and 10.5 cm at intervals, during the day.

Between 20.00 - 20.45, 50 rounds were thrown on to area in B.7.b and B.8.b. A 10.5 cm gun harassed the area B.12.a - B.12.b at intervals from 17.00 onwards.
3. GAS SHELLING. A few gas shells were reported in the vicinity of OOSTHOVE FARM.
4. MACHINE GUNS. Hostile M.Gs were noticeably quieter than during the preceding 24 hours. There was some sniping.
5. AIRCRAFT. No E.A. activity was observed.
6. BALLOONS. One H.K.B. was in position on a grid bearing of 176° from U.19.d.1.8.

(c) INTELLIGENCE.

1. FIRES AND EXPLOSIONS. Four explosions were heard from the direction of ARMENTIERES between 04.30 and 06.30

2. BOOBY TRAPS. A small French stove found in a dug out at B.7.d.9.9, which had been used by our troops the day before, blew up suddenly and was completely wrecked. Wood fuel found close by had been used to feed the stove.

Lieut-Colonel,
General Staff, 40th Division.

(Not to be taken forward of Battn H.Q.)

CONFIDENTIAL.

40th DIVISION DAILY INTELLIGENCE SUMMARY, No. 41.
Period 6 am 2nd - 6 am 3rd October, 1918.

(a) OUR OPERATIONS.

1. INFANTRY. Our troops continued to advance their line. LE BIZET was occupied by the Left Brigade and the northern outskirts of ARMENTIERES were reached without opposition.

During the night a footbridge was thrown across the River LYS at C.15.d.50.75. and portions of the original British Front Line in C.23.c were occupied.

The left bank of the LYS N. of ARMENTIERES to a line drawn through C.14.15 and 16 central is now clear of the enemy. There is no evidence that the enemy is in occupation of the trench systems on the right bank. Our patrols are pushing towards the old German front line.

The right Brigade took over the line as far South as the Corps Boundary, crossing the LYS by a pontoon bridge near ERQUINGHEM. Touch was obtained with the Brigade on our right and a line running South from road at H.6.b.8.2 to the boundary established. According to a later report our patrols have pushed forward and occupied CHAPELLE D'ARMENTIERES.

2. ARTILLERY. At the request of the Infantry batteries of the right Brigade did not fire. 18 pdrs harassed the area East of ARMENTIERES at intervals during the day.

3. AIRCRAFT. Usual formations were observed. Scouts flew low over ARMENTIERES this morning (3rd) without drawing fire.

(b) ENEMY OPERATIONS.

1. INFANTRY. Nil.
2. ARTILLERY. Hostile artillery was very quiet during the period and was chiefly confined to light and scattered shelling by 7.7 cm and 10.5 cm of areas B.8.a, B.10.a & c, B.11.d and B.15.b. At 18.15 LE BIZET received 10 rounds from a 10 cm gun. ARMENTIERES was shelled by 5.9 cm between 15.00 and 16.00. NIEPPE was also shelled by a 10 cm H.V. gun at intervals of five minutes between 22.30 and 00.05.
3. AIRCRAFT. 5 E.As attempted to cross our lines during the day but were engaged and driven off by A.A. fire.
4. MACHINE GUNS. Inactive.
5. GAS SHELLS. Occasional gas shells fell in B.22.a.
6. BALLOONS. One balloon was observed a long way back on a G.B. of 163° from B.11.d.08.60.

(c) INTELLIGENCE.

1. FIRES. Several explosions and many fires were observed in ARMENTIERES and in rear of the enemy's lines during the day and night.

2. MOVEMENT. Individual movement was observed at B.30.b.6.9 and C.19.c.26.72 during the morning.

LATER.

SITUATION. The latest line now reported is the old British front line from the River LYS in C.16.b to I.11.a. Some rifle and M.G. fire is being encountered.

for Lieut-Colonel,
General Staff, 40th Division.

(Not to be taken forward of Battn.)
CONFIDENTIAL.

40th DIVISION DAILY INTELLIGENCE SUMMARY No.42.
Period 6 am 3rd - 6 am 4th October, 1918.

(a) OUR OPERATIONS.

1. INFANTRY. Our troops continued to follow up the retirement of the enemy, and now occupy the old British front line from the LYS to reaches in C.29.a.0.0. From there the line runs along QUEENSLAND ROAD thence along I.4.a - 3.d & 9.b. we occupied

It was previously reported that/the whole of the British front line as far as the railway in I.10.b, but on the situation being cleared up this is found to be not the case. Touch has now been established between our right and left brigades.

2. ARTILLERY. Our Artillery supporting the left Infantry Brigade moved during the morning to forward positions to support better our new line.

Harassing fire was carried out on enemy forward positions throughout the period.

3. AIRCRAFT. Normal. Strong formations were observed to cross the enemy lines meeting with heavy A.A. fire.

4. MACHINE GUNS. Normal activity.

(b) ENEMY OPERATIONS.

1. INFANTRY. A strong patrol operating in C. 17.e. was surprised by our troops at about 6 am to-day. Casualties were inflicted and 11 the prisoners taken.

2. ARTILLERY. Hostile artillery was active in the morning on our new forward area, especially at the crossings of the LYS. At 12.00 LE BIZET received a few rounds from a 10.5 cm gun.

Many concentrations were put down on our forward area during the afternoon and evening. Generally, hostile activity was more pronounced N. of ARMENTIERES.

ARMENTIERES was shelled at intervals throughout the day.

3. AIRCRAFT. Active throughout the period. At 11.00 a low flying machine was observed over ARMENTIERES.

At 14.30 four E.As crossed our lines and brought down a balloon on the left of the Divisional Front sector. Several low flying E.A. were observed between 5 & 7 pm.

4. MACHINE GUNS. Considerable M.G. opposition was encountered by the right brigade during their advance, from I.3.d & B and I.2.d. Steps are being taken to deal with these. One gun was active from I.10.b.7.5. during the night.

5. TRENCH MORTARS. Trench mortars were reported firing from I.10.b.7.5.

(c) INTELLIGENCE.

1. FIRES & EXPLOSIONS. Many fires and dense clouds of smoke were observed opposite our front. A large fire burned all night on a true bearing of 152° from B.17.d.58.20.

Many fires observed East of ARMENTIERES. 3 mines blew up in ARMENTIERES during the evening. Fires/observed at following Grid Bearings from B.27.d.70.05 :- 140° 146° 153° 158° 166° 173°.

*GENERAL. During the morning an Officer and one other rank encountered a strong working party dismantling railway in I.9 and 10. Three of the enemy were shot. The Officer and 1 O.R. withdrew being outnumbered. The working party dispersed.

2. IDENTIFICATIONS. 1 Officer (wounded) and 10 O.R. (3 wounded) were captured this morning.

The following identifications were obtained :-
    4th Company - I.R. 88 - 56th Division.
    10th Company - I.R. 88 - 56th Division.

METHOD.

2.

METHOD of CAPTURE.
A patrol of 1 Officer and about 20 O.R. of the 1st Battalion I.R. 88 was sent forward to reconnoitre our positions in C.17.c and C.23.a this morning and if possible to occupy HOBBS FARM. They were surprised by our troops and M.G and rifle fire was opened on them from both flanks. The patrol scattered, several casualties were inflicted and 1 Officer and 10 O.R. surrendered. Of this number 2 belonging to the 3rd Battalion (10th Coy) were sent out later to bring in their wounded.

2. ORDER of BATTLE.
N. to S.   I.R. 118   56th Division.
           I.R. 88   56th Division.
           I.R. 140   4th Division.

3. DISPOSITIONS. The 3rd Battalion I.R.88 is holding the old German front line with 3 Companies. The 10th Company had two forward posts in their sector consisting each of one group (8 men).
The 1st Battalion is in support about 5 kilometres behind the line probably near PERENCHIES. Whereabouts of the 2nd Battalion unknown.

4. Company Strengths.
Trench Strength 4th Coy. - 80
"   "   10th " - 75

5. RELIEFS. The 1st Battalion withdrew from the bank of the LYS West of ARMENTIERES on the night of 1/2nd instant and the 3rd Battalion took up the front line position in the old German system.

INTENTIONS. Prisoners had no knowledge of enemy intentions with the exception of one who believes the withdrawal is to be continued as far as LILLE.

for Lieut-Colonel,
General Staff, 40th Division.

(Not to be taken forward of Battn H.Q.)
CONFIDENTIAL.
40th DIVISION DAILY INTELLIGENCE SUMMARY, No.43.
Period 06.00 4th - 06.00 5th October, 1918.

(a) OUR OPERATIONS.

1. **INFANTRY.**
During the evening patrols proceeded down the old British front line from C.29. No enemy were met with as far as I.5.c.2.1. where a M.G. post was located. This is covered by another M.G. from a position in the old German front line. A number of the enemy were seen.
The line of our right Brigade now runs - I.9.b.3.7. - I.9.b.60.45 - I.9.b.55.20 - I.9.c.9.0. where touch has been established with troops on our right. At 16.00 patrols gained touch with the left Brigade at I.3.d.3.0.
According to a later report our troops have occupied Gd.PORTE EGAL FARM (I.10.b.)

2. **ARTILLERY.**
Area North of the Railway in I.10.b. and I.11.a. was engaged by field guns between 15.15 and 16.00 at the request of the infantry.
Harassing and searching fire was also carried out on I.6.,12 and 18. during the night.

3. **AIRCRAFT.** Active throughout the period. Hostile A.A. fire was heavy

4. **MACHINE GUNS.** Two guns were moved forward to I.2.central to assist in dealing with enemy M.G. active in I.3.d.

(b) ENEMY OPERATIONS

1. **INFANTRY.** During the night the enemy attempted to enter our front line about C.29.a.3.5. but was driven off.
Two men were seen earlier in the afternoon apparently reconnoitring this locality and were fired at.

2. **ARTILLERY.** Normal, increasing activity being displayed on the left Brigade front during the afternoon. Desultory shelling of ARMENTIERES and LE BIZET during the afternoon is reported. Other targets included CHAPELLE D'ARMENTIERES, the railway in I.1. and HOUPLINES SWITCH. Forward areas were subjected to scattered shelling by 7.7 cm and 4.2 cm throughout the period.

3. **AIRCRAFT.** Active. Formations were observed at 08.55, 09.00 and 10.05. Attempts to cross our lines were made by single E.A. during the day but were driven off by A.A. fire.

4. **M.G's & T.M's.** Nest of M.G's and T.M's in I.10.b. were dealt with by artillery.
Occasional bursts of M.G. fire were fired from the direction of FRELINGHIEN.

5. **GAS SHELLS.** B.16.c. was shelled with mixed H.E. and Gas at 23.00

6. **BALLOONS.** One hostile balloon was observed on a G.B. of 108° from C.14.c.8.9. Two H.K.B. E. of ARMENTIERES were brought down at about 17.00.

C.....

(c) <u>INTELLIGENCE.</u>

1. <u>FIRES.</u> Several fires were observed opposite our front during the period.

2. <u>LIGHTS.</u> A few Very Lights were put up at 21.00 from about I.4.d.6.6.

signature
for Lieut. Colonel,
General Staff, 40th Division.

******

(Not to be taken forward of Battalion H.Qrs.)
CONFIDENTIAL.

40th DIVISION DAILY INTELLIGENCE SUMMARY, No.44.
Period 06.00 5th to 06.00 6th Oct.1918.

(a) Our operations.

1. **INFANTRY** At 18.00 the forward Company of our right Brigade advanced along CENTRAL AVENUE and occupied HEADQUARTERS WALK from I.10.b.3.5. to I.10.a.9.0. A further advance was rendered impossible owing to heavy M.G. fire.
During the night patrols were pushed forward to reconnoitre enemy positions: they report that INCARNATE TRENCH is strongly held by the enemy.

2. **ARTILLERY.** At 18.15 a 3-minute hurricane bombardment was put down by all batteries of the Left Group on the enemy main line in C.29.a. & c, and the enemy Support Line in C.30.a. & c. was subjected to an intense bombardment of 10 minutes duration. At 04.55 batteries covering the left Brigade fired on their S.O.S. lines in reply to S.O.S. rocket.
Two registrations were carried out.

3. **AIRCRAFT.** Normal activity. Usual formations were observed throughout the day.

4. **MACHINE GUNS.** 3,000 rounds were fired at low flying E.A.

(b) Enemy Operations.

1. **INFANTRY.** Nil.

2. **ARTILLERY.** Hostile artillery displayed somewhat increased activity on the left sector. On the right, hostile fire was below normal. HOUPLINES, LE BIZET and ARMENTIERES were shelled at intervals during the period.
At 05.30 a barrage was put down on our support line from C.29.a. to HOUPLINES. After 40 minutes the barrage, which consisted of H.E., Shrapnel and Gas, was placed along the road from HOUPLINES to C.22.a.5.7. No enemy infantry action followed.

3. **AIRCRAFT.** Normal activity. Low flying 'planes crossed our lines at 08.45, 13.15 and 15.00 and were heavily engaged with A.A. and M.G. fire.

4. **MACHINE GUNS.** Active on Support lines, firing from approximately C.17.c.

(c) Intelligence.

1. **FIRES.** Two fires were observed in a South-Easterly direction.

for Lt.Col.
General Staff, 40th Division.

CONFIDENTIAL.   Not to be taken forward of Battn H.Q.)

40th DIVISION DAILY INTELLIGENCE SUMMARY, No.45
Period 06.00 6th - 06.00 7th October, 1918.

(a) OUR OPERATIONS.

1. INFANTRY. During the night our outpost line on the left flank was withdrawn to the Support line of the old British System running S. from the LYS to the Redoubt in C.28.c.6.2. Thence our outpost line runs along AVENUE ROAD to GRANDE PORTE EGAL FARM.

2. ARTILLERY.

At the request of the Infantry our Batteries did not shoot. 10 rounds were expended in registration of farm at C.18.d.2.1. No aeroplane calls were received.

3. MACHINE GUNS.

At 20.20 guns on left flank fired at/and dispersed enemy working party.

(b) ENEMY OPERATIONS.

1. INFANTRY. The enemy raided one of the posts at C.23.a.1.6 about 05.00 (6th Oct). A few of our men are missing. One dead German was found in the post.

2. ARTILLERY.

Hostile artillery was much quieter during the period than on previous days. LE BIZET Church was registered by 15 cm How at 15.45. A little activity during the day in the vicinity of HOUPLINES is reported.

3. AIRCRAFT.

Below normal. At 17.15 two E.A. patrolled our lines for 20 minutes at a great height. At 17.45 one 1 E.A. flying very low crossed our lines, but was driven off by A.A. fire. At 23.00 a hostile plane flew over ERQUINGHEM.

4. MACHINE GUNS.

Active during night in C.28 a & b. Very active against our Aircraft in forward areas at 06.00

5. GAS SHELLING.

A few gas shells fell in HOUPLINES at 16.00.

(c) INTELLIGENCE.

1. FIRES & EXPLOSIONS. A fire (probably dump) was observed between 19.00 and 21.00 behind the enemy's lines.

2. IDENTIFICATIONS. A dead German belonging to I.R.118 was found in the post at C.23.a.1.6.

Lieut-Colonel,
General Staff, 40th Division.

(Not to be taken forward of Battn H.Q.)
CONFIDENTIAL.

40th DIVISION DAILY INTELLIGENCE SUMMARY No. 46
Period 06.00 7th – 06.00 8th October, 1918.

(a) OUR OPERATIONS.

1. INFANTRY. At 12.00 a patrol proceeded along SPAIN AVENUE to reconnoitre road in at C.28.b.70.46. Report enemy seen at C.28.b.cent. During the period posts were established as follows :-

L.G.	Infantry.
C.16.c.75.05	C.22.b.10.45
C.22.c.95.80	C.28.b.10.35
C.28.a.95.95	I.5.c.20.20
C.28.c.90.90	I.11.a.00.60

Since then a post has been established at I.11.a.4.4 which is in touch with left post of Division on our right.

2. ARTILLERY. Normal. During the night our Artillery carried out harassing fire on areas and communications likely to be occupied or used by the enemy.
   No aeroplane calls were received.

3. MACHINE GUNS. Normal.

4. AIRCRAFT. Usual artillery observers, but no strong formations were seen.

(b) ENEMY OPERATIONS.

1. INFANTRY. Nil.

2. ARTILLERY. Below normal. Forward areas harassed during the day and back areas during the night.
   ARMENTIERES received about 20 rounds 15 cm How. during the night.

3. AIRCRAFT. About 6 single machines noticed during the period. All were driven off by A.A. fire.

4. MACHINE GUNS. Active after dusk on roads and tracks in forward area.

5. GAS SHELLING. A few gas shells on NIEPPE between 22.00 and 23.00.
   C.27.d received a few Blue Cross at 21.00.

(c) INTELLIGENCE.

1. Hostile A.A. guns appear to be further back than before and the shells burst very low and forward of our support line.

Lieut-Colonel,
General Staff, 40th Division.

8-10-18.

CONFIDENTIAL.   (Not to be taken forward of Battn H.Q.)
40th DIVISION DAILY INTELLIGENCE SUMMARY, No.47.
Period 06.00 8th - 06.00 9th October 1918.
****

(a) OUR OPERATIONS.

1. INFANTRY. A patrol consisting of one Officer and three other ranks proceeded along EDMEADE AVENUE as far as C.22.b.85.45 without encountering opposition.
The following posts have been established :-

      L.G.   Infantry.
  C.22.b.40.45   C.22.a.95.60

2. ARTILLERY. 18 pdrs and 4.5" hows. carried out harassing fire on selected roads and tracks during the period. Houses and buildings in enemy forward areas were also engaged and registration carried out.
Three N.F. calls from the air were replied to.

3. AIRCRAFT. Active. Strong formations were observed during the day. Increased enemy A.A. fire, especially in forward areas was noticed.

4. MACHINE GUNS. Usual harassing fire was carried out on suspected enemy positions, roads and tracks during the night. Our guns were active against E.A. during the day.

(b) ENEMY OPERATIONS.

1. INFANTRY. Nil.

2. ARTILLERY. Increased activity was displayed by hostile artillery on our left sector, particularly during the night and early morning. Activity on right sector was normal.
ARMENTIERES and ARMENTIERES Station were shelled intermittently by 10.5 cm and 15 cm during the day. During the afternoon 21 cm hows and 15 cm hows appeared to be registering on LE BIZET Church and Convent. Other areas receiving much attention were C.21.b and d - I.3.d - I.4.d.
Normal activity during the day.

3. AIRCRAFT. As the result of an aerial encounter this morning between two scouts and an enemy two seater, one of our scouts crashed and the E.A. made a forced landing at LOWER FARM, having been shot through the petrol tank. The machine contained 2 occupants, an Officer observer (wounded) and a Sergeant pilot. The latter states that they belong to Abteilung 13 - Aerodrome near LILLE, and that their detachment is engaged principally in long distance reconnaissance and photography.

4. MACHINE GUNS. Active on our forward areas throughout the night. Suspected M.G. position at I.11.a.6.6.

5. GAS SHELLING. Between 01.45 and 02.45 the road in C.27.a and d was shelled with a mixture of gas and H.E.

6. BALLOONS. Three balloons were observed during the day on T.Bs of 60° 69° and 130° from I.2.a.10.48.

for Lieut-Colonel,
General Staff, 40th Division.

9-10-18.

(Not to be taken forward of Battn H.Q.)
CONFIDENTIAL.
40th DIVISION DAILY INTELLIGENCE SUMMARY, No. 48.
Period 06.00 9th - 06.00 10th October, 1918.

(a) OUR OPERATIONS.

1. INFANTRY. Patrolling was carried out during the night, but no hostile movement was observed.

2. ARTILLERY. Normal harassing fire was carried out at night on enemy roads and tracks. Trenches in C.24.a were also harassed and houses in I.6.a & d engaged. Two N.F. calls were answered.

3. AIRCRAFT. Active.

4. MACHINE GUNS. M.G. positions to cover artillery have been established as follows :-

I.1.c.4.4 ... 2 guns.
H.12.b.9.5 ... 2 guns.

Enemy forward areas were swept at intervals during the night.

(b) ENEMY OPERATIONS.

1. INFANTRY. Nil.

2. ARTILLERY. Very active throughout the period. Forward areas were harassed with 7.7 cm and 10.5 cm including some gas.
Increased activity was displayed on back areas, LE BIZET, GASOMETER CORNER, C.8.a & c were shelled throughout the evening and night with guns of heavy calibre 15 cm Hows. and 21 cm Hows. PONT de NIEPPE and ERQUINGHEM received attention at intervals and RUEMARLE was shelled between 08.00 and 10.00 by a H.V. gun.

3. AIRCRAFT. Increased activity was observed as compared with previous days. Single E.As crossed our lines at intervals during the day and were engaged by A.A. fire. At 15.00 a strong formation of 11 E.A. flew over our lines at a great height.

4. MACHINE GUNS. Intermittent harassing fire on our forward areas during the night.

5. GAS SHELLING. About 50 gas shells fell in H.6.d between 14.30 and 15.3
Areas C.20.b and C.21.a were also subjected to gas shelling during the night.

for Lieut-Colonel, Lt.
General Staff, 40th Division.

(Not to be taken forward of Battn H.Q.)

CONFIDENTIAL.

40th DIVISION DAILY INTELLIGENCE SUMMARY, No.49.
Period 0600 10th – 0600 11th October, 1918.

(a) OUR OPERATIONS.

1. INFANTRY. Active patrolling was carried out during the night and touch was maintained with the enemy

Patrols. (i) A patrol consisting of 1 Officer and 13 O.R. left our lines at C.28.b.1.7 with the object of locating enemy posts.
On reaching C.28.b.6.4 very lights were fired from C.29.a.2.5 and C.29.c.2.9 whereupon fire was opened by M.Gs from C.28.b.9.9, C.29.a.00.35 and C.29.c.8.7; lights being fired continuously.
(ii) A patrol consisting of 1 Officer and 10 O.R. proceeded along SUSSEX AVENUE at 02.30 as far as C.16.d.4.1 without encountering opposition. Proceeding in a S.E. direction they reached C.22.d.8.8 where they drew M.G. and rifle fi.

A sniper's post was located in tree at C.17.d.8.8.

2. ARTILLERY. The usual harassing fire was maintained during the night on roads, tracks and trenches in enemy forward and support areas. Houses in I.12.a, I.6.a and C.30.d were shelled and enemy positions I.5.d.8.0 – I.5.b.8.0 and I.6.b.8.0 – C.29.d.5.0 engaged at Infantry's request. 4.5" hows took part in Chinese barrage fired by the Division on our left by firing on the wooded area in 0.5.cent.
3. AIRCRAFT. Below normal owing to poor visibility.
4. MACHINE GUNS. Quiet.

(b) ENEMY OPERATIONS.

1. INFANTRY. Our patrols found the enemy on the alert. He appears to be holding the old British front and support lines in C.28.
An enemy patrol in front of our right Company was engaged by Lewis Gun fire.
2. ARTILLERY. Hostile artillery was less active during the day time than on previous day. LE BIZET was harassed by field guns and 10.5 cm hows. During the night forward areas were fairly quiet but heavy and continuous shelling of LE BIZET and surrounding area is reported. HOUPLINES and PONT de NIEPPE also received attention and ERQUINGHEM was shelled with a H.V. gun between 18.30 and 21.30.
The enemy again put down a barrage on the front line system of left front from 04.30 to 05.30. This has now been repeated for 3 mornings in succession and is thought to be his counter preparation.
3. AIRCRAFT. Active at 09.00. Below normal during the day.
4. MACHINE GUNS. (See above under Infantry).
5. BALLOONS. One balloon was observed in position from 16.45 to 17.50 on a T.B. of 62° from I.4.a.60.90

(c) INTELLIGENCE.

1. FIRES. A large fire was observed behind enemy's lines on a T.B. of 52° from I.4.a.60.90.
2. EXPLOSIONS. A big explosion was heard in the direction of LILLE at 15.30.

D.G. Rylings
for Lieut-Colonel,
General Staff, 40th Division.

CONFIDENTIAL.

(Not to be taken forward of Battn H.Q.)

40th DIVISION DAILY INTELLIGENCE SUMMARY, No.50
Period 0600 11th October - 0600 12th Oct. 1918.

(a) OUR OPERATIONS.

1. **INFANTRY.** As the result of a minor operation carried out this morning by a company of the K.O.S.B. our line has been slightly advanced and now runs as follows :-
North of Railway from I.11.a.6.3. along INCANDESCENT TRENCH to road at I.5.d.3.6. Posts have been pushed out in the direction of L'EPINETTE to join up with the Cameron Hrs and further posts are being pushed into INCANDESCENT SUPPORT.
No identifications were obtained as the enemy left his trenches and withdrew directly our advance was perceived.

2. **ARTILLERY.** The usual programme of night harassing fire on roads tracks and buildings was carried out.
The whole of the Advanced Guard Artillery fired a lifting barrage of 44 minutes duration in support of the above minor operation. One 18-pdr battery of the Division on our right co-operated.

3. **AIRCRAFT.** Owing to unfavourable weather conditions little flying was possible.

4. **MACHINE GUNS.** M.G's co-operated in our minor operation, 4,000 rounds being fired on INANE ALLEY in I.12.a. between 05.15 - 05.59.

TRENCH MORTARS. Fired during infantry operation.

(b) ENEMY OPERATIONS.

1. **INFANTRY.**
See above.

2. **ARTILLERY.** Activity normal with exception of reply to our barrage.
Little activity was noticed on battery and front line areas during the daytime. LE BIZET area was shelled with 7.7 cm H.E. and Gas during the night. Road running through C.21.c.9.9. to C.22.a.5.5. was constantly shelled throughout the period by 7.7 cm. H.V. guns were active on C.21.b. & d. and C.20.b. intermittently throughout the period.
The enemy's reply to our barrage was weak and consisted of 7.7 cm and 5.9" on our front line. LE BIZET and HOUPLINES were fairly heavily shelled from 0530 to 0700.

3. **GAS SHELLING.** 12 gas shells fell in C.14.a. at 09.30 and a few blue cross are reported in H.6.d. during the night.

4. **MACHINE GUNS.** Normal. Our infantry met with fairly heavy M.G. fire from flanks.

5. **AIRCRAFT.** No E.A. activity reported.

(c) INTELLIGENCE.

1. **LIGHTS.** A single red light was fired on our barrage opening at 05.15 followed about 10 minutes afterwards by a double green light.

for Lieut. Colonel,
General Staff, 40th Division.

12/10/18.

CONFIDENTIAL.
(Not to be taken forward of Battn H.Q.)
40th DIVISION DAILY INTELLIGENCE SUMMARY, No.55.
Period 0800 16th - 0800 17th October, 1918.

(a) OUR OPERATIONS.

1. INFANTRY.   Our troops have continued to advance to-day and at the time of writing are known to have reached the line of the Railway from QUESNOY STATION in D.16.a to D.30.d.9.8. No opposition of any kind has been encountered.
    Troops are now pushing forward with a view to gaining the Line of the LA BASSE DEULE CANAL from K.9.a. to K.3.a.2.0 thence along light railway to northern divisional boundary at E.15.a.3.0.

2. CIVILIANS. French civilians found in houses between D.30.d.9.8 and D.30.a.3.9 report that the enemy retired hurriedly at 0400 this morning. Civilians who entered the lines of the Corps on our right also state that LILLE was evacuated at the same hour.

3 AIRCRAFT Contact planes have been active, working in co-operation with the Infantry. Aeroplanes flew over the towns of ROUBAIX and TOURCOING this morning at a height of 800 feet without drawing A.A. or M.G. fire. Civilians in the towns waved to the machines.

GENERAL SITUATION.

    The enemy has retired hastily along the whole front. Air observers report ROUBAIX, TOURCOING and LILLE evacuated.
    There are at present no indications as to where the enemy intends to make a stand.

Major,
General Staff, 40th Division.

(Not to be taken forward of Battn H.Q.)

CONFIDENTIAL. 40th DIVISION DAILY INTELLIGENCE SUMMARY No. 56
Period 0600 26th - 0600 27th October, 1918.
****

(a) Our Operations.

1. INFANTRY. Nil.
2. ARTILLERY. Harassing fire carried out on selected targets.
3. AIRCRAFT. Our aircraft carried out low flying reconnaissances of E. side of SCHELDT during whole of the day, in spite of considerable A.A. fire.
4. M.G. & T.M. Nil.

(b) ENEMY OPERATIONS.

1. INFANTRY. Nil.
2. ARTILLERY. During the morning, enemy intermittently shelled WARCOING and PECQ with 5.9's. Intermittent shelling with 5.9's along Battalion front during whole of the night.
3. GAS SHELLING. Heavy gas shell bombardment of areas H.6.c. and d between 1810 and 1825.- Green and blue cross shells. Intermittent gas shelling of whole front line during the night - high explosive and phosgene.
4. MACHINE GUNS. Machine guns were active against our right Company posts in I.2.a and c. Occasional bursts of fire on roads in and around WARCOING.
5. TRENCH MORTAR. Enemy T.M. fairly active during the day. SUGAR FACTORY and Chateau in WARCOING receiving most attention by heavy T.M. Location of this Battery is uncertain, probably in gardens of houses in HERINNES. Inactive during the night.
6. AIRCRAFT. Several enemy planes attempted to cross our lines over PECQ at 1715 hours but were driven off by our A.A. fire.

(c) INTELLIGENCE.

1. MOVEMENT. Air observers report individual movement around HERINNES Church, also in field E. of village and Railway in C.21 Enemy transport heard moving through streets in HERINNES between 2350 and 0130 hours.
2. FIRES. House was observed to be burning last night in C.21.b.
3. DEFENCES. Air observers report houses occupied at C.28.a.50.05 and C.27.b.50.25.
4. BALLOONS. Enemy balloon brought down by our aeroplane at 0940 in direction of C.28.

INFORMATION FROM AEROPLANE PHOTOGRAPHS. STATE of COUNTRY. - The country between the ESCAUT Canal and the LANNOY-LEAUCOURT road in the Corps front is for the most part more or less badly flooded.
COMMUNICATIONS.- All the bridges over the ESCAUT have been destroyed and craters blown in the Causeway from PECQ through I.2.b and I.3.a. and in the road from C.20.d.4.7. S. of the SLUICE to HERINNES, rendering them impassable: the road along the E. bank of the ESCAUT and the road from C.15.d.0.8 to HERINNES are intact; the latter appears to be the only road through the marshes passable on the Corps front.
ENEMY DEFENCES. Consist mainly of isolated trench lengths and M.G posts, on the left Divisional front both along the E. bank of the canal and in the village of LANNOY, and on the right Divisional front more especially in the village of HERINNES. Wire has been erected chiefly in front of the above trench lengths: a certain amount of what may be wire is visible at various places on the photographs; this may, however, be only sodden tracks.

NOTE.- The hilly area E. of the TOURNAI - RENAIX Railway was not sufficiently covered to form an idea of the defences.

D G Hydings
for Lieut-Colonel,
General Staff, 40th Division.

CONFIDENTIAL. (Not to be taken forward of Battn H.Q.)

40th DIVISION DAILY INTELLIGENCE SUMMARY, No. 57.
Period 0600 27th - 0600 28th October, 1918.

(a) OUR OPERATIONS.

1. **INFANTRY.** Patrols. At 0900 a daylight patrol consisting of 1 Officer and a section attempted to proceed along LE RIVAGE, with a view to establishing a post as far along it as possible. The patrol left our lines at I.2.c.7.9 and proceeded along the causeway from I.2.a.6.2 to I.2.a.8.3, at this point they encountered M.G. fire from I.3.a.7.9 and I.3.c.7.2 and T.M. fire from C.27.c.95.65 which compelled them to withdraw to the west bank of the river.
These posts are being dealt with by Artillery.
2. **ARTILLERY.** MONT ST.AUBERT was shelled by heavy artillery during the afternoon.
3. **AIRCRAFT.** Our Aircraft were active during the fine intervals Two H.K.Bs opposite this Divisional Front were attacked and brought down at 0725 and 0940 respectively.
4. **MACHINE GUNS.** Harassing fire was carried out on enemy posts along the West side of the road running through C.21.b & d

(b) ENEMY OPERATIONS.

1. **INFANTRY.** Nil.
2. **ARTILLERY.** From 0800 onwards farm at B.30.a.6.3 was subjected to intermittent shelling by 15 cm and 10.5 cm. WARCOING was shelled occasionally by 15 cm how and PECQ and the PECQ - WARCOING road were harassed at intervals during the night with 10.5 cm and 7.7 cm.
3. **GAS SHELLING.** A few 7.7 cm gas shells fell in H.15.d, ESTAIMBOURG and forward areas.
4. **MACHINE GUNS.** Machine guns were active at intervals during the day from positions along the west side of the road from HERINNES through C.27.b & d.
During the night WARCOING - PECQ road was harassed. M.Gs were also located at I.3.a.7.9 - I.3.c.7.2 and C.9.d.6.4
5. **SNIPERS.** An enemy sniper was located firing from a crater in the centre of LA RIVAGE.
6. **TRENCH MORTARS.** Occasional rounds were fired on WARCOING and the bridge at PECQ. This Trench Mortar is believed to be firing from C.27.c.95.65.
7. **AIRCRAFT.** Hostile planes attempting to cross our lines at 0830 and 1020 were driven off by A.A. fire.

(c) INTELLIGENCE.

1. **MOVEMENT.** At 1405 two men were observed walking along the road at C.27 cent.
At 1415 individual movement was observed along the road at I.3.a., 9.5.
2. **A.A.FIRE.** Hostile A.A. fire was much less this morning (28th) than on previous days.

Lieut-Colonel,
General Staff, 40th Division.

CONFIDENTIAL.   (Not to be taken forward of Battn H.Q.)
                40th DIVISION DAILY INTELLIGENCE SUMMARY, No. 58.
                   Period 0600 28th - 0600 29th October, 1918.

                             (a) OUR OPERATIONS.
1. INFANTRY.
            An R.E. working party attempted to throw footbridge across the River in C.20.d., but were unable to do so on account of heavy M.G and Artillery fire, which was directed against them.
2. ARTILLERY. In the morning a shoot was carried out on suspected M.G. positions in houses at C.27.b.5.6 and T.M. emplacement in I.3.a., several direct hits being obtained.
3. MACHINE GUNS   Nil.
4. AIRCRAFT. Normal activity. Two of our planes were brought down in the afternoon by enemy aircraft on the east side of the river in C.20.c. One wounded pilot was safely brought into our lines by an Officer from the left subsector. The pilot of the other machine swam the river.
            Very little A.A. fire was noticed against our low flying planes.
5. TRENCH MORTARS. Our trench mortars shelled a sniper's post located in a crater at I.2.b.70.35.

                             (b) ENEMY OPERATIONS.
1. INFANTRY. Nil.
2. ARTILLERY. During the period the chief activity was displayed by 10.5 cm and 15 cm hows apparently firing at long range. The chief areas shelled were PECQ, WARCOING, C.1, H.6.a and B.24.c. ESTAIMBOURG was harassed by heavy shrapnel during the night.
3. AIRCRAFT. Several enemy planes flew over our lines during the afternoon, one group of which was engaged by our planes.
4. MACHINE GUNS. M.Gs were active from positions along East side of HERINNES. A decrease in M.G. activity as compared with previous days was noticed.
5. TRENCH MORTARS. 5 rounds were fired on PECQ bridge at 0900. Between 1730 and 2200 WARCOING was heavily shelled with about 90 shells and about 20 T.M. shells fell near the SUGAR FACTORY between 2350 and 0200.

                             (c) INTELLIGENCE.
1. MOVEMENT. Individual movement was observed on roads in C.27 a.1.3.
2. CIVILIANS. Considerable movement of civilians in HERINNES was observed, who were removing bedding etc., on wheelbarrows.
3. ENEMY DEFENCES. An enemy post is reported at C.11.d.3.6.

INFORMATION FROM PHOTOS.
            Six rifle pits are visible in front of the farm house at C.16.c. 3.5. Small craters are also shown at cross roads C.16.c.95.30 and C.16.d.10.52 (20Q K 34.81).
            Trench lengths are shown from C.27.a.95.10 to C.27.c.83.69 and C.27.d.18.90 to C.27.d.35.71. Wire is visible in front of the latter as far as C.27.d.2.6.
            A little digging is apparent at C.27.b.50.68 (possibly shelters). Three small craters have been blown across the railway at C.21.b.88.15. (20S K 34.82).
            Holes have been prepared along the hedges on the W. side of the HERINNES-LANNOY Road in C.15.d and 16 c and at C.16.c.72.39

                                        for Lieut-Colonel,
                                    General Staff, 40th Division.

CONFIDENTIAL. (Not to be taken forward of Battn H.Q.)

40th DIVISION DAILY INTELLIGENCE SUMMARY, No.59.
Period 0600 29th - 0600 30th October, 1918.

(a) OUR OPERATIONS.

1. INFANTRY. A daylight patrol consisting of 2 men proceeded along LE RIVAGE causeway at 1500 on 29th for a distance of about 500 yards in order to bring in the body of a Sergeant who had previously proceeded along the Causeway and been shot. A sniper's post was located in a trench at I.2.b.4.3. The patrol returned safely with the body which had been stripped.

During the night a patrol crossed the river by the bridge at C.20.c.7.5 and patrolled the East bank of the river from C.20.c.3.0 to C.20.d.8.6. No hostile opposition was encountered.

A footbridge was erected during the night by an R.E. working party at C.20.c.7.5.

2. ARTILLERY. At 1500 a shoot was carried out on a house at C.20.d.1.6 which was suspected to have been used by the enemy as a M.G. position by night. Five direct hits were obtained.

Between 1800 and 2200 our artillery carried out destructive fire on houses in I.3, I.4 and I.9.

3. AIRCRAFT. At 1700 our aeroplanes engaged a hostile patrol consisting of 12 machines which crossed our lines at PECQ. During the engagement 1 machine (nationality uncertain) was seen to fall.

4. MACHINE GUNS. Harassing fire was carried out by night on the cross roads in I.3.a.8.4.

5. TRENCH MORTARS. At 1500 the snipers post at I.2.b.4.3 was engaged by our trench mortars.

(b) ENEMY OPERATIONS.

1. INFANTRY. The attitude of the enemy remains quiet. A decrease of shelling and M.G. fire was noticeable.

2. ARTILLERY. Chief activity was again displayed by 15 cm hows. During the evening the area between ESTAIMBOURG and BAILLEUL was intermittently harassed by 15 cm. Slight harassing fire was directed on ST LEGER - WARCOING-PETIT LANNOY and PECQ during the period.

3. AIRCRAFT. Several patrols were engaged by our machines during the afternoon and failed to penetrate behind our front line. A hostile machine dropped 5 bombs in B.18.b.2.3 at 1845.

4. MACHINE GUNS. During the day enemy M.G. fire was directed chiefly against our aircraft. A M.G. was active during the night from C.21.b. 2 M.G. emplacements were located at I.2.b.7.4 and I.3.b.4.1.

5. TRENCH MORTARS. Heavy T.Ms shelled WARCOING between 2230-2300.

6. GAS SHELLING. Nil.

(c) INTELLIGENCE.

1. MOVEMENT. Considerable individual movement was observed in HERINNES and its outskirts.

Civilians in HERINNES were again seen to be evacuating.

Horse transport was heard in direction of C.16.a at 0100.

for Lieut-Colonel,
General Staff, 40th Division.

CONFIDENTIAL.

(Not to be taken forward of Battn H.Q.)
40th DIVISION DAILY INTELLIGENCE SUMMARY, No. 80
Period 0600 30th - 0600 31st October, 1918.

(a) OUR OPERATIONS.

1. INFANTRY. Patrols. A daylight patrol consisting of 2 Officers and 12 O.R. with a L.G. crossed the River by the bridge at C.20.c.7.5 at 1600 yesterday, and proceeded along the road in C.20.d covered by fire from our L.G. A post was located at C.20.d.6.7,- the man on guard being shot and remaining three of the post taken prisoners. M.G. fire was opened on our patrol from the direction of C.21.a.3.7.

The patrol returned to our lines with 4 prisoners, having 1 O.R. casualty.

A second patrol crossed the river at C.20.b.6.0 at 0445 to patrol road in C.20.d - C.21.c. An enemy party seen at C.20.d.7.7 was dispersed by the patrol with L.G. and rifle fire. Road clear to C.21.c.0.5.

At 1430 a patrol consisting of 1 N.C.O and 6 O.R. was pushed forward and reached about I.2.b.4.3 where they were fired on from trench or shell hole across the road. The patrol was compelled to return.

A patrol consisting of 1 N.C.O. and 3 O.R. left our lines at 2215 and proceeded along the causeway for 250 yards when they heard voices and movement near the house on right of the causeway. The Patrol then crept forward and threw several bombs at the enemy, who immediately opened fire on them with 2 M.Gs. The patrol withdrew to W. side of the river at 0330. The strength of the enemy who had posts on both sides of the road was estimated about 30-40.

2. ARTILLERY. In Counter Battery Work 100 rounds were fired on each of the following targets :- C.23.c.83.63; C.23.a.15.92 - 07.84.
3. AIRCRAFT. Usual activity.
4. MACHINE GUNS. 250 rounds were fired on the post on the road at I.2.b.
5. TRENCH MORTARS. 8 rounds were fired on the above post by our T.M.s.

(b) ENEMY OPERATIONS.

1. INFANTRY. See above.
2. ARTILLERY. WARCOING and PECQ and the area H.11.d and H.12.c. was harassed intermittently during the night by 150 mm, 105 mm and 77 mm. During the evening the area between B.23.a, B.29.d. and B.30.a was occasionally shelled with 105 mm.

At 0530 a few 105 mm and 150 mm gas shells fell in H.6.a.
3. AIRCRAFT. At 0540 two E.A. flew over our lines. At 1940 one enemy bombing plane flew over WARCOING and PECQ dropping 6 bombs in vicinity of PECQ. Two attempts to cross our lines at 0800 and 0900 failed owing to our A.A. fire.
4. TRENCH MORTARS. WARCOING was shelled with T.Ms after our daylight raid.
5. MACHINE GUNS. Quiet, except against our patrols.
6. GAS SHELLING. At 1915 PECQ was shelled with 5 tear gas shells. The area about H.11.a was subjected to 25 gas shells at 0530 this morning.

(c) INTELLIGENCE.

MOVEMENT. Several men were seen crouching past house in C.28.a.8.9. Individual movement observed in HERINNES. Movement was seen in the post on the causeway at I.2.b.4.3.
2. DEFENCES. New wire was observed to have been put up last night in front of the trench at C.27.a.80.05.

An enemy party of 6 were seen wiring in early morning at C.27.B.8.8, and a hole has been knocked in a wall behind, which would act as a loophole for M.G.
3. IDENTIFICATIONS. 4 prisoners who were captured yesterday belonged to 8th Coy. of 26th Bav.I.R., 12th Reserve Division. (See App.attached).
4. BALLOONS. A Hostile Balloon was in the air at 0715 on a G.B. 126 from C.7.d.2.8.

Lieut-Colonel,
General Staff, 40th Division.

EXAMINATION OF PRISONERS OF 8th Coy.
26th Bav. Inf. Regt., 12th Bavarian Division.

METHOD OF CAPTURE. Prisoners were surprised whilst on outpost duty by a daylight patrol.

ORDER OF BATTLE. N. to S. 26th Bav. Inf. Regt.
27th " " "

DISPOSITIONS. The 2nd Battalion of the 26th Bav. I.R. is in line with two companies forward and one in support. The 8th Coy holds a front of about 500 yards with two infantry groups and 2 light M.G's in the outpost line, the remainder being in houses in HERINNES. At night a further group with M.G. is pushed forward.

RELIEFS. On the night of the 25th/26th the 2nd Bn. Bav. I.R. 27 relieved a Prussian Battalion (believed to be the 23rd I.R.) in the HERINNES Sector.

STRENGTHS. All battalions have been reduced to 3 companies per battalion.

	Trench strength.	Ration strength.
6th Coy.	30 O.R.	-
7th Coy.	40 O.R.	120
8th Coy.	40/45 O.R.	120/140

No drafts had been received by the 2nd Battalion since end of August.

INTENTIONS. All prisoners state that there is talk of a further early withdrawal, but nothing of a definite nature was known nor was it known what line would be taken up. They had heard that Pioneers were preparing roads in back areas for demolitions.

REST BILLETS. The 2nd Bn: of Bav. I.R. 26 was in rest at MOLEMBAIX which is still full of civilians.

GENERAL. Owing to artillery fire the house at C.20.d.1.8. which was occupied by the enemy had been vacated.

31/10/18.

AA.

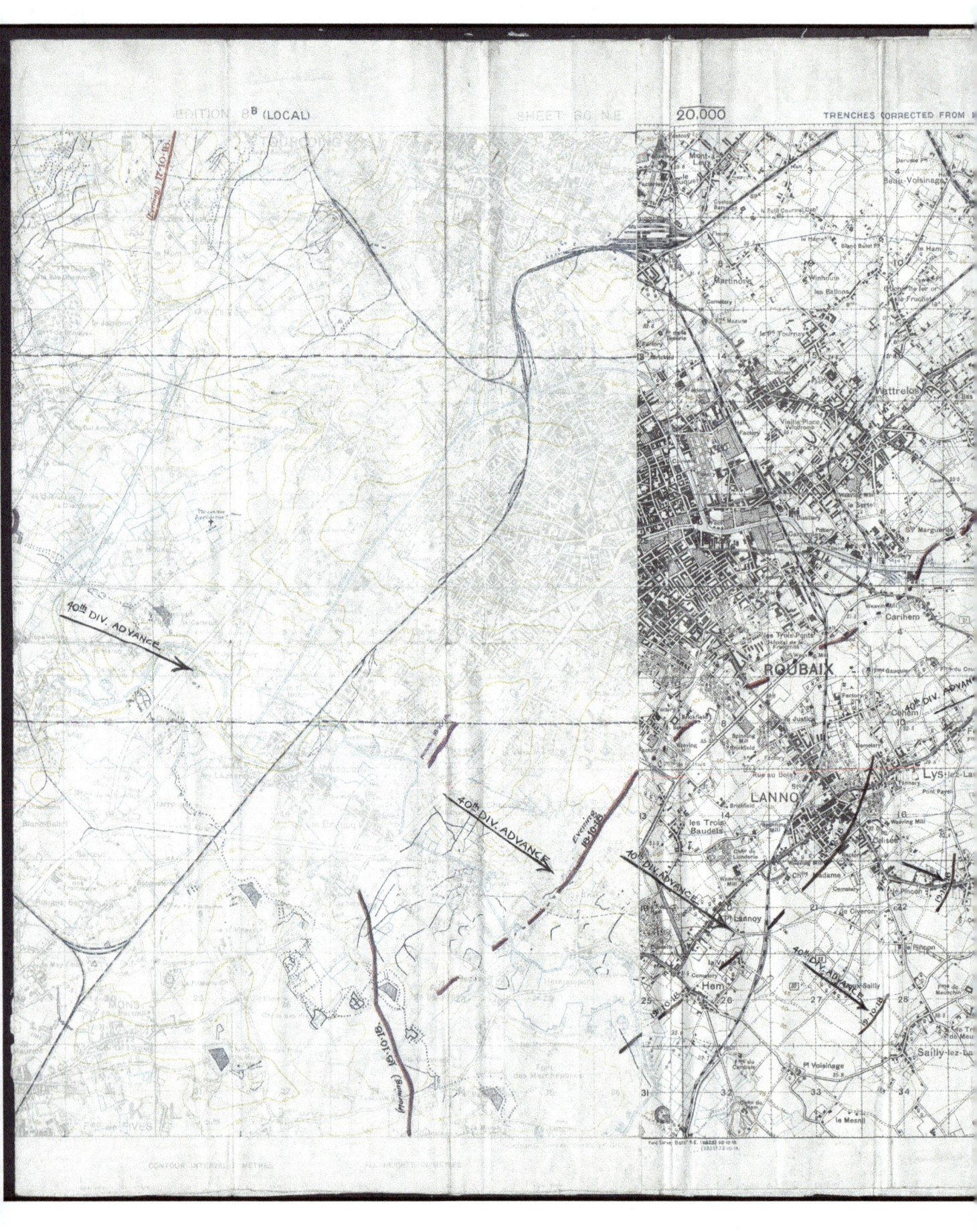

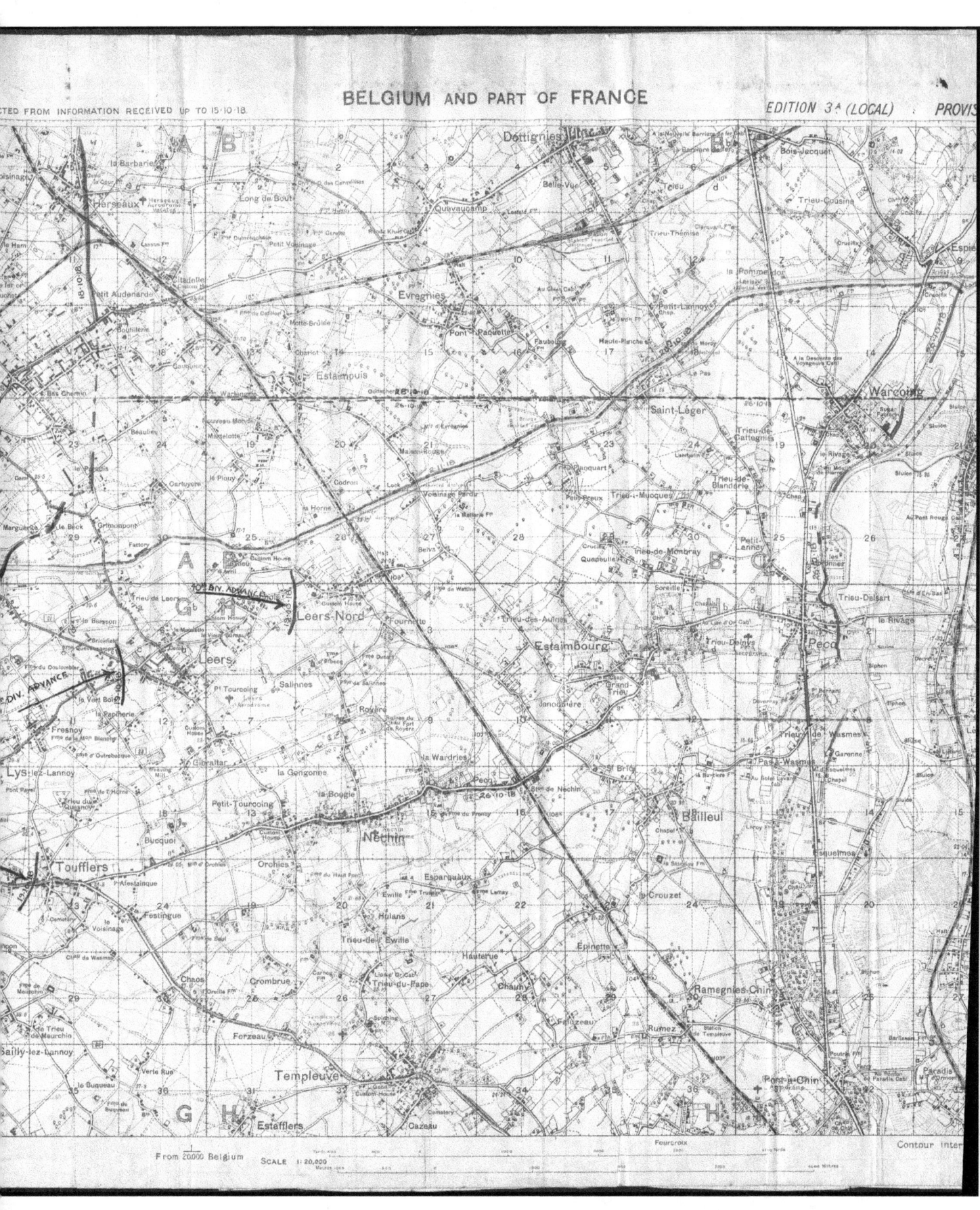

Bassin de radoub	Dry dock.
Bateau phare	Light-ship.
Blanchisserie	Laundry.
B.M. (borne milliaire)	Mile stone.
B^e (borne kilométrique)	
Boulonnerie	
Fab^e de boulons	Bolt Factory.
Bouée	Buoy.
Brasserie, Brass^ie	Brewery.
Briqueterie, Briq^ie	Brickfield.
Brise-lames	Breakwater.
Bureau de poste	Post office.
" de douane	Custom house.
Butte	Butt, Mound.
Cabane	Hut.
Cabaret, Cab^t	Inn.
Câble sous-marin	Submarine cable.
Calvaire, Calv^e	Calvary.
Canal de dessèchement	Drainage canal.
Canal d'irrigation	Irrigation canal.
Fab^e de caoutchouc	Rubber factory.
Carrière, Carr^e	Quarry.
" de gravier	Gravel-pit.
Caserne	Barracks.
Champ de courses	Race-course.
" manœuvres	Drill-ground.
" tir	Rifle range.
Chantier	Building yard. Ship yard. Dock yard.
Chantier de construction	Slip-way.
Chapelle, Ch^le	Chapel.
Charbonnage	Colliery.
Château d'eau	Water tower.
Chaussée	Causeway. Highway.
Chemin de fer	Railway.
Cheminée, Ch^ée	Chimney.
Chêne	Oak tree.
Cimetière, Cim^re	Cemetery.
Clocher	Belfry.
Clouterie	Nail factory.
Colombier	Dove-cot.

Coron	Workmen's dwellings.
Cour des marchandises	Goods yard.
Couvent	Convent.
Crassier	Slag heap.
Croix	Cross.
Darse	Inner dock.
Démoli-e	Destroyed.
Détruit-e, Dét^e	
Déversoir	Weir.
Digue	Dyke, causeway.
Distillerie, Dist^ie	Distillery.
Douane	
Bureau de douane	Custom-house.
Entrepôt de douane	Custom warehouse.
Dynamitière, Dynam^re	Dynamite magazine.
Dynamiterie	Dynamite factory.
Écluse	Sluice, Lock.
Éclusette, Ecl^te	Sluice.
École	School.
Écurie	Stable.
Église	Church.
Émaillerie	Enamel works.
Embarcadère, Emb^re	Landing-place.
Estaminet, Estam^t	Inn.
Étang	Pond.
Fabrique, Fab^e	Factory.
Fab^e de produits chimiques	Chemical works.
Fab^e de faïence Faïencerie	Pottery.
Ferme, F^me	Farm.
Filature, Fil^re	Spinning mill.
Fonderie, Fond^ie	Foundry.
Fontaine, Font^ne	Spring, fountain.
Forêt	Forest
Forme de radoub	Dry dock.
Forge	Smithy.
Fosse	Mine, Pit.
Fossé	Moat, Ditch.
Four	Kiln.
" à chaux	Lime-kiln.

Four à coke	Coke oven.
Ganterie	Glove Factory.
Gare	Station.
Garenne	Warren.
Garnison	Garrison.
Gazomètre	Gasometer.
Glacerie	
Fab^e de glaces	Mirror Factory.
Glacière	Ice factory.
Grue	Crane.
Gué	Ford.
Guérite	Sentry-box, Turret.
" à signaux	Signal-box (Ry.)
Halte	Halt.
Hangar	Shed, Hangar.
Hôpital	Hospital.
Hôtel-de-Ville	Town hall.
Houillère	Colliery.
Huilerie	Oil factory.
Imprimerie, Impr^ie	Printing works.
Jetée	Pier.
Laminerie	Rolling mills.
Ligne de haute	High water mark.
Laisse marée	
" de basse marée	Low " "
Maison Forestière M^on F^re	Forester's house.
Malterie	Malt-house.
Marbrerie	Marble works.
Marais	Marsh.
Marais salant	Saltern, Salt marsh.
Marché	Market.
Mare	Pool.
Meule	Rick.
Minière	Mine.
Monastère	Monastery.
Moulin, M^in	Mill.
" à vapeur	Steam mill.
Mur	Wall.
" crénelé	Loop-holed wall.

Army Form C. 2118.

WAR DIARY

INTELLIGENCE SUMMARY

40th DIVISION (Erase heading not required.) NOVEMBER, 1918.

Instructions regarding War Diaries and Intelligence Summaries are contained in F. S. Regs., Part II. and the Staff Manual respectively. Title pages will be prepared in manuscript.

Place	Date	Hour	Summary of Events and Information	Remarks and references to Appendices
LANNOY. (Continued).	9.		now without opposition), and occupied the high ground running N. and S. through L.4. and C.22 by 02.00 hours. The advance continued, CHEMIN VERT being entered at 06.30. hours and patrols pushed towards BUTOR and MOULEMBAIX. CLIPET, J.10.b was entered at 09.00 hours and HENHART, J.5.a. and road in D. 29 reached by 11.45 hours, patrols finally entering VELAINES, K.13.a. at 15.00 hours.	
			One Company, Corps Cyclists was attached to the Advanced Guard Brigade for these operations and cyclist patrols were sent in advance along the VELAINES-CORDES road; total advance made since daybreak was just under 7 miles. One 10 cm. gun abandoned by the enemy was captured.	
			A pack mule bridge at WARCOING and a pontoon bridge at PECQ were completed by 17.00 hours and 19.30. hours respectively.	
"	10.		Order No. 230 (regarding withdrawal of 40th Division from the line owing to convergence of Corps on right and left) issued. Appendix 7.	Appex 7.
			The line was extended Northwards along the VELAINES – CORDES road. Cyclists crossed the River RHOSNES, K.17.d. and reached the railway, F.26. One prisoner (7th Bav. Cavalry Regt.) wounded by an aeroplane bomb was taken. The Division was withdrawn from the line.	
"	11.		Message received from G.H.Q. regarding "CESSATION OF HOSTILITIES" 11.00 hours, Appendix 8.	Appex.8.
			40th Div. No. 224 G. (instructions in connection with the ARMISTICE) issued. Appendix 9.	Appex.9.
			40th Div. Order No. 231 (moves of 119th and 120th Infantry Bdes) issued. Appendix 10.	Appex.10.
"	12.		119th Infantry Bde. moved to HERINNES area, 120th Infantry Bde. to TOUFFLERS-NECHIN area.	
"	13.		Division resting, training and employed on road repair.	
"	14.		40th Div. Order No. 232 (move of Artillery to WAMBRECHIES) issued, Appendix 11.	Appex.11.

Army Form C. 2118.

WAR DIARY
or
~~INTELLIGENCE SUMMARY~~

40th DIVISION.   NOVEMBER, 1918.

(Erase heading not required.)

Instructions regarding War Diaries and Intelligence Summaries are contained in F. S. Regs., Part II. and the Staff Manual respectively. Title pages will be prepared in manuscript.

Place	Date	Hour	Summary of Events and Information	Remarks and references to Appendices
LANNOY	15th.		Order No. 233 (move of 119th Infantry Brigade to CROIX Area.) issued. 40th Divl. Artillery and 64th Army Brigade R.F.A. moved to WAMBRECHIES area.	App.12
	16th.		119th Infantry Brigade moved to CROIX. Instruction No. 14 (reference advance of Second Army to German frontier and transference of 113th Army Brigade R.F.A. from 40th Div.) issued.	App.13
	17th.		Division training. Schemes were introduced whereby a portion of the day should be devoted to Educational and Recreational Training for the troops.	
	18th.			
	19th.			
	20th.			
	21st.			
	22nd.			
	23rd.			
	24th.		Order No. 234 (move of D.H.Q. to ROUBAIX) issued.	App.14.
ROUBAIX	25th.		D.H.Q. moved to ROUBAIX.	
	26th.		Lectures were given on various subjects of Educational interest, classes arranged and reading rooms opened.	
	27th.			
	28th.			
	29th.			
	30th.			

[signature]   Lieut. Colonel,
General Staff, 40th Division.

******

"A" Form.
MESSAGES AND SIGNALS.

Army Form C. 2121

Prefix	Code	m.	Words.	Charge.			Recd. at ...... m.
Office of Origin and Service Instructions.					This message is on a/c of:		
DRLS			Sent At.........m.		............Service.		Date............ From
			To		(Signature of "Franking Officer.")		By
			By				

TO	121st Infantry Brigade.		CRA
	CRE		14th Div.

Sender's Number.	Day of Month.	In reply to Number.	
Gc 736	1		AAA

121st Brigade will establish posts night 2nd/3rd November East of the River in G.15 and 21 to prevent the enemy approaching our positions through the gap of dry ground between the Inundated areas in C.21. and C.15 aaa The C.R.E. will arrange in conjunction with 121st Brigade for a footbridge to be constructed about C.15.central and placed in position as soon as patrols are East of River and can cover its erection aaa Arrangements for use of footbridge in C.9.d. if required will be made between 121st Bde and 41st Brigade aaa Acknowledge aaa Addressed 121st Brigade C.R.E. repeated C.R.A. and 14th Division.

From	40th Division.
Place	
Time	

The above may be forwarded as now corrected.   (Z)

(sd) C.H.G.BLACK,

Censor.   Signature of Addressor or person authorised to telegraph in his name.

*This line, except **AAA**, should be erased if not required. Lt. Col. G.S.

SECRET.   Copy No. 29

40th DIVISION ORDER NO. 227.   2/11/18.

1. The 119th Infantry Brigade will relieve the 121st Infantry Brigade on night 4th/5th November.

2. All details will be arranged between the Brigadiers concerned.

3. Command will pass at 10.00 on 5th November.

4. ACKNOWLEDGE.

                                   [signature]   Lieut. Colonel,
Issued at...23.00 hrs.   General Staff, 40th Division.

Copy No. 1 to G.O.C.
      2   119th Infantry Brigade.
      3   120th   ,,
      4   121st   ,,
      5   C.R.E.
      6   40th Div. Artillery.
      7   17th Worc. R. (P).
      8   Div. Signal Coy.
      9   39th Bn: M.G.C.
     10   S.A.A. Section.
     11   Divl. Train.
     12   S.S.O.
     13   M.T. Coy.
     14   "Q"
     15   A.D.M.S.
     16   D.A.D.V.S.
     17   D.A.D.O.S.
     18   D.A.P.M.
     19   Div. Gas Officer.
     20   Div. Claims Officer.
     21   Div. Reception Camp.
     22   Div. Employment Coy.
     23   14th Division.
     24   59th Division.
     25   XV Corps G.
     26   ,,   Q.
     27   ,,   R.A.
     28   ,,   H.A.
     29   War Diary
     30   ,,
     31   File

SECRET.   Copy No. 29

            40th DIVISION ORDER NO.228. 3/11/18.
            ****

1. The 121st Infantry Brigade and the 120th Infantry
   Brigade will change places on the 6th instant.

2. All details will be arranged between the Brigadiers
   concerned.

3. ACKNOWLEDGE.

                                              Lieut. Colonel,
Issued at. 19.45   General Staff, 40th Division.

                         ******

Copy No. 1 to G.O.C.
         2   119th Infantry Brigade.
         3   120th   ,,
         4   121st   ,,
         5   C.R.E.
         6   40th Div. Artillery.
         7   17th Worc. R. (P).
         8   Signals
         9   59th Bn: M.G.C.
        10   S.A.A.Sect.
        11   Train
        12   S.S.O.
        13   M.T.Coy.
        14   "Q"
        15   A.D.M.S.
        16   D.A.D.V.S.
        17   D.A.D.O.S.
        18   D.A.P.M.
        19   D.Gas Off.
        20   Div. Claims Off.
        21   Div. Reception Camp.
        22   Div. Empl. Coy.
        23   14th Div.
        24   59th Div.
        25   XV Corps G.
        26   ,,   Q.
        27   ,,   R.A.
        28   ,,   H.A.
   29 & 30.   War Diary
        31.   File

40th Div. No. 184/14(G).   SECRET.

40th DIVISION INSTRUCTION NO. 15.

In the event of the enemy's defence of the River SCHELDT weakening and a general advance taking place, the preliminary action to be taken by this Division will be as follows :-

1. **The Advanced Guard Brigade.**
Strong patrols will be pushed out by the Right and Left Forward Battalions, crossing the SCHELDT respectively at PECQ and WARCOING. On getting East of the Inundations they will push on immediately and establish posts along the ridge running Northwards from I.4.c. to C.22.c.
The strong patrols will be followed by mopping-up parties, who on reaching the LEAUCOURT - HERINNES Road will turn right and left and examine (and if necessary mop up) all houses, shelters, dugouts etc., along that road and between it and the railway. Liaison patrols will gain touch with the Left Battalion of the Division on right at LEAUCOURT and with the Right Battalion of the Division on left at the road junction at C.10.d.7.0.
These patrols and mopping-up parties will absorb the two forward battalions of the Advanced Guard and the Reserve Battalion will then cross the River at PECQ and assemble under cover of the Woods in I.3.b. and I.4.a. with a view to making a further bound forward to the ridge running N.E. from I.11.b. to D.20.b. The original front line battalions will reform and follow up and support the vanguard battalion, moving respectively by roads running through I.4., 5, and 6 and through C.22, 23, and 24.
Liaison patrols from these battalions will gain touch with the left battalion of the division on right at the South-western corner of the Wood in I.11.b. and with the right battalion of the division on left at LE GRAND BAILLI FARM in D.20.a.
Such artillery support as may be necessary will be given by 178th and 64th Brigades R.F.A. who will be under the orders of the Advanced Guard Commander. An echelon of guns consisting of advanced sections of all batteries of one Brigade will be prepared to move forward across the River as soon as the state of the Causeways permit (probably 12 hours after the commencement of the operation).

2. **Support Brigade.** As soon as the Reserve battalion of the Advanced Guard Brigade moves across the SCHELDT the Support Brigade will move up two battalions to the River line, keeping one battalion in reserve in ESTAIMBOURG.

3. **Reserve Brigade.** This Brigade will probably be moved forward to the line NECHIN - LEERS NORD as soon as the Support Brigade moves up to the River line.

4. The MACHINE GUN BN: has 1 company attached to the Advanced Guard Brigade. It will hold another company in readiness to attach to the Support Brigade when this Brigade moves up to the River line. Headquarters and two companies will remain at LEERS NORD until further orders.

5......

-ii-

5. As soon as the Advanced Guard Headquarters cross the River SCHELDT, Divisional Headquarters will move up to ESTAIMBOURG. Separate orders have been issued regarding the maintenance of communications.

6. <u>C.R.E.</u> will be prepared to throw over a Welden trestle bridge at <u>PECQ</u> and a Pack mule bridge at WARCOING directly the strong patrols of the Advanced Guard move out. He will also have a collection of bridging and other material ready for the repair of the causeways and roads on the other side of the river.

7. ACKNOWLEDGE.

                                 Lieut. Colonel,
4/11/18.   General Staff, 40th Division.

```
G.O.C.
119th I.Bde.
120th I.Bde.
121st I.Bde.
C.R.A.
C.R.E.
17th Worc. R. (P).
O/C.Signals.
39th Bn: M.G.C.
S.A.A.Section.
Divl. Train.
S.S.O.
40th Div. M.T.Coy.
"Q".
A.D.M.S.
D.A.D.V.S.
D.A.D.O.S.
D.A.P.M.
Camp Commandant.
Div. Gas Officer.
Div. Claims Officer.
Div. Reception Camp.
Div. Employment Coy.
14th Division.
59th Division.
XV Corps G.
  ,,,    Q.
  ,,,    R.A.
  ,,,    H.A.
```

SECRET   Copy No. 19

40th DIVISION ORDER NO. 229.   6/11/18.

1. The 40th Div. front will be re-adjusted to-night, 6th/7th instant, as follows :-

2. 119th Infantry Brigade will hand over their front from the ESPIERRES Canal to C.15.c.7.3. to the Brigade on their left. Command of front handed over passes to 14th Division at 06.00 on 7th instant.

3. On completion of relief the Northern boundary will run C.15.c.7.3. to Bridge B.18.c.5.9. (inclusive to 14th Division) and thence along present boundary.

4. All details to be arranged between Brigadier Generals concerned.

5. Re-distribution of Divl. Artillery to cover the front and necessary M.G. reliefs will be arranged direct by C.R.A's and O.s C. M.G.Battalions concerned.

6. ACKNOWLEDGE.

                                                                      Lieut. Colonel,
Issued at 12.30   General Staff, 40th Division.

Copy No. 1 to G.O.C.
        2   119th I.B.
        3   120th I.B.
        4   121st I.B.
        5   C.R.E.
        6   40th D.A.
        7   17th Worc. R. (P).
        8   Signals
        9   39th Bn: M.G.C.
      10   "Q"
      11   A.D.M.S.
      12   D.A.P.M.
      13   14th Div.
      14   59th Div.
      15   XV Corps G.
      16   "   Q.
      17   "   R.A.
      18   "   H.A.
  19 & 20   War Diary
      21   File

SECRET.

App 6

40th Div. No. 4/170 G.

119th Inf. Bde.	39th M.G. Bn.
120th Inf. Bde.	"Q"
121st Inf. Bde.	A.D.M.S.,
C.R.A.,	D.A.P.M.,
C.R.E.,	D.A.D.O.S.,
17th Worc. R (P)	Div. Train.
O.C. Signals.	Div. Receptn Camp.
Div. Gas Officer.	Div. Claims Officer.

****

1. The 113th Army Brigade R.F.A., moves from LINSELLES to LEERS to-morrow 7th November, and on arrival comes under the orders of C.R.A., Division.

2. Route - CROIX BLANCHE - MOUVAIX - GRAND PLACE ROUBAIX.
To be clear of Cross Roads in F.7.d by 10.15.

3. Billets are being obtained from Area Commandant, LANNOY.

        sd. C.H.G. BLACK, Lieut-Colonel,
   General Staff, 40th Division.

6-11-18.

SECRET.   Copy No. 29

40th DIVISION ORDER NO. 250.   9/11/18.
****

1. As a result of the forward movement of the XIth and Xth Corps in an Easterly and South-Easterly direction respectively, the XVth Corps will probably become 'squeezed out' to-morrow.

2. In this event, the 40th Division will billet in depth between LANNOY and CHEMIN VERT and the 14th Division between HERSEAUX and REJET DE SEBLE.

3. When therefore the 59th and 29th Divisions join hands N. of VELAINES, the 119th Infantry Brigade will concentrate and billet in the area CHEMIN VERT - GRAND REJET - BOIS-DE-CHIN, but will keep touch with the situation by means of cyclist patrols.

4. The 14th Division is to have priority over 40th Division for traffic on WARCOING Bridge.

5. The 120th Infantry Brigade and the 121st Infantry Brigade will remain where they are, i.e. in the PECQ and LANNOY areas respectively.

6. The Divisional Artillery and attached Artillery Brigades will stand fast until further orders.

7. ACKNOWLEDGE.

                                    (H.E.Black.)   Lieut. Col.

Issued at..23.30   General Staff, 40th Division.

                                        ****

Copy No.1 to	G.O.C.	17	D.A.D.O.S.
2	119th I.B.	18	D.A.P.M.
3	120th I.B.	19	Div. Gas Off.
4	121st I.B.	20	Div. Claims Off.
5	C.R.E.	21	Div. Recept. Camp.
6	40th Div. Arty.	22	Div. Empl. Coy.
7	17th Worc. R(P).	23	14th Div.
8	Signals.	24	59th Div.
9	39th Bn:M.G.C.	25	XV Corps G.
10	S.A.A.Sect.	26	" Q.
11	Div.Train.	27	" R.A.
12	S.S.O.	28	" H.A.
13	40th Div.M.T.Coy.	29	War Diary
14	"Q".	30	"
15	A.D.M.S.	31	File
16	D.A.D.V.S.	32	29th Div.

```
Go 866        11
Following   message     from        G.H.Q.
begins      aaa         Hostilities will
cease       11.00       Nov. 11th   aaa
Troops      will        stand       fast
on          the         line        reached
at          that        hour        aaa
Defensive   precautions will        be
maintained  aaa         There       will
be          no          intercourse of
any         description with        the
enemy       until       receipt     of
instructions from       G.H.Q.      Further
instructions follow     aaa         ends
```

40th Division

               Capt.
               G.S.

40th Div. No. 224 G.   S E C R E T.

    The following instructions are issued in connection with the Armistice which came into force at 11.00 hours to-day:-

1. Troops in the line will continue to hold the outpost line occupied at the time.

2. The comfort of the troops will be the first consideration in locating all units, except those actually on outpost duty.

3. No officer, N.C.O. or man will be permitted on any pretext whatsoever to go in advance of the PICQUET LINE.
    Any man breaking the Armistice is liable to become a prisoner of war.
    All units will remain in a state of preparedness for action as before the declaration of the Armistice.

4. Fraternization with the enemy is forbidden.

5. Examining posts will be established on all main roads and will be under the command of an Officer.

6. Any hostile parties approaching the outpost line will be challenged and halted. Any messengers to be taken to the nearest examining post where a receipt for the message will be given and the bearer returned to his own lines.

7. Any civilians approaching the outpost line will be taken to the nearest examining post where they will be examined under Divisional arrangements.

8. Civilian traffic from West to East will be regulated by a line of posts in rear of the outpost line and will be allowed as far forward as the outpost line at the discretion of the Divisional Commanders. No civilians will be allowed to proceed East of the Outpost line.

9. All batteries in action will leave their guns in position, and personnel, with the exception of the necessary guards, will be withdrawn to the nearest billets in the vicinity.

                                           Lieut. Colonel,
11/11/18.   General Staff, 40th Division.

119th Infantry Brigade.	D.A.P.M.
120th ,,	Div. Train.
121st ,,	D.A.D.V.S.
C.R.E.	D.Gas Off.
C.R.A.	French Mission
17th Worc. R. (P).	Belgian Mission.
Signals	
39th Bn: M.G.C.	
"Q".	
A.D.M.S.	

SECRET   Copy No. 27

40th DIVISION ORDER NO. 231.   11/11/18.

1. 120th Infantry Brigade will move by march route on 12th November to billets as follows:-

   120th I.Bde. H.Q. } TOUFFLERS
   1 Battalion   }

   1 Battalion   BUCQUOI (G.18.central).
   1 Battalion   Western end of NECHIN.

   To be clear of PECQ by 11.00 hours.

2. Accommodation will be obtained from Town Major, TOUFFLERS and Billet Warden NECHIN.

3. 119th Infantry Brigade will move by march route on 12th Nov. to billets vacated by 120th Infantry Brigade, namely -

   Brigade H.Qrs.   } HERINNES.
   2 Battalions   }

   1 Battalion   WARCOING

   Not to enter HERINNES or to cross the PECQ RIVAGE road before 11.00.

4. ACKNOWLEDGE.

for *[signature]* Capt
Lieut. Colonel,

Issued at 16.20   General Staff, 40th Division.

****

1	to G.O.C.	17	D.A.D.O.S.
2	119th Inf. Bde.	18	D.A.P.M.
3	120th Inf. Bde.	19	Div. Gas Officer.
4	121st Inf. Bde.	20	Div. Claims Officer.
5	C.R.E.	21	Div. Reception Camp.
6	C.R.A.	22	Div. Employ. Coy.
7	17th Worc. R.(P).	23	XV Corps G.
8	Signals	24	,, Q.
9	39th Bn: M.G.C.	25	,, R.A.
10	S.A.A.Section.	26	,, H.A.
11	Div. Train.	27	War Diary
12	S.S.O.	28	,,
13	40th Div. M.T.Coy.	29	File
14	"Q".		
15	A.D.M.S.		
16	D.A.D.V.S.		

SECRET   Copy No. 27

40th DIVISION ORDER NO. 232.   14/11/18.
❋❋❋❋❋❋❋❋❋❋❋❋❋❋❋❋❋❋❋❋❋❋❋❋❋

Ref. map 1/40,000
Sheets 36 and 37.

The following moves will take place to-morrow 15th instant:-

1. 40th Divl. Artillery (including 40th D.A.C. and 64th (Army) Brigade R.F.A.) will move to WAMBRECHIES.

2. 113th (Army) Brigade R.F.A. ceases to be under the command of 40th Division from 09.00 on the 15th instant.

3. 229th Field Coy R.E. will move to the area F.25.
   231st Field Coy. R.E. will move to LA MADELEINE.

4. 1 Coy. 17th Bn: Worc. R. (P) will move from HERINNES to LANNOY.

5. ACKNOWLEDGE.

                                          Lieut. Col.
Issued at 18.30.   General Staff, 40th Division.

                    ❋❋❋❋❋❋❋

Copy No. 1 to G.O.C.   15 to A.D.M.S.
       2   119 I.B.   16   D.A.D.V.S.
       3   120 I.B.   17   D.A.D.O.S.
       4   121 I.B.   18   D.A.P.M.
       5   G.R.E.   19   Div. Gas Officer.
       6   C.R.A.   20   Div. Claims Off.
       7   17th Worc.   21   Div. Reception Camp.
       8   Signals   22   Div. Employ. Coy.
       9   39th Bn: 23   XV Corps G.
            M.G.C.   24   ,,   Q.
      10   S.A.A.Sect.   25   ,,   R.A.
      11   Div. Train   26   ,,   H.A.
      12   S.S.O.   27   War Diary
      13   M.T.Coy.   28   ,,
      14   "Q"   29   File

SECRET.   Copy N°.....

    40th DIVISION ORDER NO. 233.   15/11/18.
    ****
Ref.map
1/40,000. Sheets 36 & 37.

1. 119th Infantry Brigade will move from HERINNES Area to CROIX area on 16th instant.

2. No restrictions as to time or route.

3. ACKNOWLEDGE.

         [signature]   Lb. Col.
Issued to Signals at...   General Staff, 40th Division.
         ****

Copy No.1 to A.D.C.
   2   G
   3   Q
   4   C.R.A.
   5   C.R.E.
   6   119th Infantry Brigade.
   7   120th   "
   8   121st   "
   9   17th Worc. R." (P).
   10   39th Bn: M.G.C.
   11   Div. Train.
   12   Signals
   13   A.D.M.S.
   14   D.A.D.V.S.
   15   D.A.P.M.
   16   D.A.D.O.S.
   17   XV Corps "G"
   18   "   "Q"
   19   War Diary
   20   "
   21   File

SECRET   40th Div. No. 184 (G).

40th DIVISION INSTRUCTIONS NO. 14.

1. In accordance with the terms of the Armistice, the occupied portion of FRANCE, BELGIUM and LUXEMBURG are to be evacuated by the enemy on the 25th November.
   A further withdrawal to the east of the RHINE will take place at a later date.

2. The Allied Forces are to commence the advance on the 17th November.
   The Second Army composed as below is to take part in this advance and is to reach the German Frontier on 2nd December.

         Cavalry Corps (less one Division).
         II, III, XXII Corps.
         Canadian Corps.

3. The XVth Corps (including the 40th Division) is being transferred from Second Army to Fifth Army 'in situ' at 12.00 on the 16th November.

4. 113th (Army) Brigade R.F.A. is being transferred to II Corps at 12.00 on the 16th November.

   Orders have been issued separately.

                                               [signature]
                                               for Lieut. Col.
16/11/18.   General Staff, 40th Division.

Copies to :-

A.D.C.	A.D.M.S.
"G"	D.A.D.V.S.
"Q"	D.A.P.M.
C.R.A.	D.A.D.O.S.
C.R.E.	S.C.F.(D.C.G)
119th Inf Bde	C.C.F.(R.C.D)
120th " "	Div. Employ Coy.
121st " "	
17th Worcester (P)	
39th Bn M.G.C.	
Div. Train.	
Signals.	

SECRET.   Copy No. 78

            40th DIVISION ORDER No.234.   20-11-18.

Ref. Map.
1/40,000
Sheets 36 & 37.

1.   Headquarters 40th Division will close at LANNOY at
1200 on 22nd November, 1918 and re-open at RUE DE LILLE,-
ROUBAIX at the same hour.

2.   ACKNOWLEDGE.

                                        W.B.J. Gray, Major
        Issued at 1930.   for
                                        Lieut-Colonel,
                                        General Staff, 40th Division.

    Copy No. 1 to A.D.C. to G.O.C.,
            2   "G"
            3   "Q"
            4   40th D.A.
            5   119th Inf. Bde.
            6   120th Inf. Bde.
            7   121st Inf. Bde.
            8   17th Worc. R. (P)
            9   39th M.G.Bn.
           10.   Div. Train.
           11   Div. Sig. Coy.
           12   C.R.E.,
           13   A.D.M.S.,
           14   D.A.P.M.,
           15   D.A.D.V.S.,
           16   D.A.D.O.S.,
           17   S.C.F. (D.C.G.)
           18   S.C.F. (P.C.D)
           19   Div. Gas Officer.
           20   Div. Claims Officer.
           21   Div. Salvage Officer.
           22   Div. Empl. Coy.
           23   Camp Commandant.
           24   French Mission.
           25   Div. Reception Op.
           26   XV Corps "G".
           27   XV Corps "Q".
      28 & 29   War Diary.
           30   File.

O.

To all recipients of 40th Division Order No. 254.

The move of Headquarters 40th Division is temporarily postponed; date of the move will be notified later.

for Lieut-Colonel.
General Staff, 40th Division.

21/11/18.

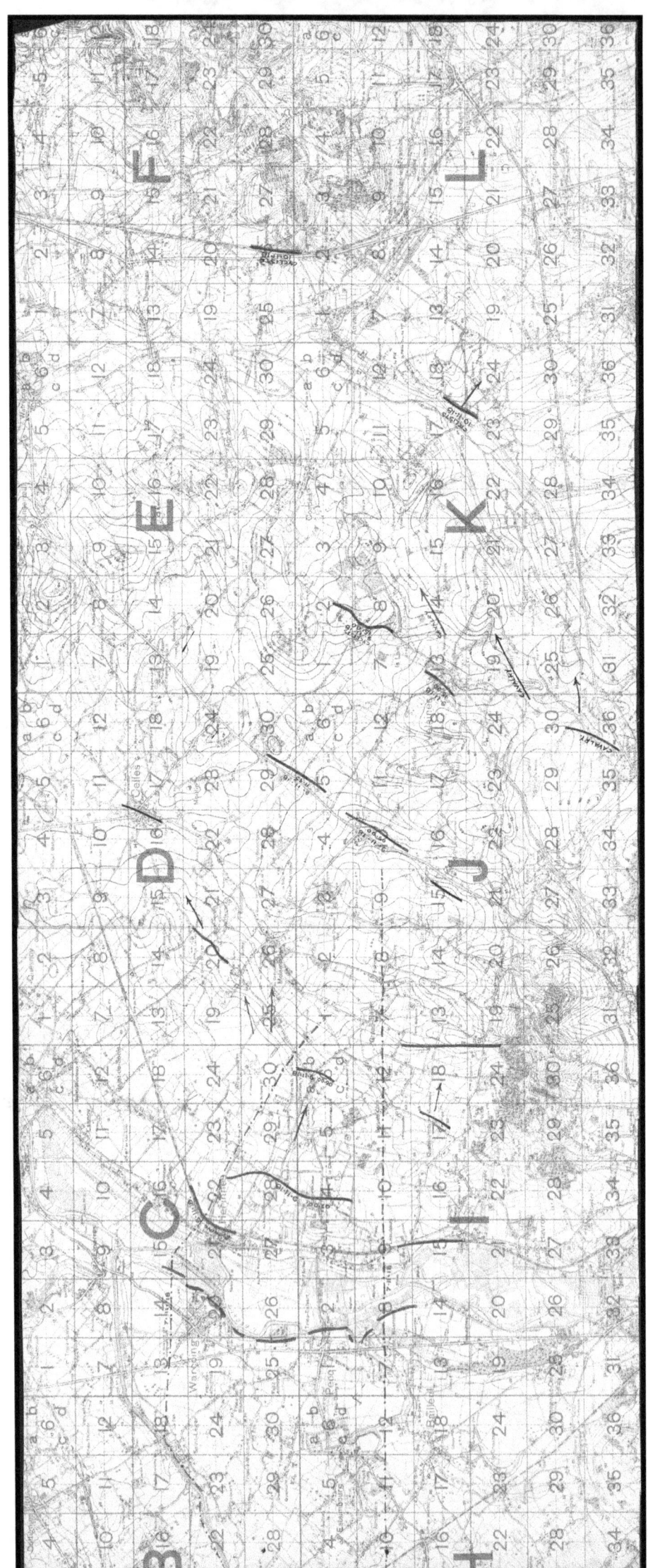

CONFIDENTIAL. ORIGINAL.

WAR DIARY.

GENERAL STAFF.

40th DIVISION.

VOL : XXXI

FROM :- 1st December, 1918.
TO :- 31st December, 1918.

Brigadier-Gen.
Commanding 40th Division.

Army Form W.3091.

Cover for Documents.

Nature of Enclosures.

Notes, or Letters written.

SECRET.   40th Division No. 34 (A).

D. A. G.,
    3rd Echelon.

         In continuation of this Office No. 34 (A) dated 19/1/19.
    Herewith original and duplicate War Diaries of "G" Branch,
    40th Divisional Headquarters, for period 1st - 31st December, 1919.

21st January, 1919.   Brig-General,
WB.   Commanding 40th Division.

Army Form C. 2118.

WAR DIARY
or
INTELLIGENCE SUMMARY

(Erase heading not required.)

Instructions regarding War Diaries and Intelligence Summaries are contained in F. S. Regs., Part II. and the Staff Manual respectively. Title pages will be prepared in manuscript.

40th DIVISION

DECEMBER, 1918.

Place	Date	Hour	Summary of Events and Information	Remarks and references to Appendices
ROUBAIX			The month was occupied in Educational and Recreational Training.	
			A Divisional School for giving refresher Courses for Carpenters, Blacksmiths, Tinsmiths, Plumbers, and Bricklayers was opened on 2nd December at WAMBRECHIES.	
			Twenty Lectures on "DEMOBILISATION" and subjects of General interest were delivered by G. H. Q. Lecturers to the Division.	
			Recreational Training consisted in :-	
			(a) An Association Football League, which was won by 10th King's Own Scottish Borderers, of 120th Infantry Brigade with 178th Brigade, Royal Field Artillery as runners up.	
			(b) Cross Country Run of teams of 12 from all units in the Division, won by 178th Brigade, Royal Field Artillery with 13th Royal Inniskilling Fusiliers second.	
			(c) A Boxing Tournament was held on 7th and 8th December.	
			13 entries for Officers' Events (3 weights)	
			42 entries for Other Ranks' Events (5 weights)	

W. A. Greymayer
for Lieut. Colonel,
General Staff, 40th Division.

ORIGINAL

WAR DIARY
****

40th Div.

General   Staff   Branch

VOL. XXXII

1st Jan. 1919 to
31st Jan. 1919.   [signature] Major General,
                        Commanding 40th Division.

(6392) Wt. W6192/P875 1,500,000 4/18 McA & W Ltd (E 2815) Forms W3091/4. Army Form W.3091.

Cover for Documents.

Nature of Enclosures.

Notes, or Letters written.

Army Form C. 2118.

WAR DIARY
or
INTELLIGENCE SUMMARY.

(Erase heading not required.)

40th DIVISION.　　　　　January, 1919.

Instructions regarding War Diaries and Intelligence Summaries are contained in F. S. Regs., Part II. and the Staff Manual respectively. Title pages will be prepared in manuscript.

Place	Date	Hour	Summary of Events and Information	Remarks and references to Appendices
ROUBAIX.			Educational and Recreational Training continued throughout the month.	
			The Divisional School at WAMBRECHIES for refresher courses for Carpenters, Builders, Blacksmiths, etc. continued.	
			A Divisional School was opened at LE TRIEZ on 2nd January at which 36 Other Ranks are receiving instruction in wireless.	
			The Divisional Class in Spanish which started on 12th December and originally consisted of 20 students, has, owing to demobilization and other causes, gradually dwindled to 6.	
			A number of Lectures in general subjects have been delivered by G. H. Q. Lecturers.	
			Recreational Training. No events of special importance occurred during the month.	

1st February, 1919.

[signature]
Lieut. Colonel,
General Staff, 40th Division.

==*=*=*=*=*=*=*=*=*=*=*

CONFIDENTIAL.   ORIGINAL.

WAR DIARY.

=== 40th DIVISION. ===

GENERAL STAFF BRANCH.

VOL : XXVIII.

FROM :- 1st February, 1919.
TO   :- 28th February, 1919.

Major-General,
Commanding 40th Division.

****

(6392) Wt. W6192/P875 1,500,000 4/18 McA & W Ltd (E 2815) Forms W3091/4.   Army Form W.3091.

Cover for Documents.

Nature of Enclosures.

Notes, or Letters written.

Army Form C. 2118.

WAR DIARY
~~INTELLIGENCE SUMMARY~~

40th DIVISION *(Erase heading not required.)* FEBRUARY, 1919.

Instructions regarding War Diaries and Intelligence Summaries are contained in F. S. Regs., Part II. and the Staff Manual respectively. Title pages will be prepared in manuscript.

Place	Date	Hour	Summary of Events and Information	Remarks and references to Appendices
ROUBAIX	1st to 28th Feb. 1919.		Military Training, Education and Recreational Training continued throughout the month. Owing to rapid demobilization it was found necessary to close the Divisional R.E., Schools of Instruction at WAMBRECHIES and the Divisional Wireless School at LA TRIEZ. The Spanish Class at Divisional Headquarters also ceased to exist. 28-2-19. *[signature]* Lieut-Colonel, General Staff, 40th Division.	

CONFIDENTIAL.   ORIGINAL.

WAR DIARY.

OF

40th DIVISION.

(GENERAL STAFF BRANCH.)

VOL : XXXIV.

FROM :- 1st March, 1919.
TO   :- 31st March, 1919.

Brig-General,
Commanding 40th Divisional Cadres.

1st April, 1919.

(6392) Wt. W6192/P875 1,500,000 4/18 McA & W Ltd (E 2815) Forms W3091/4.   Army Form W.3091.

Cover for Documents.

Nature of Enclosures.

Notes, or Letters written.

Army Form C. 2118.

WAR DIARY
INTELLIGENCE SUMMARY

(Erase heading not required.)

40th DIVISION.

MARCH, 1919.

Place	Date	Hour	Summary of Events and Information	Remarks and references to Appendices
ROUBAIX.	1/3/19. to 24/3/19.		All units proceeded with reduction to Cadre Strength. Major-General Sir W. E. Peyton, K.C.B., K.C.V.O., D.S.O. relinquished the command of the Division on 24th March. The Divisional Headquarters was reduced to cadre strength on 24/3/19.	
CROIX.	25.		Divisional Cadre Headquarters moved to CROIX.	
,,	,,		Brigadier-General F. P. Crozier, C.M.G., D.S.O., assumed command of 40th Division Cadre Groups.	
,,			Training, both military and recreational, continued throughout the month. An Inter.-Cadre Association Football League was inaugurated. 31 teams composed of personnel on the cadre strength of units are competing.	

1st April, 1919.

Borne Name
Captain.
a/ D. A. Q. M. G., 40th Division.